Feminism and the Servant Problem

In the early twentieth century, women fought for the right to professional employment and political influence outside the home. Yet if liberation from household 'drudgery' meant employing another woman to do it, where did this leave domestic servants?

Both inspired and frustrated by the growing feminist movement, servants began forming their own trade unions, demanding better conditions and rights at work. *Feminism and the Servant Problem* is the first history of how these militant maids and their mistresses joined forces in the struggle for the vote but also clashed over competing class interests. Laura Schwartz uncovers a forgotten history of domestic worker organising and early feminist thinking on reproductive labour, and offers a new perspective on the class politics of the suffrage movement, challenging traditional notions of who made up the British working class.

LAURA SCHWARTZ is Associate Professor of Modern British History at the University of Warwick. She has published widely on the history of British feminism, and is the author of *A Serious Endeavour: Gender Education and Community at St Hugh's, 1886–2011* (2011) and *Infidel Feminism: Secularism, Religion and Women's Emancipation in England 1830–1914* (2013).

T0382156

Feminism and the Servant Problem

Class and Domestic Labour in the Women's Suffrage Movement

Laura Schwartz

University of Warwick

CAMBRIDGE
UNIVERSITY PRESS

CAMBRIDGE
UNIVERSITY PRESS

University Printing House, Cambridge CB2 8BS, United Kingdom

One Liberty Plaza, 20th Floor, New York, NY 10006, USA

477 Williamstown Road, Port Melbourne, VIC 3207, Australia

314-321, 3rd Floor, Plot 3, Splendor Forum, Jasola District Centre, New Delhi - 110025, India

79 Anson Road, #06-04/06, Singapore 079906

Cambridge University Press is part of the University of Cambridge.

It furthers the University's mission by disseminating knowledge in the pursuit of education, learning and research at the highest international levels of excellence.

www.cambridge.org
Information on this title: www.cambridge.org/9781108457743
DOI: 10.1017/9781108603263

First published 2019
First paperback edition 2020

A catalogue record for this publication is available from the British Library

Library of Congress Cataloging in Publication data
Names: Schwartz, Laura, author.
Title: Feminism and the servant problem : class and domestic labour in the
    women's suffrage movement / Laura Schwartz.
Description: 1 Edition. | New York : Cambridge University Press, 2019. |
    Includes bibliographical references and index.
Identifiers: LCCN 2019007311 | ISBN 9781108471336 (hardback) |
    ISBN 9781108457743 (paperback)
Subjects: LCSH: Household employees–Great Britain–History–20th century. |
    Feminism–Great Britain–History–20th century. | Social conflict–Great
    Britain–History–20th century. | BISAC: HISTORY / Europe / Great Britain.
Classification: LCC HD8039.D52 .G79 2019 |
    DDC 331.4/864094109041–dc23
LC record available at https://lccn.loc.gov/2019007311

ISBN   978-1-108-47133-6   Hardback
ISBN   978-1-108-45774-3   Paperback

Contents

Figures

Acknowledgements

The research for this book was supported by an Institute of Advanced Study postdoctoral fellowship at the University of Warwick, and then by Warwick's History Department where I feel lucky to have found an intellectual home. Rosa Campbell, Lyndsey Jenkins, Tara Morton, Sandra Stanley Holton, Michael Meeuwis, Carolyn Steedman and Barbara Taylor read chapters at various stages of preparation. Marc Calvini Lefebvre, Alison Light, Mark Philp, Aditya Sarkar and Mathew Thomson commented on a draft of the whole manuscript. I'm hugely grateful that, despite the pressures of the neo-liberal university, they all took the time to do this. The book is much better as a result, and all errors remain my own. Thanks also go to Eileen Boris, Lucy Delap, Jack Elliott, Amy Galvin, Barbara Green, Daniel Grey, Vanessa May, Premilla Nadasen, Sarah Richardson, Mari Takayanagi and Padraig Yeates for their expertise and help with queries. Audrey Canning shared her knowledge of Jessie Stephen; Fae Dussart offered insights on domestic service and colonialism; Anna Hajkova co-convened the Feminist History Group at Warwick, providing a crucial forum in which to develop ideas; Karen Hunt and Theresa Moriarty helped me track Grace Neal in Dublin; Sybil Oldfield gave over a whole day to talking to me about Mary Sheepshanks; and Sandra Stanley Holton was unfailingly generous in guiding me through the Priestman Bright Clark family networks. All of them provided intellectual inspiration, to which the notes to this book are testament. I am indebted to staff at all the archives I visited, especially Alfred Gillett Trust in Street and The Women's Library at the London School of Economics. Also to Freda Roberts and Colin Frayling for talking to me about and showing me around Eagle House, Batheaston.

Clare Bielby turned up during the book's conclusion, providing at first a delightful distraction and then the strength to finish it under difficult circumstances. My father, Michael Schwartz, did not live to see it published and probably wouldn't have read it even if he had. It is nonetheless because of him that I have never once had to question whether one could be both a kitchen-porter and a radical, a night-cleaner and a story-teller, a road-sweeper and an artist. *Feminism and the Servant Problem* belongs to the comrades who, over the last decade or so, have been in and around Feminist Fightback. Gabriella Alberti, Camille Barbagallo, Sofie Buckland, Rosa Campbell, Esme Cleall, Katie Cruz, Erin Cullen, Anna Davies, Kiran Dhami, Albane Duvillier, Rachael Ferguson, Frances Grahl, Rebecca Galbraith, Kate Hardy, Lydia Harris, Claire English, Gwyneth Lonergan, Roisin McDowell, Ziggy Melamed, Cathy Nugent, Anne-Marie O'Reilly, Mary Partington, Alice Robson, Laura Rogers, Millie Wild and Anna Wolmuth – thank you for everything you have taught me about sisterhood, workplace organising and the political imperative of the cleaning rota.

Introduction
Whose Problem Was the 'Servant Problem'?

In November 1911 the suffragist newspaper the *Common Cause* published a letter from a woman who had worked in service since the age
of thirteen. Identifying herself only as 'Another Servant', she objected not
only to hard working conditions and harsh employers, but also to the
complacency of the suffrage movement. 'Why don't suffragists begin
their reform work at home ...?', she demanded, 'why don't they try in
some way to relieve the monotonous life of the domestic servant? If they
want equality with men, why cannot they put servants on twelve hours a
day shift, like the majority of workmen[?]'[1] The *Common Cause* was in
fact quite open to discussing the 'servant problem', publishing many
letters from readers who were both servants and mistresses. A month
later, a cook general named Kathlyn Oliver (1884–1953), who had
founded the Domestic Workers' Union almost two years earlier, wrote
offering a more optimistic perspective on the relationship between servant militancy and women's emancipation, insisting, 'This servant agitation belongs to the feminist movement.'[2]

This book is about how feminists thought about domestic service, and
how servants thought about feminism. It is about a moment in history
when these two groups of women were sometimes united – when servants became feminists – and sometimes at odds with one another –
when feminists employed servants. I examine how all of these women
grappled with the question of what it meant to employ another woman to
do a form of work that you yourself would rather not. My focus is the
early twentieth-century suffrage movement and how it responded to a
perceived shortage of competent, reliable and obedient domestic
workers – what was referred to at the time as the 'servant problem'.[3]
Feminism and the Servant Problem is also a history of the British working

---

[1] *Common Cause* 9 Nov. 1911, p. 543.   [2] *Common Cause* 7 Dec. 1911, pp. 621–622.
[3] In 1911 the *Concise Oxford English Dictionary* defined this problem as one of the 'getting
and controlling of servants'; Selina Todd, *The People: The Rise and Fall of the Working
Class, 1910–2010* (London: John Murray, 2014), p. 21.

class, one that rejects masculine models of class formation to look not only at women workers but at a hyper-feminised form of work in the private sphere of the home. Feminism is therefore both my subject and my methodology, though I also aim to uncover its historical limitations and their theoretical legacies. Combining feminist history with labour history, *Feminism and the Servant Problem* examines class relations between women in the home and explores a subject matter – servant militancy in general and the Domestic Workers' Union in particular – that has tended to fall outside both histories of the women's movement and histories of trade unionism.

This dual interest has led me to focus mainly on the first decade and a half of the twentieth century, when both the struggle for the suffrage and working-class militancy were at their height. Following the establishment of the National Union of Women's Suffrage Societies in 1897 and the Women's Social and Political Union in 1903, the campaign for the vote turned more towards grassroots organising and mass protest, involving greater numbers of working-class women than ever before. Meanwhile, the New Unionism that had begun in the 1880s was gaining ground, reaching out beyond heavy industry to many female-dominated work-places. Women workers came to play an important role in the unprecedented levels of industrial action known as the Great Unrest of 1907–1914. The suffrage and the workers' movements often overlapped, sometimes working together, sometimes coming into conflict, and this complex relationship created fertile ground for the growth of servant agitation. It is no coincidence that middle-class anxiety about the 'servant problem' also peaked during these years. The relatively short period of social and political ferment with which this book concerns itself was interrupted by the outbreak of war in 1914. Most suffrage organisations suspended their campaigns, labour disputes were curtailed, and industry was radically reorganised. In particular, hundreds of thousands of women left domestic service to take up jobs vacated by men now fighting at the front. In 1918 some women were finally granted the parliamentary vote, and the disbandment of the suffrage movement is usually seen to mark the end of the 'first wave' of feminism in Britain. Yet live-in domestic servants remained disenfranchised until 1928, the struggle for women's rights was far from over, and the 'servant problem' remained a pressing issue throughout the interwar years. The chronological scope of *Feminism and the Servant Problem* is not, therefore, intended to impose a definitive periodisation, but rather to allow for an in-depth exploration of the extraordinary amount of thought and activity relating to women's emancipation, work and domestic service generated in the years leading up to the First World War.

I argue that the 'servant problem' should be understood as a distinctively feminist problem. Domestic labour was at this time invariably perceived as the work of women, whether they be housewives, servants or mistresses. The possibility of men doing their fair share was very rarely voiced even within the women's movement. Middle-class suffrage activists were especially reliant upon servants to take responsibility for the smooth running of their households while they dedicated themselves to the struggle for the vote. At the same time, servants were also involved in the suffrage movement, and were inspired by both feminism and trade unionism to stand up to their female employers. Some of them joined the Domestic Workers' Union, a grassroots organisation formed by servants for servants, and it is their story that forms the heart of this book. Class conflict between women is an important element of this history, as are the intellectual and political limitations of a movement with a predominantly middle-class leadership. Yet the story of suffrage and the 'servant problem' cannot be narrated solely in terms of the exclusion or marginalisation of working-class women. To the contrary, I have encountered servants as an active force in the movement's history, answering back and attempting to define on their own terms feminist debates about housework, domestic service and what it meant to be a 'free woman'.

This book argues that the 'servant problem' should not be dismissed as a trivial middle-class gripe but that it pointed to deeper and widespread social anxiety over rising worker militancy, the strengthening of the women's movement and the changing relationship between the domestic sphere and the world of work. The 'servant problem' can be traced back to the second half of the nineteenth century, coinciding with, and in part provoked by, the entry of middle-class women into professional work outside the home and growing demands for emancipation among women of all classes.[4] A shortage of people willing and able to perform the reproductive labour of the home was a genuine problem, and *Feminism and the Servant Problem* asks why this situation came about and what women activists at the time had to say about it. The 'servant problem' consisted not just of 'irritable mistresses' but also 'irritated servants', and throughout the book I explore the problem from the perspective of domestic workers themselves: as a problem of low wages, terrible working conditions and authoritarian employers.[5] The employer class was increasingly

---

[4] Between 1890 and 1919 British newspapers referred to the 'servant problem' and the 'servant question' 5,118 times, its popularity as a discussion item coinciding with a peak in the number of times that women's suffrage was mentioned. Data derived from keyword search of 602 digitised newspapers in the British Newspaper Archive, www.britishnewspaperarchive.co.uk.

[5] Ellen W. Darwin, 'Domestic Service', *Nineteenth Century*, 28 (1890), 286–296, p. 287.

confronted with the uncomfortable realisation that the 'servant problem' was, at least in part, driven by ever more vocal dissatisfaction among that section of the working class who resided within their own homes.

The 'servant problem' was of direct interest to the women's suffrage movement not only because so many of them employed servants, but also because domestic service was still by far the most common form of work for women. Feminists were therefore compelled to consider how this problem might be solved to the satisfaction of both mistress and maid. If individual liberation from housework meant employing other women to do it, what did this imply about the scope of the feminist project? Was domestic labour inherently inferior to masculine forms of work? And if so, were women who worked as domestic servants capable of living up to feminist ideals of modern and emancipated womanhood? Many of these questions remain unresolved in the twenty-first century, despite fundamental changes to women's role in society and their relationship to waged work and the home. One hundred years on from the events of this book, longer working hours, a diminished welfare state, the need for at least two incomes to adequately support a family and the rise of a global domestic labour market have contributed towards a new 'crisis of care'.[6] Both women and men are not simply unwilling but often unable to undertake necessary housework and care for their families. This book, then, is a history of how we got to where we are today – an exploration not only of feminism's past but also its future possibilities.

Servants and the 'Servant Problem'

This is my life – getting up at 6 o'clock, toiling on until 11 p.m. often later; liberty – a few hours at the end of the month ... For the sake of supporting an elderly mother and myself I am in truth a slave, like many others, to idle gadabouts whose entertainment at afternoon tea consists of talking of our ignorance and dissecting our character.

Letter from 'Justice' to the *Glasgow Herald* (1913)[7]

In 1893 the suffragist and labour organiser Clementina Black affirmed that 'most young women of the working class dislike domestic service'.[8] Three years earlier, former Cambridge University lecturer Ellen Wordsworth Darwin had drawn her readers' attention to 'one great and

---

[6] Feminist Fightback, 'Cuts Are a Feminist Issue', *Soundings,* 49 (Winter 2011), 73–83; Nancy Fraser, 'Contradictions of Capital and Care', *New Left Review,* 100 (July–Aug. 2016), 99–117.
[7] *Glasgow Herald* 23 Sept. 1913, p. 3.
[8] Clementina Black, 'The Dislike to Domestic Service', *Nineteenth Century,* 33:193 (1893), 454–456, p. 454.

significant fact', that in 'manufacturing districts where there is ample employment' barely any young women chose to go into service.[9] In 1903, the Women's Industrial Council deemed the problem to be worthy of a 'systematic inquiry' and concluded that domestic service was – the title of their report – 'An Unpopular Industry'.[10] Another more extensive inquiry carried out by the Council just before the First World War and published in 1916 likewise admitted that although happy servants and mistresses did exist, they were by far the minority.[11] While not all contemporaries agreed upon the universal unpopularity of domestic service,[12] historians have corroborated a growing reluctance among young working-class women to take it up. In 1881 there had been 218 female domestic servants to every 1,000 families in England and Wales, but by 1911 this had fallen to 170. Even Wales, where service comprised over 50 per cent of female employment at the turn of the century, saw a decline from 1891 onwards. In Scotland, the percentage of the female workforce in domestic service declined from around 30 per cent in 1891 to around 23 per cent in 1911. Domestic service remained the most common form of female employment, accounting for between one-third and one-quarter of all women workers in the first decade of the twentieth century. The 1911 census recorded about 1.3 million women in private service in England and Wales and 135,052 in Scotland, but demand outstripped supply.[13] Employers also complained bitterly about

---

[9] Darwin, 'Domestic Service', p. 287.

[10] Catherine Webb, 'An Unpopular Industry', *Nineteenth Century*, 53 (June 1903), 989–1001.

[11] C. Violet Butler, *Domestic Service: An Enquiry by the Women's Industrial Council* (New York: Garland, 1980 [first published 1916]), p. 9. The report was based upon questionnaires drawn up by the Women's Industrial Council (WIC); 708 replies were returned from employers, 566 from servants. It also drew upon a few hundred letters, addressed to the WIC either privately or through the press.

[12] For example, M. E. Benson, 'In Defence of Domestic Service: A Reply', *Nineteenth Century*, 28 (Oct. 1890), 616–626.

[13] Pamela Horn, *The Rise and Fall of the Victorian Servant* (Stroud: Alan Sutton Publishing, 1990), pp. 28, 171–172; Eleanor Gordon, *Women and the Labour Movement in Scotland, 1850–1914* (Oxford: Clarendon Press, 1991), p. 25; Carys Howell, 'Wales' Hidden Industry: Domestic Service in South Wales, 1871–1921', PhD thesis, University of Swansea (2014), p. 14. Horn notes that the overall numbers of female domestic servants did not decline in this period, but rather there was a 'dramatic slowing down in the rate of expansion'. Whereas earlier historiography suggested that the decline in the servant population was due to the emergence of more modest housekeeping practices among the late Victorian middle class, leading to a reduction in the demand for servants, there is now a consensus that demand remained high, Edward Higgs, 'Domestic Servants and Households in Victorian England', *Social History*, 8:2 (May 1983), 201–210, pp. 204–205; Sian Pooley, 'Domestic Servants and Their Urban Employers: A Case Study of Lancaster, 1880–1914', *Economic History Review*, 62:2 (2009), 405–429, p. 426.

servants refusing to stay in their posts long term, and simply moving on when they became bored or unhappy.[14] Kathlyn Oliver, for example, changed jobs seven times in less than two years before she found a position that suited her.[15] This national picture was subject to significant regional variation, but overall contributed to a widespread sense of panic over servant 'shortages', and a very real problem for large numbers of middle-class women attempting to run households without adequate labour power.[16]

Who were these supposedly troublesome servants, and what kind of people entered domestic service during this period? The vast majority of them were women. Male servants were relatively unusual by the second half of the nineteenth century, and by 1900 only extremely wealthy families employed them in the capacity of butler or footman.[17] Female servants were also young (about one-third of them aged between fifteen and twenty) but literate (the beneficiaries of the introduction of state-funded and then compulsory education from the 1870s onwards). Improved standards of education were often remarked upon, and sometimes lamented, as one of the causes of a growing unwillingness to pursue domestic employment.[18] It nevertheless remained common practice for working-class families to send school-educated daughters into service as a way of supplementing family income.[19] Jessie Stephen (1893–1979), founder of the Scottish Federation of Domestic Workers, was the eldest of ten children whose father struggled to support his family on his earnings as a tailor. Her autobiography recalls how she had once accidentally walked in on her mother praying out loud to God for help with the rent arrears.

Later on, when I left school, memories like these had a decisive influence when I had to choose between taking jobs which ran between half a crown and four

---

[14] Horn, *The Rise and Fall of the Victorian Servant*, pp. 135–136.
[15] *Woman Worker* 4 May 1910, pp. 942–943.
[16] For regional variation, see Horn, *The Rise and Fall of the Victorian Servant*, pp. 32–34; Pooley, 'Domestic Servants and Their Urban Employers'. For the tendency of census data to mask such regional variation, and the inherently flawed nature of the 1891 census data on domestic workers, see Higgs, 'Domestic Servants and Households'.
[17] Wales had a higher than average proportion of male servants, with one in ten male workers employed in service between 1871 and 1901 compared with the British average of one in twenty-two, Howell, 'Wales' Hidden Industry', p. 7.
[18] Margaret Bondfield, 'Women as Domestic Workers', in Ellen Malos (ed.), *The Politics of Housework* (London: Alison & Busby, 1980 [first published 1919]), 83–87, p. 84; Horn, *The Rise and Fall of the Victorian Servant*, p. 28.
[19] Theresa McBride, *The Domestic Revolution: The Modernisation of Household Service in England and France 1820–1920* (London: CroomHelm, 1976), p. 50; Samuel Mullins and Gareth Griffiths, *Cap and Apron: An Oral History of Domestic Service in the Shires, 1880–1950* (Leicester: Leicestershire Museums, Art Galleries and Records Service, 1986), p. 1.

shillings a week and the prospect of domestic service where board and lodging helped the money wage.

Watching his eldest daughter compelled into service was a 'blow' to her father, who had high hopes for his daughter when she excelled at school and won a scholarship to train as a pupil teacher. But economic necessity won out, for while she continued to live at home she was but an extra mouth to feed.[20]

Compulsion was an even stronger factor in the case of girls growing up in orphanages, reformatories or workhouses, who were routinely sent directly into service once they reached their middle teens. Even before entering formal domestic employment they were often used as unpaid servants in their institutional homes under the guise of 'industrial training'. Once in service, girls from institutional care were more vulnerable to mistreatment since they lacked wider support networks and did not have a family to return to if they wished to leave a post quickly. Institutions thus played an important role in mitigating the effects of the 'servant problem' by ensuring a ready supply of cheap, though not necessarily willing, domestic labour.[21]

With greater or lesser degrees of enthusiasm, many working-class women across Britain saw domestic service as an inevitable stage of early adult life, which would end only in marriage.[22] Recent historiography has nuanced earlier narratives of service as a universally dislocating and isolating experience. Not all servants were young girls separated from their families and uprooted from their homes in the countryside. Although this was some women's experience, there were also servants who took up places close to their families, or used networks to ensure they were posted near friends or siblings.[23] The most common form of service was as a maid of all work (often known as a 'general') in a household that employed only one or two servants.[24] This meant that although considerable variations existed between different grades of domestic worker – a lady's maid and a kitchen-maid for example – such

---

[20] Working Class Movement Library (hereafter WCML), Salford, Jessie Stephen, 'Submission Is for Slaves' (unpublished manuscript), pp. 9–10, 15.

[21] Pamela Horn, *Life below Stairs in the Twentieth Century* (Stroud: Amberley, 2001), pp. 3–4, 90–96; Alison Light, *Mrs Woolf and the Servants* (London: Penguin Books, 2008), pp. 85–108; Lucy Delap, *Knowing Their Place: Domestic Service in Twentieth Century Britain* (Oxford: Oxford University Press, 2011), pp. 33–35.

[22] McBride, *The Domestic Revolution,* p. 9.

[23] Pooley, 'Domestic Servants and Their Urban Employers'; Delap, *Knowing Their Place.* For a contemporary critique of the perceived 'isolation' of domestic servants, see Benson, 'In Defence of Domestic Service', pp. 620–621.

[24] In 1911, 80 per cent of households employing servants employed only one or two, Horn, *The Rise and Fall of the Victorian Servant,* pp. 19–26.

hierarchies were not particularly significant to the majority of servants at this time who had a shared experience of life as a general, or perhaps a cook or parlour-maid working alongside each other and sharing the housework between them.

Most servants were not employed by the very wealthy but by a wide spectrum of the middle classes. Jessie Stephen, for example, was employed by a concert pianist (one who needed to supplement his income by giving private singing lessons); then in the much grander household of Sir John Chisholm, former Provost of Glasgow; then by an artist called David Gould, who lived with his wife in a flat; then as a 'daily maid' for the secretary of a Chinese missionary society. She also joined the domestic staff in a nursing home and in a hotel, reminding us that institutional service in hospitals, colleges and schools, for example, was also an important component of the industry in this period.[25] The lower middle classes (shopkeepers and clerks, anyone not engaged in manual labour) also frequently employed at least one servant.[26] The suffragette and socialist Hannah Mitchell (1872–1956), for example, worked as a general maid for a schoolmaster's family.[27] Less well-off employers might also have relied upon a charwoman to come in for a set number of hours each week, and this more casual form of domestic service was on the rise in the first decade of the century.[28] Millions of women in this period, therefore, would have had experience of either employing a servant or working as one.[29] Even single women living alone needed help with the housework, and the question of how to cater for the domestic needs of single professional 'ladies' was a pressing one for the suffrage movement. Kathlyn Oliver worked alongside just one house-maid as a cook general for Mary Sheepshanks (1872–1960), whose job as principal of Morley College in South London, in addition to her active support for the suffrage movement, kept her too busy to run her own household.[30]

One important aspect of the labour performed by Britain's domestic servants was looking after children. In upper- and upper middle-class homes a nanny and perhaps also a nurse-maid freed up the mother from daily care of infants, whereas in lower middle-class households a single

[25] For domestic service in an Oxbridge women's college, Laura Schwartz, *A Serious Endeavour: Gender, Education and Community at St Hugh's, 1886–2011* (London: Profile Books, 2011), chapter 4.
[26] Girls from institutional care often went to less well-off employers such as small trades people; Horn, *Life below Stairs*, p. 91.
[27] Hannah Mitchell, *The Hard Way Up: The Autobiography of Hannah Mitchell, Suffragette and Rebel* (London: Virago, 1977), pp. 67–70.
[28] Delap, *Knowing Their Place*, pp. 35–41.   [29] Light, *Mrs Woolf and the Servants*, p. xv.
[30] England and Wales Census (1911), 1 Barton Street, Westminster, London.

servant might be expected to help with any resident small children in between her other chores.[31] Childcare thus made up a significant element of domestic service, and yet it received very little mention in discussions of the 'servant problem'. This is probably due to the belief that the care of children was, at the very least, conceptually different from cooking and cleaning. Although it was often difficult in practice to separate out childcare from other kinds of housework, and the former undoubtedly created more of the latter,[32] by the turn of the twentieth century a distinction was increasingly being made between the care of children and the 'dirty' work of the home. New ideas about parenting, informed by the emerging disciplines of psychology and eugenics as well as concerns about infant mortality and the future of the imperial 'race', placed greater value and expectations upon motherhood.[33]

This distinction between childcare and housework was also reflected in increasingly rigid stratifications within the domestic labour force. The nurse or nanny became more professionalised by training institutions and qualifications, so that by the interwar period she was often separated from the rest of the servant class even if she hailed from the same social background.[34] In 1911, even women working as nurse-maids at the much lower end of the market, for the same wages they would have received as kitchen-maids, were said to view childcare as more 'genteel' than cleaning.[35] The 'servant' of the 'servant problem' was widely understood to be a 'general', a house-maid, a parlour-maid or a cook rather than a nanny or a nurse-maid.

The servants who feature in this book were mainly white and British-born. Before the First World War, only small numbers of Black, other

---

[31] Leonore Davidoff, *Worlds Between: Historical Perspectives on Gender and Class* (Cambridge: Polity Press, 1995), p. 109; Leonore Davidoff, Megan Doolittle, Janet Fink and Katherine Holden, *The Family Story: Blood, Contract and Intimacy, 1830–1960* (Harlow: Longman, 1999), p. 168.

[32] Ellen Ross, *Love and Toil: Motherhood in Outcast London, 1870–1918* (Oxford: Oxford University Press, 1993).

[33] Anna Davin, 'Imperialism and Motherhood', *History Workshop Journal*, 5 (1978), 9–65, Ross, *Love and Toil*, pp. 21–26. New ideas about motherhood applied to middle- and working-class mothers in very different ways, and historians have debated the degree to which they were taken up and internalised by individual families in the years before the First World War; Sian Pooley, 'Parenthood, Child-Rearing and Fertility in England, 1850–1914', *The History of the Family*, 18:1 (2013), 83–106, p. 92.

[34] Delap, *Knowing Their Place*, pp. 108–109; Katherine Holden, *Nanny Knows Best: The History of the British Nanny* (Stroud: History Press, 2013), p. 79, chapter 4.

[35] This was one of the conclusions drawn from an investigation by the WIC into 'the supply and demand for nurses for small children' for which 100 servants' registries were visited across the United Kingdom; *Women's Industrial News* June 1911, pp. 95–104.

European and Indian servants worked in Britain.[36] Emigration was
more common than immigration, with many British servants moving
to Canada, Australia and New Zealand in search of better wages and
higher status.[37] This did not mean that ideas of race and Empire had no
effect upon domestic service in Britain, where throughout the nineteenth
century the working class had often been constructed as a racialised
'other' and Empire exerted its influence on everyday culture. The
devaluing of women's domestic labour in Britain paralleled that of male
and female workers from the colonised territories.[38] The idealised qualities of mistresshood with which middle- to upper-class women were
inculcated as a birthright – responsibility for one's 'inferiors', the inherent right of command, the sanctity of service as the foundation of the
nation – were central to the imperialist frame of mind.[39] I have not,
however, come across any direct influence of colonial ideas of service
in the Indian subcontinent or Africa on articulations of the British

[36] Caroline Bressey, 'Black Women and Work in England, 1880–1920', in Mary Davis
(ed.), *Class and Gender in British Labour History: Renewing the Debate (or Starting It?)*
(Pontypool: Merlin Press, 2011), 117–132; Horn, *Life below Stairs*, 222–246; Olivia
Robinson, 'Out of Sight and Over Here: Foreign Female Domestic Servants in
London 1880–1939', unpublished conference poster presented at the Social History
Society Conference, University of Lancaster, 2016; Rozina Visram, *Ayahs, Lascars and
Princes: Indians in Britain 1700–1947* (London: Pluto Press, 1986), chapter 2; Holden,
Nanny Knows Best, pp. 83–86; Olivia Robinson, 'Travelling Ayahs of the Nineteenth and
Twentieth Centuries: Global Networks and Mobilisation of Agency', *History Workshop
Journal*, 86 (2018), 44–66.
[37] Horn, *Life below Stairs*, pp. 211–222.
[38] Anne McClintock, *Imperial Leather: Race, Gender, and Sexuality in the Colonial Contest*
(London: Routledge, 1995), p. 138; Leonore Davidoff, *Worlds Between*, chapter 4.
[39] Anne Summers, 'Public Functions, Private Premises: Female Professional Identity and
the Domestic-Service Paradigm in Britain, c. 1850–1930', in Billie Melman (ed.),
Borderlines: Genders and Identities in War and Peace, 1870–1930 (London: Routledge,
1998), 353–376; Light, *Mrs Woolf and the Servants*, p. 37. Historians of colonial India
have argued that ideas of domesticity and service were central to forming the identities of
coloniser and colonised; Nupur Chaudhuri, 'Memsahibs and Their Servants in
Nineteenth-Century India', *Women's History Review*, 3:4 (1994), 549–562; E. M.
Collingham, *Imperial Bodies: The Physical Experience of the Raj, c. 1800–1947* (Oxford:
Polity Press, 2001), pp. 103–113; Mary A. Procida, *Married to the Empire: Gender Politics
and Imperialism in India, 1883–1947* (Manchester: Manchester University Press, 2002),
chapter 3; Elizabeth Buettner, *Empire Families: Britons and Late Imperial India* (Oxford:
Oxford University Press, 2004); Fae Dussart, 'The Servant/Employer Relationship in
Nineteenth Century India and England', PhD thesis, University College London
(2005); Fae Dussart, '"To Glut a Menial's Grudge": Domestic Servants and the Ilbert
Bill Controversy of 1883', *Journal of Colonialism and Colonial History*, 14:1 (2013), n.p.;
Fae Dussart, '"Strictly Legal Means": Assault, Abuse and the Limits of Acceptable
Behaviour in the Servant–Employer Relationship in Metropole and Colony
1850–1890', in Victoria K. Haskins and Claire Lowrie (eds.), *Colonisation and Domestic
Service: Historical and Contemporary Perspectives* (Abingdon: Routledge, 2015), 153–171.

'servant problem'.[40] This might seem strange to a twenty-first-century audience living through a resurgence in waged domestic labour so evidently structured by unequal global power relations.[41] Yet the racial divisions and migration patterns that characterise today's domestic labour market cannot be mapped onto late nineteenth- and early twentieth-century Britain. Rural to urban migration within and between the 'four nations' was a more significant factor in shaping encounters between servants and employers of different ethnic and cultural backgrounds. Women from Ireland (still under British rule at this time) comprised 2.7 per cent of the British domestic workforce in 1881 and around 4 per cent of indoor domestic servants in the interwar period. Both 'white' and racialised, they could become the targets of racist and anti-Catholic prejudice, and some mistresses were hesitant about having Irish servants live in rather than working for them as charwomen.[42] Large numbers of Welsh servants also travelled to England in search of employment, and were sometimes stereotyped as sloppy in their work.[43]

The 'servant problem' may have been first identified and widely discussed by the employer class, but servants were quick to intervene in these debates and to define the problem as lying not with them but with

[40] The main findings of the above scholarship have been to show how colonisers' ideas about servants were imported into India, shaping the way they related not only to domestic workers but also to Indian people in general, rather than demonstrating how the experience of Empire affected domestic service in Britain; Dussart, 'The Servant/Employer Relationship', p. 28.

[41] Victoria K. Haskins and Claire Lowrie, 'Introduction: Decolonising Domestic Service: Introducing a New Agenda', in Victoria K. Haskins and Claire Lowrie (eds.), *Colonisation and Domestic Service*, 1–18, pp. 4–6. See also Antoinette Fauve-Chamoux (ed.), *Domestic Service and the Formation of European Identity: Understanding the Globalisation of Domestic Work, 16th–21st Centuries* (Bern: Peter Lang, 2004); Dirk Hoerder, Elise van Nederveen Meerkerk and Silke Neunsinger (eds.), *Towards a Global History of Domestic and Caregiving Workers* (Leiden: Brill, 2015).

[42] Bronwen Walter, 'Strangers on the Inside: Irish Women Servants in England, 1881', *Immigrants and Minorities*, 27:2/3 (2009), 279–299; Bronwen Walter, 'Irish Domestic Servants and English National Identity', in Fauve-Chamoux (ed.), *Domestic Service and the Formation of European Identity*, 471–488; Delap, *Knowing Their Place*, p. 38. British working-class Jewish women, also both 'white' and racialised, rarely entered service, but in the 1930s domestic servants' visas became one of the few ways in which Jewish women fleeing the rise of fascism in Europe could gain entry to the United Kingdom; Bronwen Walter, 'Irish/Jewish Diasporic Intersections in the East End of London: Paradoxes and Shared Locations', in M. Prum (ed.), *La Place de l'Autre Paris* (Paris: L'Harmattan Press, 2010), 53–67, p. 59; Rose Holmes, 'Love, Labour, Loss: Women, Refugees and the Servant Crisis in Britain, 1933–1939', *Women's History Review*, 27:2 (2017), 288–309.

[43] Emrys Jones, 'Victorian Heyday', in E. Jones (ed.), *The Welsh in London 1500–2000* (Cardiff: University of Wales Press, 2001), 110–126, pp. 122–126; Mari A. Williams, '"The New London Welsh": Domestic Servants 1918–1939', *Transactions of the Honourable Society Cymmrodorion*, 9 (2003), 135–151; Howell, 'Wales' Hidden Industry', pp. 198–199.

the conditions under which they were compelled to labour. The focus of this book is on politicised servants, especially those who engaged with the women's movement, and they should not be seen as typical of the entire profession. I do, however, maintain that the prevalence of attacks on service by domestic workers themselves, appearing not just in the left-wing press but also in local and sometimes national newspapers in this period, should be seen as indicative of a more generalised and possibly less clearly formulated discontent among the domestic workforce as a whole. When women such as Clementina Black, Catherine Webb and Margaret Bondfield penned articles proclaiming the widespread unpopularity of domestic service, they were basing this conclusion upon their long-standing experience of investigating women's employment, supporting women's trade unions, and campaigning alongside working-class women's organisations such as the Women's Labour League and the Women's Co-operative Guild. To some degree the declining numbers of domestic servants from the late nineteenth century onwards speak for themselves; whenever alternative forms of female employment were available, young women chose them over domestic service. And as office work, shop work and light manufacturing expanded, they began to overtake domestic service as the most common female entry-level job.[44]

I argue that it is possible to see such developments as driven in part by the actions and decisions of domestic workers themselves. This was certainly the view of Jessie Stephen, who, looking back in the late 1970s, maintained that although her efforts to create a domestic workers' union had never succeeded in recruiting but a tiny fraction of the servant population, the efforts of her and fellow comrades ultimately had long-term and widespread effects. They represented only the most visible form of, in Stephen's words, a 'process … going on quietly all the time': conversations in kitchens, pantries and backyards in which servants articulated an increasing 'reluctance to accept Victorian conditions of employment'.[45] As a lifelong socialist and trade unionist Jessie Stephen had her own reasons for wanting to present what she called the 'march of time' in such a manner. Kathlyn Oliver, after a year spent getting the Domestic Workers' Union off the ground, was less optimistic and began to express reservations about servants' capacity to bring about change entirely through self-organisation and unionisation.[46] Yet membership of trade unions is not the only means by which people assert their identities

[44] Horn, *The Rise and Fall of the Victorian Servant*, p. 28; Delap, *Knowing Their Place*, p. 240.
[45] WCML, Stephen, 'Submission Is for Slaves', p. 154.
[46] *Labour Leader* 2 Dec. 1910, p. 765.

as workers or build collective resistance in their workplaces. If we conceptualise overtly political and militant projects such as the Domestic Workers' Union as the tip of the iceberg, or as a barometer of developments in workplace organising and growing class consciousness more broadly defined, then it becomes possible to identify a more collective and more politicised context to the individual acts of resistance recorded in existing historiography.

The 'Servant Problem' as a Feminist Problem

Around 1900, most British women were either members of households that employed servants, or servants themselves. Domestic service was, moreover, the only large-scale industry that took place within the home – one of the very few places in which women could legitimately exercise authority. From the early nineteenth century onwards, the home had been naturalised as woman's sphere and equated with her special moral influence. The role of the mistress, and her supposed duty to protect, educate and elevate the servants who fell under her spiritual stewardship, was central to Christian constructions of middle-class womanhood, which had a very strong influence upon 'first wave' feminism.[47] No wonder, then, that many suffrage activists turned their attention to the 'servant problem'. In 1911 the editors of the National Union of Women's Suffrage Societies' newspaper, the *Common Cause*, went so far as to declare that 'Nothing could be of greater advantage to the status of women than to raise domestic work to a skilled trade with proper conditions ... protected by unions.'[48] Lucy Delap's more general cultural history of twentieth-century service noted in passing how the position of domestic workers was used by feminists as an 'index' by which to attend to the condition of women in society more generally.[49] I explore this in much more depth, arguing that domestic service became the framework for discussion of a wide range of feminist concerns during this period – a vision of female subordination and confinement but also a persistent and discomforting reminder of the domestic sphere from which many, if not all, in the suffrage movement sought liberation. Feminist politics and organisational networks supported women such

---

[47] Summers, 'Public Functions, Private Premises'; Light, *Mrs Woolf and the Servants*, pp. 23–26. For an overview of Christianity's relationship with British feminism, see Laura Schwartz, *Infidel Feminism: Secularism, Religion and Women's Emancipation, England c. 1830–1914*, introduction.
[48] *Common Cause* 19 Oct. 1911, p. 484.   [49] Delap, *Knowing Their Place*, p. 2.

as Clara Collett and the Women's Industrial Council in their investigations into conditions in domestic service.[50] The rights and wrongs of service were widely discussed in the suffrage press, though there was much disagreement among readers and journalists as to both the nature of the 'servant problem' and how to solve it. One of the main issues that the suffrage movement had to wrestle with is neatly illustrated within a single copy of newspapers such as the *Common Cause* or the Women's Social and Political Union's *Votes for Women*, which might carry an article or letter sympathetic to the poorly treated domestic worker in its front matter, while posting in its classified columns advertisements seeking housekeepers or 'a good cook general'.[51]

Middle-class suffrage activists' support for domestic servants was fundamentally complicated by the fact that they, perhaps even more than other women of their class, *needed* servants. Not only did their political work take them out of the home, they were also more likely to be among the increasing numbers of middle-class women entering professional employment. The late nineteenth and early twentieth century witnessed what historians have described as a dramatic change in women's relationship to home and work. Whereas in the mid-nineteenth century it was unusual for middle-class women to work outside the home, by the eve of the First World War they had become an essential part of Britain's workforce.[52] The total number of women in waged work rose from 3,349,320 in 1861 to 4,830,734 in 1911. The greatest increase was in teaching, nursing, shop and clerical work and the civil service, so that by 1911 women made up 32.9 per cent of workers in these professions.[53] Although this period also witnessed the entry of women into well-paid and what had once been exclusively male professions such as medicine and academia, it was the 'white blouse' sector that was the most numerically significant. These non-manual jobs, requiring some level of formal education, were taken up by lower middle-class women benefiting from the expansion of state schooling and the rise of correspondence courses

---

[50] Ellen Mappen, *Helping Women at Work: The Women's Industrial Council 1889–1914* (Dover Newhaven: Hutchinson, 1989); June Hannam, 'Women's Industrial Council (est. 1894–c. 1917)', *Oxford Dictionary of National Biography*, online edn. (Oxford University Press, 2004).

[51] For example, *Votes for Women* 30 Dec. 1910, p. 219, 28 Oct. 1910, p. 63; *Common Cause* 24 Aug. 1911, p. 351.

[52] Lee Holcombe, *Victorian Ladies at Work: Middle-Class Working Women in England and Wales 1850–1914* (Hamden, CT: Archon Books, 1973), p. 20; Ellen Jordan, *The Women's Movement and Women's Employment in Nineteenth Century Britain* (London: Routledge, 1999), p. 5.

[53] Holcombe, *Victorian Ladies at Work*, pp. 213–217.

and evening classes.[54] The 'servant problem' therefore needs to be understood not only in relation to declining numbers of working-class women willing to enter service, but also in the context of growing numbers of middle-class women undertaking work outside the home. Even if we take into account those elements of housekeeping that had become commercialised (more factory-made food and shop-bought clothing, etc.), the overall amount of female labour available to undertake the work of the home was diminishing. At the same time, the growing number of professional women increased demand for workers catering to their domestic needs while they were engaged in paid work. The 'servant problem' thus also emerged because of a reduced reproductive workforce (one whose work reproduces people rather than produces commodities) and should be understood as an economic as well as a political issue. Many factors contributed to these changes in the labour market, including the expansion of commercial and administrative elements of the economy keen to recruit women who were more flexible and cheaper than their male counterparts. Feminism also played an important role as, from the 1860s onwards, the right to education and decently remunerated professional employment became key demands.[55]

The organised women's movement began to emerge in Britain in the second half of the nineteenth century, and also campaigned for legal equality (especially within marriage) and political rights (especially the parliamentary suffrage).[56] The first coordinated national campaign for votes for women was an amendment placed by John Stuart Mill MP to the first Reform Bill of 1866, supported by a public petition signed by 1,499 women and men.[57] In 1867 various local committees came

[54] Gillian Sutherland, *In Search of the New Woman: Middle-Class Women and Work in Britain 1870–1914* (Cambridge: Cambridge University Press, 2015); Helen Glew, *Gender, Rhetoric and Regulation: Women's Work in the Civil Service and the London County Council, 1900–55* (Manchester: Manchester University Press, 2016).

[55] Jordan, *The Women's Movement and Women's Employment*; Jane Lewis, 'Women Clerical Workers in the Late Nineteenth and Early Twentieth Centuries', in Gregory Anderson (ed.), *The White Blouse Revolution: Female Office Workers since 1870* (Manchester: Manchester University Press, 1988), 27–47.

[56] Feminist ideas in Britain can be traced back to Mary Wollstonecraft, *A Vindication of the Rights of Women* (1793), and Owenism and Freethought in the first half of the nineteenth century, but had not yet cohered into an organised movement. Histories of feminism in Britain before 1850 include Barbara Taylor, *Mary Wollstonecraft and the Feminist Imagination* (Cambridge: Cambridge University Press, 2003); Barbara Taylor, *Eve and the New Jerusalem: Socialism and Feminism in the Nineteenth Century* (London: Virago, 1983); Kathryn Gleadle, *The Early Feminists: Radical Unitarians and the Emergence of the Women's Rights Movement, 1831–1851* (Basingstoke: Macmillan, 1995); Barbara Caine, *English Feminism, 1780–1980* (Oxford: Oxford University Press, 1997); Schwartz, *Infidel Feminism*.

[57] Prior to this the Owenites had supported women's right to vote, and some radical unitarians had pushed for it to be included in the Chartists' list of demands in the

together to form the National Society for Women's Suffrage, which began to publish its own *Women's Suffrage Journal* in 1870. An initial point of disagreement was whether to call for votes for married as well as single women, or whether to concede to the opposition's argument that a husband acted as his wife's representative in the public sphere. This was resolved by 1894 Local Government Act, which gave women the right to vote in municipal elections regardless of their marital status.

Attention shifted instead to the economic class of potential women voters. Should the movement call for votes for all women or only for propertied ladies? Was votes for women on equal terms with men the best way to formulate the demand, or should the campaign be for universal suffrage for women and men? From the late 1880s onwards, organisations such as the Women's Franchise League (est. 1889) and the Women's Emancipation Union (est. 1891) had been arguing for a move away from a tactical focus on private negotiations with individual MPs and towards more large-scale public demonstrations with the aim of generating mass support. Despite the growing numbers of working-class and socialist women involved in the suffrage movement by the beginning of the twentieth century, the issue of the property qualification was never resolved, and the 1918 Representation of the People Act not only excluded women under thirty but also a further two million working-class women who did not meet the property qualification.[58] One of the main concerns of this book is to show that many servants were actively involved in the struggle for the vote, although their contribution has been hidden from history, in part due to their erasure from suffrage spectacle and propaganda. Their precarious position within the movement is most definitively indicated by the fact that after 1918 even live-in servants over the new voting age did not qualify for the franchise.

Whereas in the nineteenth century the demand for enfranchisement had been but one of many equally important campaigns pursued by the women's movement, by the twentieth century it had begun to supersede and encompass all other demands.[59] This was in part because campaigners in other areas were beginning to feel they had achieved all they could without having a voice in Parliament. But it was also due to the shift

1830s; Taylor, *Eve and the New Jerusalem*, pp. 180, 218–219, 70; Gleadle, *The Early Feminists*, pp. 140–141.

[58] Cheryl Law, *Suffrage and Power: The Women's Movement 1918–1928* (London: I. B. Tauris, 1997); Anna Muggeridge, 'The Missing Two Million: The Exclusion of Working-Class Women from the 1918 Representation of the People Act', *Revue Française de Civilisation Britannique*, 23:1 (2018), 1–15.

[59] Ray Strachey, 'Changes in Employment', in Ray Strachey (ed.), *Our Freedom and Its Results* (London: Hogarth Press, 1936), 117–172, p. 123.

towards much more publicity-seeking tactics. In 1903 Emmeline Pan-khurst set up the Women's Social and Political Union (WSPU), initially based in Manchester, in the belief that alliance with progressive and labour movement forces, especially the Independent Labour Party, would prove more effective than non-partisan lobbying which, after forty years, had still not achieved its goal. The WSPU was also notable for being women only, whereas the National Union of Women's Suffrage Societies (NUWSS, est. 1897), led by Millicent Garrett Fawcett, was mixed sex. The NUWSS was also regrouping around this time and reconsidering its tactics. Following a conference in 1903 they began to turn away from Parliament towards building support on the ground across constituencies, campaigning for local MPs who promised to vote for female suffrage. In 1905 the WSPU announced its intention to embrace so-called militant tactics, ushering in a mass campaign of civil disobedience that lasted until the outbreak of the First World War. Militancy ranged from breaking up meetings of male political parties to 'rushing' Parliament, smashing windows, acid-bombing letterboxes, refusing to pay taxes, dodging the 1911 census, and, in a few cases after 1910, attacking stately homes and setting fire to churches. The NUWSS remained committed to 'constitutional' or 'law-abiding' practices, and after 1910 began to strengthen its ties with the Labour Party and other 'democratic suffragists', in contrast to the WSPU which formally separated from the Independent Labour Party in 1907. Historians have cautioned against too polarised an understanding of militants versus constitutionalists, since direct action tactics such as mass public meetings and demonstrations could be traced back before the WSPU to earlier generations of radical suffragists, while many individuals remained members of both the WSPU and the NUWSS. Other national suffrage organisations included the militant Women's Freedom League, founded in 1907 as a more democratic split from the WSPU and supported by Hannah Mitchell, and the People's Suffrage Federation, founded in 1909 as a campaign for full adult suffrage and supported by Kathlyn Oliver.[60] By 1913 suffrage societies affiliated to one or other of these

---

[60] The historiography of the suffrage movement is vast. The overview provided here is indebted to Sandra Stanley Holton, *Feminism and Democracy: Women's Suffrage and Reform Politics in Britain 1900–1918* (Cambridge: Cambridge University Press, 1986). For the WSPU, see the work of June Purvis, especially *Emmeline Pankhurst: A Biography* (London: Routledge, 2002) and *Christabel Pankhurst: A Biography* (London: Routledge, 2018). For Britain beyond England, see Leah Leneman, *A Guid Cause: The Women's Suffrage Movement in Scotland* (Aberdeen: Aberdeen University Press, 1991); Ryland Wallace, *The Women's Suffrage Movement in Wales* (Cardiff: University of Wales Press, 2009). Other works will be referred to throughout in the context of their specific contributions.

organisations existed in almost every town across Britain, with the Suffrage Annual recording 460 branches of the NUWSS, 90 affiliated to the WSPU, 61 to the WFL and 68 to the Conservative and Unionist Women's Franchise Association (est. 1908).[61]

This book focuses on the suffrage movement but situates it as part of a broader tradition of 'first wave' feminism, examining not just suffrage societies but also a wider range of women's organisations supportive of, but not directly dedicated to, women's enfranchisement. In the early years of the twentieth century the struggle for the vote came to represent a much more general support for women's rights and dominated the overall identity of the feminist movement, even while wider campaigns continued. Suffrage societies developed in dialogue and shared members with other political networks, including those concerned with women's position in the workplace and/or working-class women's organisations. This relationship fostered the diversification and rapid expansion of the women's movement, and the early twentieth-century upsurge in suffrage activism coincided with the high point of 'first wave' feminism as whole. The words 'feminism' and 'feminist' were not coined in English until the 1890s, and did not come into common use until the early 1900s. Not all suffrage supporters would have called themselves feminists, and a few feminists sought to disassociate themselves from suffragism.[62] I, like a number of historians, nonetheless find it useful to use the term 'feminism' more broadly, if anachronistically, to describe an awareness of women's structural oppression and a desire to act collectively to change that. My use of the term 'first wave' feminism is intended primarily as chronological shorthand to refer to a period of women's rights activism beginning in the 1860s and finishing in 1918. It is not a label that can be usefully deployed to describe a particular type of feminism nor any one political agenda, since 'first wave' feminism was an ideologically diverse and eclectic movement that encouraged debate and co-operation amongst different currents. Nor does my focus on the 'first wave' imply that feminist activity ended in Britain after 1918. The war and the Representation of the People Act marked an important watershed, since, without the unifying demand for the vote, women's organisations were compelled to reorganise and reorientate. Nevertheless, a variety of

---

[61] A.J.R., *The Suffrage Annual and Women's Who's Who* (London: Stanley Paul, 1913).

[62] Nancy F. Cott, *The Grounding of Modern Feminism* (New Haven: Yale University Press, 1987); Karen Offen, 'Defining Feminism: A Comparative Historical Approach', in Gisela Bock and Susan James (eds.), *Beyond Equality and Difference: Citizenship, Feminist Politics and Female Subjectivity* (London: Routledge, 1992), 69–88; Caine, *English Feminism*; Lucy Delap, 'Feminist and Anti-Feminist Encounters in Edwardian Britain', *Historical Research*, 78:201 (August 2005), 377–399.

campaign work continued in the interwar period, with some feminists focusing on women's rights as mothers while others emphasised the need for equal pay and the right to work.[63]

By examining how the suffrage movement was enmeshed within this wider political context, this book is less concerned with the campaign for the vote – there are many fine histories of this already – but with the movement's wider interests and intellectual culture. Suffrage was not a single-issue campaign. The suffrage press provided a platform for women's trade unionism, religious debate, reflection upon female sexuality and same-sex desire, women's housing, and any number of legal and personal abuses against women. It is entirely wrong, therefore, to portray either 'first wave' feminism or the suffrage movement as solely concerned with formal political and legal reform. As much as the Women's Liberation Movement seventy years later, 'first wave' feminists understood that the personal was political and set about transforming the conditions of everyday life. My interest is in how the British women's suffrage movement grappled with the 'everyday' problem of housework, of who should do it, and how it related to the forging of a newly emancipated womanhood. The 'servant problem' was frequently attributed to a wider and more fundamental problem of housework. Chapters 3 and 4 examine a diverse range of feminist thinking on the home, housework as labour and the feminist work ethic. Such debates offered servants a political vocabulary with which to describe their particular experience of exploitation, while at the same time making it difficult for them to lay claim to a feminist identity. Both servants and mistresses found themselves caught between their wish, on the one hand, to re-value domestic labour and, on the other, to liberate themselves from such work. Servants resisted simplistic analyses of housework as women's shared oppression, just as their involvement in the struggle for the vote complicated attempts to represent it as a cross-class movement by bringing the question of women's competing class interests uncomfortably close to home.

Servants and the Working Class

The 'servant problem' also emerged in the context of an upsurge in labour militancy beginning with the New Unionism of the 1880s and culminating in the Great Unrest between 1907 and 1914. Between 1888 and 1918, trade unions grew at a faster rate than any other time

---

[63] For a seminal critique of waves theory, and especially the idea that little happened between the 'first' and the 'second wave', see Dale Spender, *There's Always Been a Women's Movement This Century* (London: Pandora Press, 1983).

in their history – an expansion that incorporated 'unskilled' and previously unorganised workers into general unions made up of multiple trades.[64] Women played an important part in the unrest, going on strike and joining trade unions in greater numbers than ever before. After 1906 much of this activity occurred under the auspices of the National Federation of Women Workers, a general trade union for women.[65] Many people at the time understood the 'servant problem' in relation to this rise in worker militancy. In 1916 the Women's Industrial Council's report into the conditions of domestic service concluded that:

> Although domestic servants often speak sadly of themselves as a class apart, they are by no means cut off from the remainder of the industrial community. The fathers and brothers of many of them have been on strike in recent years, and they have read the newspapers. Industrial unrest … [has] reached the minds of those servants who think, and … helped to focus the resentment of those who have room in their minds only for their own grievances.[66]

In placing domestic service at the centre of a history of pre–First World War workers' militancy, this book seeks to contribute to a rewriting of the history of the British working class. Until recently, domestic servants were seldom the subject of more than a few lines in labour movement histories, and when they do appear they have often been portrayed as cut off from wider class-conscious communities of working people.[67] This has been attributed to the relative isolation of domestic servants working alone in private houses and the tendency to identify with the interests of

---

[64] Mary Davis, '1880–1914: TUC History Online', www.unionhistory.info/timeline/1880_1914.php.

[65] Deborah Thom, 'The Bundle of Sticks: Women, Trade Unionists and Collective Organisations before 1918', in Angela V. John (ed.), *Unequal Opportunities: Women's Employment in England 1800–1918* (Oxford: Basil Blackwell, 1986), 261–289; Cathy Hunt, *The National Federation of Women Workers, 1906–1921* (Basingstoke: Palgrave Macmillan, 2014), pp. 49–54. See also Barbara Drake, *Women in Trade Unions* (London: Virago, 1984 [first published 1920]), chapter 4; Sheila Lewenhak, *Women and Trade Unions: An Outline History of Women in the British Trade Union Movement* (New York: St. Martin's Press, 1977); Gerry Holloway, *Women and Work in Britain since 1840* (London: Routledge, 2005); Sarah Boston, *Women Workers and the Trade Unions* (London: Lawrence & Wishart, 2015).

[66] Butler, *Report of the Women's Industrial Council*, p. 11. See also Amy Bulley, 'Domestic Service: A Social Study', *Westminster Review*, 135:2 (1891), 177–186, pp. 177–178.

[67] For a discussion of this historiography, see Holloway, *Women and Work*, p. 20; Light, *Mrs Woolf and the Servants*, p. 3; Steedman, *Labours Lost*, p. xv; Anna Clark, 'E. P. Thompson and Domestic Service', *Labor: Studies in Working-Class History of the Americas*, 10:3 (2013), 41–44; Selina Todd, 'People Matter', *History Workshop Journal*, 77 (Autumn 2013), 259–265. For a rare exception to the general exclusion of domestic servants from labour histories, see Bressey, 'Black Women and Work in England'.

wealthy and paternalistic employers rather than their own class.[68] Such an assessment, however, owes as much to the way in which the working class has been defined historically, using an industrial model that excludes domestic labour, as it owes to domestic workers' failure to organise on a mass scale. Cooking, cleaning and caring took place in the private sphere of the home, (re-)producing people rather than commodities, and have therefore frequently been defined as 'non-productive'. The failure by labour historians to acknowledge such work reflects a much wider disinclination to define domestic labour as *real* work, ensuring that it was, and still is, undervalued and underpaid.[69] Feminists have long agitated for both waged and unwaged domestic work to be recognised as such, and this book likewise argues for historians to reconfigure the industrial paradigm (which has focused on white male factory workers) when writing the history of Britain's working class.[70]

Feminism and the Servant Problem is part of a recent historiographical effort to reconnect the history of servants with broader developments in labour regulation and workplace rights.[71] Chapter 1 offers a micro-history of servants' working conditions and the labour process in suffrage households, examining the interactions between the 'emotional' and the 'economic' in the mistress–maid relationship. Chapter 5 provides the first in-depth history of the Domestic Workers' Union of Great Britain and Ireland, which requires us to radically rethink preconceived notions of servants as largely untouched by working-class militancy. The Domestic Workers' Union sought to carve out a space within the broader labour

---

[68] Brian Harrison, 'Tape Recorders and the Teaching of History', *Oral History*, 1:2 (1972), 3–10, pp. 3–4; Lewenhak, *Women and Trade Unions*, p. 181; Mark Ebery and Brian Preston, *Domestic Service in Late Victorian and Edwardian England, 1871–1914* (London: George Over, 1976), p. 99.

[69] Selina Todd, 'Domestic Service and Class Relations in Britain 1900–1950', *Past and Present*, 203 (2009), 181–204, p. 183; Silvia Federici, *Revolution at Point Zero: Housework, Reproduction and Feminist Struggle* (Oakland, CA: PM Press, 2012), p. 71.

[70] The most forceful arguments for the inclusion of household workers within definitions of an economically productive working class were made in the 1970s by the Wages for Housework movement in the United Kingdom, United States and Italy; Mariarosa Dalla Costa and Selma James, *The Power of Woman and the Subversion of the Community* (Bristol: Falling Wall Press, 1975); Silvia Federici, *Wages against Housework* (New York: Falling Wall Press, 1975); Federici, *Revolution at Point Zero*; Selma James, *Sex, Race, and Class – The Perspective of Winning: A Selection of Writings 1952–2011* (Oakland, CA: PM Press, 2012). For the marginalisation of women workers in British labour history, see Mary Davis (ed.), *Class and Gender in British Labour History: Renewing the Debate (or Starting It?)* (Pontypool: Merlin Press, 2011), 1–11.

[71] In addition to the work by Delap, Dussart, Light, Todd and Steedman cited throughout, see Eileen Boris and Premilla Nadasen (eds.), Special Issue: 'Historicizing Domestic Labor: Resistance and Organizing', *International Labor and Working-Class History*, 88 (2015).

movement. These servants viewed themselves not as victims but as workers. They saw their grievances as extending beyond the individual mistress–maid relationship to connect with wider experiences of workplace exploitation. The union received a mixed response from male trade unionists, who highlighted various perceived and real obstacles to domestic worker organising, from ideas of servants as passive, to the refusal to see the home as a workplace, to the difficulties in uniting a dispersed workforce kept under the watchful eye of the employer. The history of the Domestic Workers' Union demonstrates that although it was difficult to organise workers in the 'private' sphere of the home, the impetus for collective struggle could extend beyond the 'public' workplaces of the factory, docks and office.

Class, as a historical and political category, has been both challenged and transformed over the last four decades or so, and defining such an ideologically freighted and contested concept is far from straightforward. Socialist feminists, from the late 1960s onwards, were among the first to critique the reductive deployment of class as a unitary concept. As research into women's history gained ground, numerous scholars began to point out what was becoming glaringly obvious: that women's experience could not be neatly encapsulated within or subsumed by male-orientated definitions of class.[72] Not only were class identities and experiences far more diverse than had previously been acknowledged, they were also cut across with competing systems of oppression. The working class was not only structured by economic forces from without, but also shaped by power struggles from within.[73] This feminist critique overlapped with and gave political bite to poststructuralist theories also gaining influence in the Anglophone world in the late twentieth century. The idea that language structures meaning, and that, following this, identities are contingent and unstable, not only presented a fundamental challenge to the structuralist Marxist view of class as an objective economic category, but also undermined the until then highly influential approach of New Left historian E. P. Thompson, who argued that class should be understood as a dynamic relationship between two clearly

---

[72] Key contributions to this debate include Judith L. Newton, Mary P. Ryan and Judith R. Walkowitz (eds.), *Sex and Class in Women's History* (London: Routledge & Kegan Paul, 1983); Joan Scott, *Gender and the Politics of History* (New York: Columbia University Press, 1988). These feminist interventions must be understood alongside parallel and overlapping moves within Black and postcolonial politics to critique and expand more orthodox Marxist understandings of the proletariat to include, among others, peasants, slum-dwellers and 'subalterns'.

[73] Anna Clark, *The Struggle for the Breeches: Gender and the Making of the British Working Class* (Berkeley: University of California Press, 1995).

delineated groups of people. Poststructuralists also questioned the assumption (Marxist in origin but implicit within most of the social history of the 1960s) that class consciousness emerged, if not naturally or inevitably, then at least in relation to certain economic conditions and one's location vis-à-vis the means of production.[74]

This was the theoretical and political climate in which I was trained as a historian in the first decade of the twenty-first century, and *Feminism and the Servant Problem* owes a great deal to the nuances and subtleties of feminist and poststructuralist cultural history. But I am also part of a generation of scholars who came of age not in the postmodern 1990s but during the global economic crisis of the late 2000s. Some of us are now keen to revisit categories such as class, work and materiality and more open to considering them in a dialectical relationship with 'culture' and 'discourse' rather than in opposition.[75] My work is therefore informed by heterodox modes of Marxist thought rather than a renunciation of it. It draws especially upon the work of a variety of Marxist-feminists and socialist feminists who have argued that capitalist exploitation was not limited to the realm of production, that 'capitalism also depends on domestic labour' and that the workplace of the home should be understood as a site of struggle.[76]

Throughout this book I refer to those women who employed servants as 'middle-class' and those women who worked for them as 'working-class'. The distinction between these classes was, however, never as straightforward as this shorthand implies. Even many of the late nineteenth- and early twentieth-century socialist thinkers who feature in this book and who broadly subscribed to a primarily economic definition of the proletariat (those with nothing to sell but their labour power) versus the bourgeoisie (those who profited from that labour) accepted that this was not a wholly adequate description of the social reality. Likewise, although the distinction between manual labour and intellectual labour, or between those who 'dirtied hands and face and those who did not', was a crucial dividing line in this period, there were exceptions to and gradations within these two groups.[77] The so-called middle or professional classes overlapped at one

---

[74] For useful overviews of these critiques, see Geoff Eley and Keith Nield, *The Future of Class in History: What's Left of the Social?* (Ann Arbor: University of Michigan Press, 2007); Ulrika Holgersson, *Class: Feminist and Cultural Perspectives* (Abingdon: Routledge, 2017).

[75] Eileen Boris, 'Class Returns', *Journal of Women's History*, 25:4 (Winter 2013), 74–87.

[76] This current extended well beyond the Wages for Housework movement, which was an extremely contentious demand and certainly not accepted by all Marxist and/or socialist feminists who otherwise argued for the value of reproductive labour.

[77] Sutherland, *In Search of the New Woman*, p. 89.

end of the spectrum with the propertied classes, living off a combination of financial investment and comfortable incomes, while at the other end white collar workers in offices, shops and state administration had an often precarious hold on economic security and social standing and might even earn less than the best paid factory workers. Levels of education and cultural practices thus also played a part in distinguishing groups of similar income levels from each other.[78] Significant variations also existed within the working class – the labour aristocracy in the skilled heavy industries having considerably better standards of living than the sweated workers of London's East End, for example, and regional variations were part of this. Among women, these class distinctions were complicated further, especially for those who risked losing caste and/or economic stability through their involvement in the suffrage movement.[79] Many of the mistresses featured in this book were not necessarily wealthy women, but were compelled to work for a living, earning modest incomes as teachers, social workers or secretaries, or as journalists, political organisers, writers and artists.[80] The suffrage movement often elided distinctions between these kinds of women and women manual workers, referring to them all as 'working women'. Relatively low-paid 'lady workers' employed servants nonetheless, even when they struggled to afford them, and co-operative housekeeping was frequently framed as a solution to their particular domestic needs. Lower middle-class wives, relying upon their husband's limited income, were often able to afford only a single servant and would still have had to undertake a significant share of the housework themselves.

Employing servants was still widely understood as a key indicator of class position, and the institution of domestic service functioned around perceived, if sometimes overdetermined, class difference.[81] In 1901 the

---

[78] Eric Hobsbawm, *The Age of Empire 1875–1914* (London: Weidenfeld & Nicolson, 1987), pp. 180–184.

[79] Krista Cowman, '"Incipient Toryism"? The Women's Social and Political Union And the Independent Labour Party, 1903–1914', *History Workshop Journal*, 53 (2002), 128–148, p. 133; Krista Cowman, *Women of the Right Spirit: Paid Organisers of the Women's Social and Political Union, 1904–1918* (Manchester: Manchester University Press, 2007), pp. 15–16, 19–20, 23.

[80] Sutherland, *In Search of the New Woman*, pp. 118, 126–128.

[81] Horn suggests that by the early twentieth century the minimum annual income needed to keep a resident general servant was £300. Other historians have found instances of some working-class people, or lower middle-class shopkeepers for example, who also bought in household help; Horn, *The Rise and Fall of the Victorian Servant*, pp. 17, 30; Higgs, 'Domestic Servants and Households', p. 201; Pooley, 'Domestic Servants and Their Urban Employers', pp. 405, 411–412; Howell, 'Wales' Hidden Industry', p. 186. Within working-class communities, many 'interdependent' service relationships existed whereby neighbours and strangers might periodically help each other out with housework and childcare (sometimes for a wage, sometimes not) or rent out food and lodgings to people of their own class, thus creating 'tangled relationships which cannot easily be distinguished between master/mistress versus servant or landlady and lodger';

social investigator Benjamin Seebohm Rowntree cited 'servant keeping' as 'marking the division between the working classes and those of a higher social scale'.[82] Leonore Davidoff's work on the nineteenth century has shown the central role servants played in protecting the bourgeois subject and the middle-class home from both the literal and metaphorical contamination of the working world, tradesmen, the street and their own bodily functions.[83] Judy Giles and Alison Light argue that the mistress–maid relationship continued to crystallise and symbolise class differences between women into the interwar period.[84] Yet the work of domestic servants was not *only* symbolic, and to treat it thus would be to approach them, as Marx did, as the baubles of bourgeois luxury, 'flunkies and lickspittles', different to and separate from the true proletariat.[85] Instead, an approach that recognises domestic labour as fundamental to the survival of a household and as underpinning the capitalist economy requires consideration not just of the ideological or cultural meanings of class that were embedded in the mistress–maid relationship but also of how servants' labour enabled their employers to undertake 'productive' work outside the home.[86] In Chapters 1 and 2, I pay close attention to the actual work, the day-to-day labour, undertaken by servants employed by the Blathwayt family, and trace how it contributed not only to the smooth running of the household but also to the sustainability and success of the suffrage movement. This offers another way of considering the class dynamics of the suffrage movement, in terms of not just the social backgrounds of the individuals involved but also the classed division of labour that enabled it to function.

Sources

One of the most challenging things about writing this book has been hearing servants' points of view amidst the cacophony of middle-class voices that dominated public discussion of the 'servant problem'. Working

---

Davidoff et al., *The Family Story*, pp. 160–161. Working-class employers are very rarely mentioned in debates on the 'servant problem'.

[82] Quoted in Judy Giles, *The Parlour and the Suburb: Domestic Identities, Class, Femininity and Modernity* (Oxford: Berg, 2004), pp. 94–95.

[83] Davidoff, *Worlds Between*, chapter 4.

[84] Giles, *The Parlour and the Suburb*; Alison Light, *Forever England: Femininity, Literature and Conservatism between the Wars* (London: Routledge, 1991); Light, *Mrs Woolf and the Servants*.

[85] Karl Marx, *Grundrisse* (Harmondsworth: Penguin, 1973 [first published 1939]), pp. 414, 397–398; Karl Marx, *Capital: A Critique of Political Economy*, 3 vols. (London: Penguin Books, 1976 [first published 1867]), vol. I, pp. 573–574. See also Laura Schwartz, 'Servants', in *Handbook of Marxism* (London: Sage, in press).

[86] Higgs, 'Domestic Servants and Households', pp. 203–205.

people were far less likely to write and certainly to publish their autobiographies, and those who did were mainly men. The memoirs that I draw upon of Louise Jermy's, Hannah Mitchell's, Emma Sproson's and Jessie Stephen's time in service are unusual.[87] A number of women who had worked as servants in the Edwardian period were interviewed in the 1970s and 1980s as part of oral history projects, but these did not focus on the politicised servants featured here.[88] Diary writing was a very common activity for middle-class women throughout the nineteenth and early twentieth century, and the diaries of Mary and Emily Blathwayt have provided invaluable insights into everyday life in a suffrage household from the point of view of the mistress. It would have been very difficult for a domestic servant to find the time and space to keep a detailed written record of daily life, and I have no equivalent source for servants.[89] Instead, letters written by domestic workers to local, radical and feminist newspapers provide a rare and valuable opportunity to hear militant servants describing their experiences in their own words, writing in the moment rather than as autobiographers or interviewees recalling the distant past.

In this book I examine a number of debates on the 'servant problem' that raged across several issues of a particular publication and attracted large numbers of correspondents, apparently spontaneously provoked by an initial letter or article. Such letters must of course be approached critically. The directness of tone can be seductive, and for good reason: there must have been an exhilaration in finding a public platform to express one's resentment at petty humiliations which, especially for a general servant working alone, had to be endured mainly in silence. But we should not read them simply as transparent and 'authentic' expressions of servants' experiences. They were also rhetorical performances, and sometimes themes or particular phrases in one letter were picked up and repeated in subsequent letters, woven into personal accounts. This

---

[87] Jane McDermid, 'The Making of a "Domestic" Life: Memories of a Working Woman', *Labour History Review* 73:3 (Dec. 2008), 253–268, pp. 253–254. Of 783 working-class autobiographies collected for people born between 1790 and 1900, only 23 were by women who describe their time in service; John Burnett, David Vincent and David Mayall (eds.), *The Autobiography of the Working Class: An Annotated, Critical Bibliography*, 3 vols. (Brighton: Harvester Press, 1984), vol. I.

[88] For an overview of oral histories of servants, see Delap, *Knowing Their Place*, pp. 22–25. Two interviews (one recording, one transcript) with Jessie Stephen were undertaken by historians of feminism, and focus more on her suffrage activism than on her trade union organising; The Women's Library at the London School of Economics, London, 'Oral Evidence on the Suffragist and Suffragette Movements: The Brian Harrison Interviews' (1974–1981), interview with Jessie Stephen (1977), Disc 32–33, 8SUF/B/157; Susie Fleming and Gloden Dallas, 'Jessie', *Spare Rib*, 32 (Feb. 1975), 10–13.

[89] Cullwick's diaries are exceptional in this as in so many other ways; Liz Stanley (ed.), *The Diaries of Hannah Cullwick, Victorian Housemaid* (London: Virago, 1983).

does not make them any less genuine but it does remind us that servants' sense of grievance, understandings of their exploitation and identification with a wider working class were forged not only in the workplace but also in discursive forums where the less-initiated could emulate more experienced and politicised domestic workers. Because most servants' letters were anonymous – another indication of the close surveillance and regulation of their conduct – it is impossible to reconstruct a full demographic portrait of these correspondents. It is therefore difficult to use them to gain an overall sense of the type of domestic servant who was more likely to, first, dislike their work, and, second, want to publicly communicate that dislike to both the employer class and fellow domestic servants. Nevertheless, the recently available 1911 census data have made it possible to trace a few servants who might otherwise have remained merely a name on a piece of paper, to find out where they were born, the occupations of their parents, where they worked and who employed them. On occasion I have discovered that prominent middle-class suffrage activists were often supported in their work and possibly even influenced by equally politically committed servants.[90]

Many of my other sources have to be read against the grain in order to piece together a picture of servants active in a movement whose presence was rarely remarked upon in official suffrage propaganda. Although police and magistrates' reports recording the occupation of women arrested for militant activity identify a few individuals, it is the absence of representations of servants in suffrage pageantry and imagery that is most revealing. Instead, I have had to go 'behind the scenes', to look at suffrage-supporting households via domestic ephemera such as log books and timetables, mistresses' diaries and some correspondence between servants and employers, to reveal the political contributions of servants. Thinking about how domestic labour has been conceptualised as non-productive, how in not producing commodities it does not leave a permanent mark on our material culture nor a clearly identifiable economic outcome, and how its unobtrusive performance is a measure of the domestic worker's skill and efficiency has informed my methodology. It prompted me to look for the implicit politicisation of housework in the margins of the suffrage press: in advertisements, household tips,

---

[90] The 1911 census has limitations as a suffrage source, since a number of activists (especially in the Women's Freedom League and WSPU) either evaded or resisted the census as part of a national campaign of civil disobedience. On occasion servants also participated in this, although it is difficult to establish to what degree they were acting under pressure from their employers; Jill Liddington, *Vanishing for the Vote: Suffrage, Citizenship and the Battle for the Census* (Manchester: Manchester University Press, 2014), p. 229.

competitions and short stories as well as in the more overtly 'political' content of these periodicals. The final chapter on co-operative house-keeping, and the attempt to uncover the experiences of domestic servants who undertook this supposedly more advanced and egalitarian form of domestic labour, took me away from the more fluent feminist debates about the nature of housework and the possibility of unionising domestic workers, attending instead to the built environment, architectural plans and household technology.

The variety of methods necessary to investigating a group who have been so obscured in the traditional historical record has resulted in my fusing a number of different historiographical approaches. Micro-history and the history of everyday life have been useful in finding a way into, and arguing for the political salience of, the particularities of the domestic sphere. Labour history's traditional interest in day-to-day working prac-tices, conditions and living standards prompted me to re-examine the proliferation of data collected about working-class women's lives by feminist social reformers (in many ways the pioneers of sociology and social history) at the turn of the century. The investigations conducted by, for example, the Women's Industrial Council, as well as the docu-mentary style of accounts in the suffrage press, reveal as much about the middle-class gaze as they do about their subjects. Nevertheless, some servants used the upsurge of interest in their social position as an oppor-tunity, and perhaps even provocation, to put forward their own point of view. I therefore approach the feminist public sphere not as a coherent and homogenous discourse, but one that straddled suffrage organisa-tions, the feminist and radical press and working-class women's organ-isations, incorporating many conflicting viewpoints as different perspectives and a range of political analyses jostled to be heard. This book is in part a history of feminist thought, an intellectual history concerned with tracing the formation and legacies of ideas such as 'emancipation' and 'work'. My primary interest is what happened when different women attempted to live these ideas, to put them into practice in their daily lives, and what new social and political forms and relation-ships they helped to bring to life.

1 The 'Servant Problem' and the Suffrage Home

> Wanted. – Good plain COOK, in small family where House Parlour-maid is kept. Simple cooking. Separate bedroom and servants' bathroom. Much personal liberty. Wages, £24 and washing. No beer. Excellent references required. – Apply, with full particulars, to Mrs Blathwayt, Eagle House, Batheaston, Bath.
>
> Advertisement placed in classified section of *Votes for Women* (1908)[1]

In the autumn of 1908 Elsie Harris, cook to the Blathwayt family of Bath, handed in her notice in anticipation of her coming marriage. 'We are all sorry', wrote the mistress of the house, Emily Blathwayt, knowing only too well how hard it would be to find a suitable replacement. Between 1907 and 1913, the period when the Blathwayt family were actively involved in the suffrage movement, fifteen servants passed through their household despite their only employing two live-in servants at any one time. Some stayed for a number of years, others were dismissed after a few days or weeks for a variety of reasons ('untruthfulness', 'staying out late at night', 'cookery uncertain', 'rheumatic knee' and 'dirty saucepans'), while others left of their own accord. Emily Blathwayt devoted considerable time and energy to finding her servants, taking recommendations from friends and acquaintances, applying to servants' registries and advertising in the local and national press. On each occasion she was required to contact the new servant's former employer for a 'character' (reference), while providing her own for the servant who was leaving.[2] By the time of Elsie Harris's departure, Emily Blathwayt had many years' experience of this aspect of the 'servant problem', and duly set about looking for a new cook. Her daughter, Mary Blathwayt, helped with the search, paying 2s. 6d. to place an advertisement in *Votes for Women*, which Emily Blathwayt believed to be 'the first of the kind in that paper'.[3]

---

[1] *Votes for Women* 29 Oct. 1908, p. 85.
[2] Gloucestershire Archives, Gloucester, Blathwayt Family of Dyrham Collection (hereafter GA), E. M. Blathwayt, 'Household Log Book', D2659/24/45.
[3] GA, E. M. Blathwayt, 'Diary', 21 Oct. 1908, p. 112; 28 Oct. 1908, p. 116; 3 Nov. 1908, p. 122, D2659/24/11.

Mistresses found the incessant round of searching for, hiring, training-up and getting used to a new servant, only for so many of them to move on after a short period of time, extremely irksome. Servants, on the other hand, endured poor wages, uncomfortable living and working conditions and unwarranted restriction of personal freedom. One 'Greenwich domestic' wrote to the *Common Cause* in 1911 to present this servants' view of the 'servant problem': 'I am 35 years of age and I have quite a struggle to get a wage of £26 per annum ... I wonder how women getting much better salaries would like to be boxed up in uncongenial surround-ings and to be unable to choose their friends ...?'[4] Were the suffrage-supporting mistresses reading this letter any better than the average employer? This chapter examines the 'servant problem' as it manifested in the homes of suffrage activists Mary and Emily Blathwayt of Bath, Helen Clark of Street and Mary Talbot Muirhead of London and Bir-mingham. Their feminism does seem to have encouraged a somewhat more progressive approach to servant keeping, and these mistresses sometimes shared suffrage sympathies and even occasionally forged friendships with their maids. Yet this did not prevent them from approaching the employment relationship as ultimately one of economic exchange. I therefore argue that attention to the personal, intimate and affective histories of domestic service should not obscure the significance of the wage relation with which they were always intertwined.

The Servant's View of the 'Servant Problem'

One of the most common complaints about service was its long hours, with time off usually limited to half a day on Sunday and a two-week holiday once a year. It was normal for servants to work a sixteen-hour day and many resented always being on call, at the mercy of parsimonious employers keen to ensure that every minute of their servant's time was put to good use.[5] Servants were the only kind of manual worker not protected by the Truck Acts, which outlawed the payment of wages in kind because of the potential for this system to be abused by employers.[6] Food and lodgings were considered a part of their wage, and servants frequently found these to be substandard. They were forced to sleep in

---

[4] *Common Cause* 28 Sept. 1911, p. 432.
[5] C. Violet Butler, *Domestic Service: An Enquiry by the Women's Industrial Council* (New York: Garland, 1980 [first published 1916]), p. 14.
[6] Einat Albin, 'From "Domestic Servant" to "Domestic Worker"', in J. Fudge, S. McCrystal and K. Sankaran (eds.), *Challenging the Legal Boundaries of Work Regulation* (London: Hart Publishing, 2012), 231–250, pp. 236–237. Acts were passed in 1831, 1887 and 1896.

attics and basements, sometimes in the kitchen or, in Jessie Stephen's case, a cupboard. Employers often purchased lower quality food for their servants than that enjoyed by their own family.[7] The 1916 Women's Industrial Council investigation also reported that large numbers of servants were prohibited from sharing bathrooms with their employers.[8] When Jessie Stephen worked for Lord and Lady Chisholm she was forced to heat water to wash with in a copper in the kitchen, despite the house having two fully plumbed bathrooms.[9] Even Edith Ayrton Zangwill, a prominent supporter of votes for women who professed great affection for her general maid, Florence Isabel, wrote as if it was normal to allow her to only use the bathroom as a special treat.[10]

Once excessively long hours, poor quality food and dismal lodgings were taken into account, servants' wages did not compare well to those of factory workers or shop assistants. Grace Neal, a cook general and General Secretary of the Domestic Workers' Union, calculated in 1911 that the average servant was paid only about 1d. per hour, although this was questioned by some employers on the basis that servants supposedly had periods of rest during the working day.[11] It is hard to generalise about wage levels due to considerable variation existing across not just grades of servants, but also age and region. Clara Collet's *Report on the Money Wages of Indoor Domestic Servants* (1899) found the average annual wage of a servant under sixteen working in London to be £7.9 compared with a wage of £27.8 averaged by a domestic servant over the age of forty, whereas their equivalents across the rest of England and Wales earned £7.1 and £24.7, respectively. In 1908 a large country house in Gloucestershire, employing a number of servants, paid their upper house-maids £30 per year and their under house-maids £19 and £20.[12] That same year, fifteen-year-old Jessie Stephen was paid £9 6s. in her first job in Glasgow, though she claimed she had demanded 6s. a month more than the average servant of her age due to the trade union principles instilled in her by her father. Stephen also recalled how some of the young women who entered service straight from orphanages were paid only room and board. This may have been something of an

[7] Working Class Movement Library (hereafter WCML), Salford, Jessie Stephen, 'Submission Is for Slaves' (unpublished manuscript), p. 33.
[8] Butler, *Report of the Women's Industrial Council*, p. 45.
[9] WCML, Stephen, 'Submission Is for Slaves', p. 30.
[10] *Freewoman* 23 Nov. 1911, p. 12.
[11] *Common Cause* 19 Oct. 1911, p. 486. Jessie Stephen claimed that 'the average wage of the domestic servant worked out at ¾ d. to 1 ½ d. per hour'; *Glasgow Herald* 16 Oct. 1913, p. 10.
[12] Pamela Horn, *The Rise and Fall of the Victorian Servant* (Stroud: Alan Sutton Publishing, 1990), pp. 145–146. These figures refer to the cash wage received on top of room and board.

exaggeration, since some general servants coming from workhouses are recorded as having been paid £2 10s. per year in the 1890s, while in London the Poor Law authorities began to insist upon a minimum of £5. Stephen's claim would hold, however, if she was referring to girls still in care sent out daily to work unpaid for local families, or to unmarried mothers encouraged to work for free for a year or two as recompense for the institutional support they had received during their pregnancy.[13] Servants were usually expected to pay for their own uniforms and, because they were often paid annually or quarterly rather than weekly, they often had very little ready cash and were particularly vulnerable to the threat of withholding their wages if relations with their employers broke down.[14] Servants often gave a large portion of their wage to their families, while the imperative to save, to support themselves in times of sickness and old age, further reduced their spending power. Until the National Insurance Act of 1911, servants were usually dismissed from their posts if they remained ill for longer than a week or so, while only in the rarest of cases were servants provided with a pension. Before the introduction of state pensions in 1908, former domestic servants made up a large proportion of elderly female workhouse inmates.[15]

At the turn of the twentieth century, local, radical and suffrage papers became forums in which a newly literate generation of servants publicised their dissatisfaction and a confirmed sense of injustice. They complained that their employers failed to recognise them as fully human, denying them basic needs – such as being able to eat one's meals in peace – on the basis that "'she's only the servant'".[16] In 1913 a housemaid wrote to the *Glasgow Herald* to inform mistresses that:

A domestic is not a mechanical chattel like a watch, guaranteed to be regulated to keep correct time without losing a minute in six months and kept going by the necessary supervision of winding up regularly.[17]

This objection to being treated like automata came up again and again in servants' accounts during this period. Kathlyn Oliver likewise claimed to have handed in her notice after a week in her first job, even though it had been relatively 'easy', because her mistress treated her as 'a machine', never allowing her to make up her own mind about how to organise her

---

[13] WCLM, Stephen, 'Submission Is for Slaves', p. 20; Horn, *The Rise and Fall of the Victorian Servant*, p. 144; Pamela Horn, *Life below Stairs in the Twentieth Century* (Stroud: Amberley, 2001), p. 91.

[14] Lucy Delap, *Knowing Their Place: Domestic Service in Twentieth Century Britain* (Oxford: Oxford University Press, 2011), p. 52.

[15] Horn, *The Rise and Fall of the Victorian Servant*, pp. 181–182, 186–187.

[16] *Glasgow Herald* 29 Sept. 1913, p. 5.   [17] *Glasgow Herald* 2 Oct. 1913, p. 3.

work.[18] Servants also objected to attempts to control what they did in their leisure time. 'We don't want mistresses saying, "who is that man you spoke to just now?"', wrote one servant, signing herself as 'Freedom', in a letter to the *Common Cause* in 1911: 'We want to be treated like free human beings.'[19] Perhaps one of the most extreme examples of the dehumanising aspect of service was the practice of some employers arbitrarily changing their servants' names, sometimes to avoid clashes with a family name and sometimes simply to alleviate the effort of having to remember new ones.[20]

Following a number of well-publicised cases of cruelty against servants by their employers, the Apprentice and Servants Act was passed in 1851, specifying that servants must be provided with 'necessary Food, Clothing, or Lodging'. By the beginning of the twentieth century, incidences of extreme abuse had significantly decreased, although physical chastisement had not disappeared. On questions of unfair dismissal, breach of contract and employers refusing to write references crucial to servants' future employability, the law still operated in the employer's favour. Mistresses were also perfectly within their rights to search a servant's bedroom and personal belongings without warning.[21] Hannah Mitchell and Jessie Stephen both recalled being forced by mistresses angry at their leaving for a new post, to work out their month's notice by undertaking an intensive spring clean. Hannah Mitchell 'decided to leave at once rather than be exploited in such a manner'. She managed to sneak out her belongings in advance, to prevent them being held to ransom, but could do nothing about her mistress withholding her previous month's wages.[22]

In 1911, the litany of complaints about domestic service appearing in the letters pages of the *Common Cause* prompted one mistress, Jane Uniacke, to write to the editors:

Don't you think the various 'Domestic Servants' who write to your columns make a mistake in writing of 'domestic service' as if the same conditions prevailed throughout this employment? There are numerous households known to one

---

[18] *Woman Worker* 5 Jan. 1910, p. 606. See also *Glasgow Herald* 20 Sept. 1913, p. 3; 23 Sept. 1913, p. 3; 25 Sept. 1913, p. 3; 26 Sept. 1913, p. 5, 29 Sept. 1913, p. 5; *Woman Worker* 21 July 1909, p. 54; Butler, *Report of the Women's Industrial Council*, p. 95. For a long tradition of servants as 'automata', Carolyn Steedman, *Labours Lost: Domestic Service and the Making of Modern England* (Cambridge: Cambridge University Press, 2009), p. 47.
[19] *Common Cause* 9 Nov. 1911, p. 543.
[20] Horn, *The Rise and Fall of the Victorian Servant*, pp. 126–131.
[21] Ibid., pp. 137–139; Delap, *Knowing Their Place*, p. 87.
[22] WCML, Stephen, 'Submission Is for Slaves', p. 19; Hannah Mitchell, *The Hard Way Up: The Autobiography of Hannah Mitchell, Suffragette and Rebel* (London: Virago, 1977), pp. 68–70.

personally where servants are well paid, well fed, treated with consideration, and where they get much spare time.[23]

Recent historiography has similarly emphasised variation in employers' 'authority practices' and servants' experiences at work. One of the main aims of Lucy Delap's book *Knowing Their Place* was to liberate the history of domestic workers from a 'melodramatic account of nineteenth-century service as a site of victimhood'. Focusing on the twentieth century, she sought to outline 'a far more diverse setting for domestic service than the monotony of drudgery that has predominated in histor-ical accounts'. *Knowing Their Place* insisted that not all domestic workers' experiences were of 'anomie and self-alienation' inside a 'totalising insti-tution'. Entering service could be viewed as a positive career choice: a way to build up savings without the expense of room and board, a chance to experience different ways of life in a middle-class home, or an oppor-tunity to escape from one's own unhappy family. Delap's sources also sometimes reveal 'pleasure and satisfaction and accomplishment along-side sentiments of bitterness and resentment'.[24] Sian Pooley has also called into question some of the earlier historiographical generalisations, especially with regard to the significance of class difference and class inequality. Her detailed study of a single location, Lancaster, instead revealed that 'relationships were highly diverse'.[25]

My concern is not with denying the substance of the claims made by this richly nuanced research, but with asking whether an emphasis on variety and diversity of experience can obscure what the archives have revealed, to me, as a strikingly repetitive expression of dissatisfaction among servants. A dislike of domestic service was shored up by the profound structural inequality that continued to characterise early twentieth-century Britain, despite the democratic upheavals of the period. Of course not all servants hated their jobs. Some servants also wrote to newspapers to say that they were happy in their posts.[26] Even the most militant among them acknowledged that it was possible to find a good employer. Kathlyn Oliver publicly recognised Mary Sheepshanks as one of the 'best' of mistresses, allowing her time off in the evenings so that she could pursue an education at Morley College.[27] Jessie Stephen painted an even-handed portrait of her first employers, who were 'on the

---

[23] *Common Cause* 26 Oct. 1911, p. 504.   [24] Delap, *Knowing Their Place*, pp. 4, 27–28.
[25] Sian Pooley, 'Domestic Servants and Their Urban Employers: A Case Study of Lancaster, 1880–1914', Economic History Review, 62:2 (2009), 405–429, p. 405.
[26] *Glasgow Herald* 25 Sept. 1913, p. 3; 27 Sept. 1913, p. 3.
[27] *Woman Worker* 8 Dec. 1909, p. 522.

whole a most pleasant family to work for', especially her mistress, Mrs Harvey, who was sometimes 'very kind indeed and thoughtful' although prone to 'moods'.

Such servants were also fully cognisant of the fact that kindly employers did not stop their job from being exploitative. Jessie Stephen got on very well with Mrs Harvey, who appreciated her maid's hard-working attitude – so much so that her mistress fired the second servant to save money and placed Stephen in charge of the whole house with only a small increase in her wage.[28] I aim to be precise in my use of the term 'exploitation', which I see as distinct from more generalised understandings of 'oppression'. Exploitation is not just about whether employers are nice or nasty.[29] It is, rather, a central characteristic of labour under capitalism whereby the worker is denied the full fruits of their labour, the value of which is in part appropriated by the employer. Servants did not get to eat the meals they cooked, sleep in the beds they made, or entertain in the drawing rooms they cleaned. Whether or not domestic labour produces 'surplus value' according to a classical Marxist definition, employers certainly profited from the work of their servants in that it freed them to undertake more lucrative and higher status work.[30] Servants were only affordable because their time and labour had a lower market value than that of their employers. Domestic workers may not have been legally or physically coerced into service, but they were subject to economic compulsion (the need to support themselves with few alternative employment options). They also had very little control over how their work was organised, and thus they fulfil many of the criteria for 'unfree' labour identified by Marx. Servants experienced exploitation and 'unfreedom' to different degrees.[31] The workhouse girl, for whom service was the only

[28] WCML, Stephen, 'Submission Is for Slaves', pp. 16–18, 27–28.
[29] As Marx's imaginary worker says to their employer: '"You may be a model citizen, perhaps a member of the RSPCA, and you may be in the odour of sanctity as well; but the thing you represent when you come face-to-face with me has no heart in its breast"'; Karl Marx, *Capital: A Critique of Political Economy*, 3 vols. (London: Penguin, 1990 [first published 1867]), vol. I, p. 343.
[30] Marx, *Capital*, vol. I, part 3. This has been the subject of much debate; Eva Kaluzynska, 'Wiping the Floor with Theory: A Survey of Writings on Housework', *Feminist Review*, 6 (1980), 27–54, pp. 42–45. Recently, historians have argued that it is 'analytically absurd' to deny that domestic labour produces surplus value, citing especially the role played by domestic workers in freeing up women in the global north to enter the labour market outside the home, Elise van Nederveen Meerkerk, Silke Neunsinger and Dirk Hoerder, 'Domestic Workers of the World: Histories of Domestic Workers as Global Labor History', in Hoerder, Nederveen Meerkerk and Neunsinger (eds.), *Towards a Global History of Domestic and Caregiving Workers* (Leiden: Brill, 2015), 1–24, pp. 17–18.
[31] Nancy Holmstrom, 'Exploitation', *Canadian Journal of Philosophy*, 7:2 (June 1977), 353–369; Katie Cruz, 'Beyond Liberalism: Marxist Feminism, Migrant Sex Work, and Labour Unfreedom', *Feminist Legal Studies*, 26 (2018), 65–92.

imaginable future, was markedly less 'free', and much closer to an indentured worker, than a relatively educated lady's maid, who could earn a
good living travelling the world with her mistress. The wage relation and
the nature of the employment contract nevertheless meant that some
form of exploitation structured even the most friendly and socially egalitarian of mistress–maid relationships, including those in suffrage
households.

The Blathwayts and Their Servants

The Blathwayts had lived at Eagle House in Batheaston in Somerset
since 1882, when the head of the household Colonel Linley Blathwayt
retired from service in India. They were a comfortably off family, related
to the Blathwayts of Dyrham Park – a landed estate in nearby Gloucestershire. Even as an unmarried adult Mary Blathwayt did not have to
concern herself with paid work, living off stocks and shares and an
allowance from her parents.[32] Eagle House had been rebuilt in the
1720s by the leading architect John Wood the elder, its large windows,
high ceilings and classical proportions in keeping with the elegant style of
nearby Bath. The house consisted of twenty-one rooms and two bathrooms spread over three stories, plus a basement kitchen and scullery. It
was inhabited by Emily Marion Blathwayt (c. 1852–1940), her husband
Linley, their daughter Mary (1879–1962) and, when he was not living
abroad, their adult son William.[33] Eagle House was also home to an ever-
changing staff of domestics. House- and parlour-maid Ellen Morgan was
one of the longest standing employees of this period, staying six years
from 1904 to 1910 (see Figure 1). She worked alongside the cook, Elsie
Harris, until Harris left to get married in November 1908. Harris was
briefly replaced by Helena Denny, who was found to be unsatisfactory.
She was soon replaced by Emily Hulance in December 1908, who acted
as general servant until March 1909, while Ellen Morgan was promoted
to head servant. Sarah (Kate) Hale was employed as a cook general in
June 1909, although Emily Blathwayt 'found her not up to [the] work'
and asked her to leave in October that year.[34]

[32] June Hannam, '"Suffragettes Are Splendid for Any Work': The Blathwayt Diaries as a
Source for Suffrage History', in Claire Eustance, John Ryan and Laura Ugolini (eds.),
A Suffrage Reader: Charting Directions in British Suffrage History (London: Leicester
University Press), 53–69, p. 53.

[33] England and Wales Census (1911), Eagle House, Batheaston, Bath.

[34] GA, E. M. Blathwayt, 'Diary', 4 June 1908, p. 68; 21 Oct. 1908, p. 112; 21 Nov. 1908,
p. 131; 12 Dec. 1908, pp. 138–139; 13 Dec. 1908, p. 139; 21 Dec. 1908, p. 141, D2659/
24/11; E. M. Blathwayt, 'Household Log Book', n.p., D2659/24/45.

Figure 1 'Parlourmaid at Eagle House, Batheaston' (1909). Probably
Ellen Morgan, who worked as a house-and parlour-maid at the time.
The sitter wears a brooch featuring the initial E.
Photographed by Linley Blathwayt. Bath Central Library: Private print X.50,
17390 (reproduced by permission of Bath in Time)

The arrival of Ethel Durnford as cook general in November
1909 marked the beginning of the Blathwayts' employment of a number
of Durnford sisters. They were all in their twenties, the daughters of a
Somerset farm worker and his wife, and were born and raised in various
different Somerset villages (including Mells, Chewton Mendip and Chilcompton) just over ten miles south of Batheaston.[35] Ethel Durnford left
owing to illness in June 1910, but was replaced by her sister, Ellen
Matilda Durnford (referred to in the Blathwayts' diaries as 'Nelly'),

---

[35] The England and Wales Census (1911), Eagle House, Bathaston, Bath, records Ellen
Durnford's birthplace as Mells, Somerset, and Mabel Durnford's as Chewton Mendip,
Somerset. The England and Wales Census (1901), Chilcompton, North Somerset,
records Eliza Durnford and her husband Edward living in the village of Chilcompton
with their children Arthur, Mabel, Ellen, Winifred Elsie, Horace and Daisy. Edward
Durnford's occupation is listed as 'Carter on farm, e.g. horse worker', pp. 11–12.

who departed relatively quickly in December 1910 to take another post in Bath. After Ellen Morgan was given her notice by Emily Blathwayt in March 1910, she was replaced by a general servant named May Woodham, who subsequently took on the position of cook. In January 1911 a third sister arrived, Mabel Elizabeth Durnford, working as cook general. She too did not remain in her post long term, but left in August that year. Her successor, Bessie Willis, developed 'hysteria' in December 1911 and was sent home in a taxi cab never to return, though Emily Blathwayt did provide her with a character on three future occasions. Ellen Durnford had returned to the Blathwayts by 1911, when the census records her employed as a parlour-maid. In May 1912 she was put in charge of the cooking with a plan to have a 'girl' working beneath her, although in the end this second servant was never employed. Ellen Durnford left one year later to emigrate to Canada and marry a man named Allan Keevill.[36] The Blathwayts also employed a gardener and chauffer, Moses William Rawlings, and his wife Ellen Martha Rawlings (b. 1878), who in January 1910 began charring at Eagle House. The Rawlings lived with their two young sons, Joseph and William, in a cottage in the spacious grounds of Eagle House.[37] During 1910 the Blathwayts also sent out some of their washing to a local woman named Katie Kite, though after a few months they withdrew their patronage, complaining that her work was not up to scratch.[38]

Many of the women working in the Blathwayt household during this period were supporters of votes for women, as were the Blathwayt family themselves. Mary Blathwayt was the most actively engaged through her work for the Women's Social and Political Union (WSPU), which included acting as treasurer for the Bath branch, organising public

[36] GA, E. M. Blathwayt, 'Household Log Book', n.p., D2659/24/45; England and Wales Census (1911), Eagle House, Batheaston, Bath.

[37] GA, E. M. Blathwayt, 'Diary', 8 June 1908, p. 77, D2659/24/11. Mrs Rawlings was initially paid 1s. 6d. per week for indoor cleaning on top of cleaning the brass on the motor car and the outdoor houses for which she already received 2s. per week; GA, E. M. Blathwayt, 'Household Log Book', n.p., D2659/24/45. By 1910 this was raised to 2s. per week for indoor cleaning; GA, E. M. Blathwayt, 'Diary', 24 Feb. 1910, p. 21, D2659/24/12. Mr Rawlings's wage consisted of accommodation in the cottage, the provision of coal and vegetables and 18s. per week in cash; GA, E. M. Blathwayt, 'Diary', 24 Feb. 1910, p. 21, D2659/24/12.

[38] In March 1910 Katie Kite wrote to Emily Blathwayt asking if she could give her any extra work as Kite's husband had been unemployed all winter and her daughter was home ill from service with an ulcerated stomach. Emily Blathwayt was initially sympathetic, dropping by Katie Kite's house to give her 5s. and noting her request for any of the Blathwayts' cast-off shoes, but by July the mistress of Eagle House was fed up with the low quality of Kite's work, commenting how 'she does spoil the things so and sends them back dirty'; GA, E. M. Blathwayt, 'Diary', 11 March 1910, p. 28; 13 March 1910, pp. 29–30; 13 March 1910, pp. 29–30; 25 July 1910, p. 76, D2659/24/12.

meetings, open-air speaking, and working on campaign tours in the south-west of England.[39] Linley and Emily Blathwayt also played an important role, opening their house to touring suffragette lecturers as a place to rest, recuperate and organise. Such hospitality led to close personal ties between the Blathwayts and the leaders of the WSPU, especially Annie Kenney. Many of the servants at Eagle House – Moses and Ellen Rawlings, Ellen Morgan, Elsie Harris, May Woodham and Ellen Durnford – were also supporters of women's suffrage.

We know all this because Emily and Mary Blathwayt kept extremely detailed diaries, providing an unusually rich account of the daily life and domestic organisation of a suffrage household.[40] Mary Blathwayt almost never wrote about her personal feelings or political opinions, and Emily Blathwayt did so only occasionally. Instead they recorded matters such as how much fish their household consumed each week or how frequently bedrooms needed to be vacuumed.[41] Reading these 'mundane' sources prompted me to think about how social relations and economic structures do not exist as abstract forces external to the individual, but are reproduced by experience and made manifest through everyday practices. I therefore approach the Blathwayts' accounts of apparently insignificant activities as a window into employment relations between women, the construction of gendered class identities, and how domestic labour was thought about in early twentieth-century Britain.[42]

---

[39] Mary Blathwayt was also a member of the Bath branch of the National Union of Women's Suffrage Society and was a member of its executive committee for a few months at the very end of 1907 and the beginning of 1908, combining this with fully paid-up membership of the WSPU. In April 1908, she resigned secretaryship of the NUWSS local society and became treasurer of the newly founded Bath WSPU branch. For the Blathwayt family's involvement in the suffrage movement, see Crawford, *The Women's Suffrage Movement: A Reference Guide* (London: University College London Press, 1999), pp. 64–66; Hannam, '"Suffragettes Are Splendid for Any Work"'.

[40] Linley also kept a diary, but the years 1907 to 1911 are missing from the archive; Hannam, '"Suffragettes Are Splendid for Any Work"', p. 54.

[41] Today's understanding of the diary as place to explore and construct the self was a relatively new development from the late nineteenth century onwards; Joanne E. Cooper, 'Shaping Meaning: Women's Diaries, Journals and Letters – The Old and the New', *Women's Studies International Forum*, 10:1 (1987), 95–99; Harriet Blodgett, *Centuries of Female Days: Englishwomen's Private Diaries* (Gloucester: Alan Sutton, 1989); Judy Simons, *Diaries and Journals of Literary Women from Fanny Burney to Virginia Woolf* (Basingstoke: Macmillan Press, 1990); Anne-Marie Millim, 'The Victorian Diary: Between the Public and the Private', *Literature Compass*, 7:10 (2010), 977–988.

[42] Dorothy E. Smith, *The Everyday World as Problematic: A Feminist Sociology* (Milton Keynes: Open University Press, 1988); Sandra Stanley Holton, 'Challenging Masculinism: Personal History and Microhistory in Feminist Studies of the Women's Suffrage Movement', *Women's History Review*, 20:5 (2011), 829–841, p. 837; Carolyn Steedman, *An Everyday Life of the English Working Class: Work, Self and Sociability in the Early Nineteenth Century* (Cambridge: Cambridge University Press, 2013).

Emily and Mary Blathwayt's diaries offer only the mistress' perspective on the servant–employer relationship. However, especially when placed alongside the household log book, they can be read against the grain to reveal a great deal about working conditions at Eagle House as well as some information on the servants' health, personal relationships and political loyalties. The Blathwayts appear to have paid towards the higher end of the spectrum compared with equivalent positions in their region. In the years 1907–1913, the Blathwayts' house-maid, parlour-maid and cook's wages ranged between £22 and £26 per annum. Their 'untrained' general maid started on £17 per annum, but this was raised to £18 within a few months.[43] Servants at Eagle House also had their own bedrooms and bathroom (the latter would have been a considerable boon), as well as the promise of keeping early dinner, which freed up much of their evening. The servants' accommodation and meals were 'all found', part of their wage, and they were also given washing money (one shilling per week in 1910) to pay for their laundry to be sent out. The Blathwayts did not, however, pay 'beer money' (a way of supplementing servants' wages left over from the time when servants would commonly have drunk beer rather than tea).[44] When, in January 1908, Emily Blathwayt noticed that the part of the house where they slept was 'horribly cold' with the thermometer reaching only a little over 12°F, she and Linley Blathwayt decided to convert the laundry room into a servants' hall and agreed with a builder on a plan for refurbishment at the projected cost of £700. These renovations were partly prompted by an awareness of the growing 'servant problem', and Emily Blathwayt worried that 'servants will not go to a house now unless there is a servant hall to sit in'. The Blathwayts motivation, however, was not entirely altruistic, for they were advised that the servants' new quarters could easily be converted into a separate house that would significantly increase the value of the property. Ellen Morgan and Elsie Harris moved into their new rooms in September 1908.[45]

The advertisement Mary Blathwayt placed in *Votes for Women* promised prospective servants 'much personal liberty', and this seems to have been in keeping with her mother's approach. Emily Blathwayt gave her servants time off to attend suffrage meetings, and her diary also records them visiting the local flower show and charitable entertainments while

[43] GA, E. M. Blathwayt, 'Household Log Book', D2659/24/45; Horn, *The Rise and Fall of the Victorian Servant*, pp. 145–146.
[44] GA, E. M. Blathwayt, 'Diary', 2 June 1910, pp. 56–57, D2659/24/12; 1 Nov. 1908, p. 121, D2659/24/11. For beer money, see Horn, *The Rise and Fall of the Victorian Servant*, p. 147.
[45] GA, E. M. Blathwayt, 'Diary', 10 Jan. 1908, p. 5; 17 Jan. 1908, p. 7; 5 March 1908, p. 24; 24 Sept. 1908, p. 102, D2659/24/11.

their mistress stayed home to 'keep house'. She also noted proudly that 'We always send maids out after [mid-day] dinner Sundays and do everything ourselves the rest of the day, however many are here.'[46] Emily Blathwayt felt a strong duty of care towards her servants, sending them to bed when they were unwell, sometimes for days at a time. When Ethel Durnford fell ill, Emily Blathwayt called the doctor, who put Durnford to bed on a milk diet and ordered that she have five linseed poultices over her kidneys. It is possible that Emily or Mary Blathwayt nursed her themselves, since their other maid, Ellen Morgan, had to leave the house to visit her fiancé, who was suffering from pneumonia. Ethel Durnford's mother and sister were permitted to visit, while Mary and Emily went into town to buy fish for her invalid's diet.[47] Ill health formed the backdrop to life at Eagle House, as it did for so many in Edwardian England. Emily Blathwayt's diary is full of meticulous reports of her household's every bodily twinge, cough and fever. Servants and their employers were compelled into an intimate awareness of each other's physical state, for illness immediately disrupted the smooth running of the household. Linley Blathwayt, for example, was frequently bed-ridden with lumbago and gout, requiring his wife to spend much of her time nursing him. The servants, too, were expected to rise in the middle of the night to attend to Linley Blathwayt, and an electric bell was installed in their room for this purpose. Emily Blathwayt was an especially zealous advocate of dental treatment. She frequently sent her servants to the family dentist, and once paid as much as 'four guineas' (£4 4s.) for Ellen Morgan's 'double set' (a full pair of false teeth).[48]

Emily Blathwayt was, however, quite clear that her responsibility for servants' well-being did not extend beyond the point at which they were unable to perform their work to an acceptable standard. She sought to employ only young, healthy women; asking that Mabel Durnford (who had previously been an invalid) provide a doctor's report before Blathwayt would agree to take her on and turning down a cook that had been recommended by a friend on the basis that the cook was old and could not read or write.[49] Emily Blathwayt also insisted on taking new employees

---

[46] GA, E. M. Blathwayt, 'Diary', 9 March 1908, pp. 27–29; 17 Nov. 1908, p. 128, D2659/24/11; 17 Aug. 1911, p. 160; 19 March 1911, p. 182, D2659/24/12.

[47] GA, E. M. Blathwayt, 'Diary', 10 Jan. 1910, p. 5; 12 Jan. 1910, p. 6; 13 Jan. 1910, p. 6, D2659/24/12.

[48] Though when Elsie Harris was found in need of an entirely new set of teeth, her mistress insisted that this should be her wedding present; GA, E. M. Blathwayt, 'Diary', 22 Oct. 1908, p. 113, D2659/24/11.

[49] GA, E. M. Blathwayt, 'Diary', 29 Dec. 1910, p. 144; 30 Dec. 1910, p. 144, D2659/24/12; 3 Nov. 1908, p. 122, D2659/24/11.

on a one-month trial during which failure to please meant immediate severance, even if this left the servant in a very vulnerable position. One particularly poignant example of this is the case of Helena Denny (referred to in Emily Blathwayt's diaries as Lena), who was taken on as cook in November 1908 after the boarding-house where she worked closed due to lack of business. Only three days after she arrived, her new mistress packed her off to the dentist where she had three teeth removed under gas. The procedure, however, did not agree with her and she soon began to cough up blood in the night. The Blathwayts called the doctor, put her to bed in William's old room and fed her a milk diet. However, after five days they ran out of patience. Without consulting 'Lena', they organised for her to be transferred to a hospital, which they had agreed to pay for. On hearing of this plan, Helena Denny 'made a scene', perhaps panicking at the prospect of hospital, perhaps fearful of losing her position. Eventually she agreed to return to her relatives in Plymouth and the Blathwayts paid her fare plus a month's wages and promised that they would pay for a Plymouth dentist to finish the dental work they had begun. Such kind-nesses appear to have been prompted by a sense of duty and the desire to hasten her exit, rather than personal concern. Emily Blathwayt remarked in her diary that evening: 'We are heartily glad to be rid of her ... She would have been no use to us here. She liked pleasure too much and novel reading, and was terribly untruthful.'[50]

Whether such accusations were invented by Emily Blathwayt to salve her conscience at dismissing her servant for an illness which she might have played some part in bringing on, or whether the sickness was used as an excuse to expel a woman whose character Blathwayt found unattract-ive, we do not know. It is evident, either way, that servants with less than robust physical or mental health were ultimately regarded as a burden by the Blathwayts, however assiduously they fulfilled their responsibility to provide them with medical treatment. This was even the case for long-standing servants. Ellen Morgan's fiancé's illness turned out to be not pneumonia as she had first thought, but 'consumption' (tuberculosis). Emily Blathwayt allowed her time off to help nurse him, but noted around this time that 'Ellen has been suffering from much nervous irritability and I told her today I thought it better for all that we should change.' This was certainly a euphemism for dismissal, since the next day she began advertising for a new servant. Morgan's fiancé died shortly

---

[50] GA, E. M. Blathwayt, 'Household Log Book', D2659/24/45; E. M. Blathwayt, 'Diary', 7 Dec. 1908, pp. 135–136, D2659/24/11. Helena Denny did, in fact, take up Emily Blathwayt's offer to pay for the finished dental work, so perhaps she had the last word after all.

afterwards in February 1910 but this did not prompt Blathwayt to change her mind, and Morgan left a few weeks later to take up a new post in Bath.[51] Her six years of service at Eagle House, shared political commitments and work for the WSPU were not enough to keep her in the Blathwayts' employment.

The Clark Family Servants

The Clark family archive allows us to get a little closer to servants' own voices, as it holds the letters of Eliza Oldham, a general maid, who wrote frequently to Helen Clark between 1870 and 1892, and those of Emma J. Bennett, a lady's maid, whose letters to Clark survive for the first decade of the twentieth century. Oldham and Bennett did not work for Clark directly, and thus the correspondence gives an insight into how mistresses and servants might communicate and perhaps even befriend one another outside of the employment relationship. Although the archive does not contain Helen Clark's replies, it has preserved her household accounts and lists, providing a detailed picture of how Clark organised day-to-day domestic labour and managed her own servants.

Helen Clark (1840–1927) was the eldest daughter of the Radical MP John Bright and brought up in the family home of One Ash in Rochdale. She began working for the suffrage as early as 1865 when she campaigned for women to be enfranchised under the forthcoming Reform Bill. Clark remained active in the radical liberal wing of the women's movement, supporting the reform of women's legal position within marriage and the campaign against the Contagious Disease Acts.[52] In 1911, she joined the WSPU, and in 1913 became a tax resister and honorary treasurer for the National Union of Women's Suffrage Societies (NUWSS) West of England Federation. Both Helen Clark and her husband William were Quakers. They married in 1866 and lived together in Street, Somerset, where the Clarks' large shoe and boot factory was based. Together they had two sons and four daughters, including the medical doctor Hilda Clark and the historian Alice Clark.[53]

After she married and moved to the south of England, Helen Clark maintained her relationship with Eliza Oldham (c. 1820–1892), who worked as a servant for Clark's family in Lancashire. Eliza Oldham's

[51] GA, E. M. Blathwayt, 'Diary', 17 Feb. 1910, p. 19; 18 Feb. 1910, p. 19; 25 Feb. 1910, p. 22; 26 Feb. 1910, p. 22; 8 March 1910, p. 26.

[52] Sandra Stanley Holton, *Quaker Women: Personal Life, Memory and Radicalism in the Lives of Women Friends, 1780–1930* (Abingdon: Routledge, 2007).

[53] Crawford, *The Women's Suffrage Movement*, pp. 113–114.

father, Benjamin Oldham, had been a long-standing employee in the Bright family's mill and a neighbour and friend of Helen's father. Eliza Oldham also started out as a mill hand, but at the age of about twenty-six moved to working as a general maid, first for Helen Clark's great aunt, Margaret Wood, and then for Wood's niece, Jane Crosland. Historian Sandra Stanley Holton has written of how Oldham and Clark's affectionate and long-lasting friendship began during Clark's childhood, when she often came to stay with her great-aunt in the house where Oldham worked. Helen Clark evidently felt a deep connection and responsibility towards the Oldham family, persuading her father to give Benjamin Oldham a pension of 5s. per week, which she matched from her own funds. After Benjamin's death the pension was transferred to Eliza Oldham.[54] When Helen Clark moved away from Rochdale, Eliza Oldham began a correspondence which lasted for the next thirty-five years. Oldham wrote to Clark with family news, but her letters also discussed political events, especially anything concerning the cause of women, and she too was an active supporter of women's suffrage.[55]

Helen Clark also corresponded with Emma J. Bennett (b. 1852), who worked as a lady's maid in Edinburgh for Clark's aunt, Priscilla Bright McLaren (1815–1906). Clark was particularly close to Bennett's mistress, who had looked after her in infancy and young childhood following the death of her mother.[56] Priscilla Bright McLaren had also been campaigning for women's suffrage since the 1860s. She supported the Lancashire radical suffragists in the early 1900s and sat on the executive committee of the NUWSS.[57] Emma J. Bennett first began to write to Helen in 1898 on behalf of her mistress, who, in her old age, was perhaps not well enough or lacked the eyesight to put pen to paper herself. The letters, however, were not transcribed verbatim but written in Bennett's own voice: 'Mrs McLaren's time has been much taken up. I think I may say she is fairly well.' And Bennett always signed off with a more personal greeting: 'I hope, dear Madam, you and all your family are well. I remain yours respectfully Emma J. Bennett.'[58] Priscilla Bright McLaren died in 1906, and in 1907 Emma J. Bennett took up a new post at Bodnant Hall

[54] Sandra Stanley Holton, 'Friendship and Domestic Service: The Letters of Eliza Oldham, General Maid (c. 1820–1892)', *Women's History Review*, 24:3 (2014), 429–449, pp. 440–441.

[55] Alfred Gillett Trust, Street, Millfield Papers (hereafter AGT), Oldham Correspondence (1870–1905), MIL/64/01.

[56] Scotland Census (1901), 10 Blacket Avenue, Edinburgh; Holton, *Quaker Women*, pp. 75–76.

[57] Crawford, *The Women's Suffrage Movement*, pp. 400–404.

[58] AGT, Bennett Correspondence, Emma J. Bennett to Helen Clark, 1 April 1899, MIL/62/1.

in North Wales, home to Priscilla's son Charles (a Liberal MP) and his wife, Laura McLaren. Here Bennett worked directly for Laura McLaren's elderly mother, Agnes Pochin, who came from the same affluent, radical liberal and suffragist circles as the Bright's. Pochin wrote *The Right of Women to Exercise the Elective Franchise* (1855) and had spoken at the first public women's suffrage meeting in 1868. She joined the Council of the Women's Emancipation Union in 1892, and continued to donate money to suffrage organisations into the early twentieth century.[59] Laura McLaren was also an active suffrage campaigner during the time that Bennett was employed in her household.[60] Emma Bennett kept up her correspondence with Helen Clark while working for Agnes Pochin, now writing on her own behalf rather than in the name of her mistress. Clark also stayed in touch, sending Bennett cards at Christmas and during summer holidays. It was she who found Bennett her new place with Pochin, and around this time sent the lady's maid what Bennett described as a 'handsome gift ... more than I could ever expect', advising her to put it towards her savings.[61]

The intimacy that existed between Clark and Oldham, and the more distant but nevertheless caring connection between Clark and Bennett, appears very different to the way in which Clark managed her own servants. Millfield House was an imposing sixteen-room grey stone building, built for the Clark family in the 1880s and located just outside of the village of Street. Helen Clark ran a slightly larger household than the Blathwayts, employing in 1911 a cook (Sarah Jane Butler), a parlour-maid (Annie Elizabeth Marsh), a house-maid (Louise Clark) and a kitchen-maid (Daisy Best).[62] Household lists from around 1910–1927, written in Helen Clark's hand, show Clark to have provided her servants with an extremely detailed breakdown of their working day, specifying which tasks should be performed, when and for how long.[63] Her cook, for example, should be downstairs by 7 a.m. (6:30 a.m. in the summer, 'earlier on washing mornings') and proceed like so:

---

[59] Crawford, *The Women's Suffrage Movement*, pp. 557–559.

[60] Ibid., pp. 399–400; Elizabeth Crawford, 'McLaren, Laura Elizabeth, Lady Aberconway (1854–1933)', in *Oxford Dictionary of National Biography*, online edn. (Oxford University Press, 2004).

[61] Holton, *Quaker Women*, p. 206; AGT, Bennett Correspondence, Bennett to Clark, 18 April 1907, 27 May 1907, 21 March n.d.

[62] England and Wales Census (1911), Millfield House, Street, Somerset; Holton, *Quaker Women*, p. 193.

[63] AGT, 'Tradesmans' Books and Household Lists 1910–1940', MIL/72/04. These instructions to servants are catalogued alongside other household papers belonging to Alice Clark, but the archivist Julie Mather (consulted September 2017) and myself believe that the handwriting belongs to Helen Clark.

Light kitchen fire – open hall doors and shutters – sweep hall and doorstep, shaking the mats, dust furniture and windows of hall, and light fire when needed. Dust kitchen. Prepare breakfast. Then clean boots. Kitchen breakfast. Wash up parlour and kitchen breakfast things, polishing the silver with leather. Attend to the larder – wipe anything that needs it. Take orders for dinner, help housemaid with beds.

All this was to be performed before the cook got down to her main task for the day, preparing the mid-day 'dinner'. On top of this, the cook had a different 'extra' task to perform every day except Sunday:

> **Monday**: Wash alternate weeks
> **Tuesday**: Bake, Help Iron
> **Wednesday**: Clean dish covers, iron
> **Thursday**: Clean dish covers ...
> **Friday**: Bake. Clean larder, kitchens and cupboards, blacklead the range
> **Saturday**: Clean Hall.

This indicates not only that Helen Clark expected her cook to work extremely hard, but also that this work was predetermined and rigidly timetabled by Clark herself. The supposed autonomy of the pre-industrial labourer or worker untouched by the factory system does not seem to have been enjoyed by the Millfield servants, despite frequent claims in this period that domestic service was a remnant of the feudal age. Rather, their domestic work was designed to look very similar to the industrial labour process – tasks always had to be performed in the same way, at the same time and by the right type of servant over and over again. The list of the house-maid's jobs (three times the length of the cook's) specified not only which equipment should be used and which clothes should be worn, but also the precise manner in which each individual task ought to be performed:

open the windows in damp weather only a little way – a little at the top and bottom in heat. Take-up hearth rug and move the fender. Spread a piece of coarse wrapping before the grate and clean the latter and light the fire. Rub fender and fire irons. Use housemaid's gloves and a good coarse apron tied well round to keep your dress clean. Having carried away boxes, Ashes etc, proceed to sweep the room (or go over carpet with a slightly damp cloth). Dust the furniture thoroughly with dusting brush and duster.

Helen Clark expected quality as well as quantity, insisting that servants perform their work to the highest standards. Her cook, for example, was expected (in between washing up the breakfast dishes and polishing the silver with leather) to cover for the house-maid while she was changing into her afternoon uniform and answer all bells in her place. Despite having to juggle these multiple tasks, Clark reminded her cook to 'Never go untidy to the door.' Likewise, the Clarks' house-maids were told that when sweeping the bedroom and stairs' carpets, they should take 'care that no bits are left about on them'. Helen Clark's household lists also cast doubt upon the argument, made by so many of her contemporaries, that although servants' working day was indeed longer than most other workers, it included many moments of respite when no particular task presented itself. Clark sought to maximise the labour that could be squeezed out of every minute for which her servants were employed. When their mistress wanted time alone with visitors, for example, house-maids were nevertheless expected to remain at hand in case anything was needed. While the family were eating the dinner that had been prepared by the cook, house-maids were to use this pause in their regular activity to 'dust about the drawing room', and the lull between dinner and tea was to be filled with sewing and ironing.

Helen Clark was concerned not only with the day-to-day labour of her servants, but with the household economy as a whole. Further lists written in her own hand show her calculating to the ounce how much basic food substances members of her household were expected to consume each week. An adult woman, for example, was provided with 8lbs of bread (about four loaves), while a man was allocated twice that amount. Helen also broke this down according to professional hierarchy: the two highest-ranking servants received 3oz of tea each per week, while the rest were given only 2oz. These accounts reveal a clear understanding of the monetary value of the living-in system. Clark was also aware of more hidden costs such as laundering bedclothes, and determined that her servants should receive clean sheets only once every two weeks, whereas her own family had theirs changed weekly.

Helen Clark's management practices were far from exceptional, in accordance with the advice given in a proliferation of servant-keeping manuals from the mid-nineteenth century onwards.[64] That reproducing people (keeping them clean, warm and well fed) was fundamentally a question of economics was far more evident to Victorian and Edwardian mistresses like Helen Clark than it was to later labour historians, who saw domestic service as distinct from other forms of work under capitalism. Resisting this historiographical trend, Leonore Davidoff argued that the 'rationalisation of housework' had become widespread by the second half

---

[64] Alison Light, *Mrs Woolf and the Servants* (London: Penguin Books, 2008), pp. 25–26. Jessie Stephen recalled being required to follow similarly strict and precise timetables in her first job as a general maid in Glasgow; WCML, Stephen, 'Submission Is for Slaves', pp. 16–18.

of the nineteenth century, with its origins traceable back to early Protestant sects who saw thrift in relation to both time and money as a virtue.[65] It is likely that Helen Clark's demanding and precise timetables were informed by her Quaker faith and the importance it placed upon duty and hard work. Her religious motivations intertwined with her political identification with the 'industrious classes', against the idle and parasitic landed class. Helen and her husband believed in the moral virtues of well-administered capitalism, maintaining that the regularity and mechanisation of factory labour promoted 'orderliness' within the workforce.[66] Clark's household lists, reflecting her desire to exhaust the potential of every minute in the servant's day, suggest that such thinking was also applied to the labour of the home. Davidoff's main interest in the rationalisation of housework was how it brought 'the *values* of business into the home' whereby strict codes about the placement of people and things maintained boundaries and hierarchies between different classes, between the pure and the impure, and between the public and the private sphere.[67] I argue that it is also possible to trace how the capitalist work ethic, as well as ideas about national 'efficiency' that were gaining popularity in the early twentieth century, shaped the practice of the work itself. Such values were made manifest in the domestic labour process. This in turn shaped the views of both mistresses and maids, and in particular how servants understood themselves in relation to the wider working class. By 1900 the experiences of the domestic worker and that of the industrial worker were not so very different in terms of how their time was managed and their tasks were structured.

How are we to reconcile the business-like regime that Helen Clark imposed on her own servants with the consideration and kindness she exhibited towards Eliza Oldham and Emma J. Bennett? Sandra Stanley Holton has argued that Oldham's relationship with Clark was not merely one of patronage and charity but also of friendship, suggesting that this was in part due to their particular historical, regional and political location. Both women had grown up in Lancashire, born into a radical tradition influenced by the Anti-Corn Law League and early nineteenth-century campaigns for parliamentary reform that highlighted

---

[65] Leonore Davidoff, *Worlds Between: Historical Perspectives on Gender and Class* (Cambridge: Polity Press, 1995), pp. 81–83. See also Judy Giles, *The Parlour and the Suburb: Domestic Identities, Class, Femininity and Modernity* (Oxford: Berg, 2004), pp. 21–22.

[66] Sandra Stanley Holton, 'Religion and the Meanings of Work: Four Cases from the Bright Circle of Women Quakers', in Krista Calman and Louise A. Jackson (eds.), *Women and Work Culture: Britain c. 1850–1950* (Aldershot: Ashgate, 2005), 48–69; Holton, *Quaker Women*, pp. 148–150.

[67] Davidoff, *Worlds Between*, pp. 83–94.

the common interests of the self-made capitalist class and the workers they employed in their mills and factories. This shared political outlook, with its emphasis on cross-class alliances, enabled bonds of trust and affection to develop between women of otherwise unequal social and economic standing.[68] Yet this insightful account of Clark's relationship with Oldham does not offer a framework for understanding her far more utilitarian and pragmatic approach to the employment of servants in her own household.

Was Clark simply inconsistent in valuing Oldham's friendship, or in wanting to return the care that Emma J. Bennett had shown to her aunt Priscilla, while at the same time failing to consider that her own servants might have found her stringent working conditions oppressive and exhausting? Perhaps the high levels of scrutiny and control suggested by Clark's household lists reflect the fact that, by the early twentieth century, she was managing a large household employing about five servants, a scale that necessitated more professional and less emotionally invested managerial practices. Alternatively, it could be posited that, by the 1910s, a more polarised understanding of class relations had come to dominate over that early nineteenth-century radical tradition. All these hypotheses might to some degree hold true, but I think that to properly understand Helen Clark's seemingly contradictory attitudes we also need to recognise that emotions and exploitation cannot be counter-posed. Feminists have long argued against such binaries, pointing out that care work still counts as work, and is often structured by the market, while the wage relation does not banish feelings, desires and intimacies from the workplace.[69] In fact, the intensive work regime at Millfield House was not devoid of an ethic of care: Clark took her servants to the doctor and on the occasional outing, and even offered to help pay for the education of one former servant's daughter.[70] Affection between employer and worker does not, however, erase exploitation. To argue this is not to call into question the 'genuine' nature of the connections and solidarities that did, sometimes, emerge, but rather to acknowledge that such personal bonds were always bound up with economic considerations.

Emma J. Bennett's letters show how attachment to one's mistress did not necessarily preclude either an awareness of wider class inequality or

[68] Holton, 'Friendship and Domestic Service', pp. 432, 445.
[69] Carol Wolkowitz, Rachel Lara Cohen, Teela Sanders and Kate Hardy (eds.), *Body/Sex/Work: Intimate, Embodied and Sexualised Labour* (Basingstoke: Palgrave Macmillan, 2013).
[70] Holton, *Quaker Women*, p. 143; AGT, Helen Clark, 'Diary', 9 Aug. 1902, 1 March 1909, 30 April 1909, 1 Aug. 1909, MIL/70/1; AGT, Rhoda [Churchill] to Clark, 23 Oct. 1917, MIL/64/2.

one's own interests as a worker. Bennett expressed great sadness at Priscilla Bright McLaren's death, referring to her as 'our dear Lady'. When Bennett began working for Agnes Pochin, she wrote to Helen describing how 'when I ask her if I may help her or do anything for her, she says no thank you, I can do for myself ... It seems very strange after being so much with Mrs McLaren.' By the following month, a more mournful note had crept in: 'some days she don't seem to want me at all ... She seldom ever says anything more than about the weather or her self – all the caps I make or do, she alters.' Bennett repeatedly and rather critically described Agnes Pochin as 'very independent', and she appears to have missed having someone depend upon her and perhaps even someone to serve. Bennett's need to be needed did not, however, prevent her from recognising when unreasonable levels of work were being imposed, nor from making a decision to put her own health before that of another employer. When Pochin fell ill with congestion of the lungs in the winter of 1907–1908, her lady's maid was required to visit her in bed two or three times a night. This Bennett found 'very trying', causing her to contract a 'weak head' and 'a crick in my neck for some time'. Moreover, she felt that her exertions were underappreciated by her mistress's daughter, Laura McLaren. When Agnes Pochin died in February 1908, Bennett did not express any sadness at her passing, but instead wrote to Helen Clark with a clear assertion of her own needs: she refused 'go through the same ordeal' in her next position and had decided that she would never again agree to do 'night work'.[71]

Emma J. Bennett used a correspondence begun on behalf of her mistress to develop an independent relationship with Helen Clark. At first, Bennett's letters merely conveyed her mistress's views, giving her news of the family and recounting household events, as well as commentary on developments in the suffrage movement. Soon, Bennett's own voice began to intrude, giving her own opinion on McLaren's health, and sending her personal regards to Clark's family. By 1902 Bennett was writing her own letters to Clark, which gave news of Mrs McLaren but appear to have been written at her own volition. Perhaps Bennett already had an interest in radical politics and the women's movement and this is why McLaren employed her, or perhaps she had become interested in these questions in her capacity as go-between for Clark and her aunt. Either way, by 1907 she was confident enough to bring up topics such as

---

[71] AGT, Bennett Correspondence, Bennett to Clark, 23 June 1907, 18 July 1907, 23 Feb. 1908, MIL/62/1.

colonialism and international politics and solicit Clark's opinion. Common political sympathies and a sense of their shared oppression as women did not, however, negate Bennett's awareness of the social gulf that existed between herself and women such as Clark. In 1907, a lady doctor by the name of Agnes (probably Priscilla Bright McLaren's step-daughter Agnes McLaren, another active suffrage campaigner) invited Emma J. Bennett to stay with her in Kensington. Bennett hesitated, and wrote to Clark to ask if this would be too 'presuming ... or would you advise me not to trouble her?' At times Bennett also doubted her right to a relationship with Helen Clark, adding at the end of a long letter describing her holiday in the summer of 1907, 'I hope I have not troubled you too much with things. I hope it's what you wanted to know', scrawling again on the envelope: 'I hope, Madam, I have not intruded too much.'[72] Helen Clark never stopped being 'Madam' to Emma J. Bennett, who understood clearly the asymmetry of their relationship. However friendly and affectionate their exchanges, Clark always had the advantage in terms of status, wealth and political connections. The degree to which Bennett might be able to benefit from these was wholly dependent upon Clark's goodwill.

Louise Jermy and Mary Muirhead

Louise Jermy (née Withers, c. 1877–1952) moved from Hampshire to London as a young child, to live with her father and stepmother. Her father was a labourer who then turned his hand to a number of small businesses including a fish shop, stone masonry and horse-drawn cab firm. Jermy wrote *The Memories of a Working Woman* (1934) in late middle-age, recording a long career as a domestic servant, which began in her late teens and lasted until she married John Jermy, a farm labourer, in 1911 at the age of thirty-four. Even after leaving live-in service to become a housewife, Jermy took on 'daily work' during her pregnancy, and after her husband died she did the laundry for the 'lady of the manor' in her village of Wroxham in Norfolk.[73]

Louise Jermy comes across in her autobiography as a woman of powerful passions, albeit ones carefully contained within proscribed social norms. For her, domestic service offered escape from a deeply unhappy home life dominated by her stepmother's violent bullying. Louise Jermy

---

[72] AGT, Bennett Correspondence, Bennett to Clark, 25 April 1899, 1 April 1899, 21 July 1902, 18 April 1907, 29 April 1907, 5 June 1907, 20 June 1907, 23 June 1907, MIL/62/1.
[73] Louise Jermy, *The Memories of a Working Woman* (Norwich: Goose & Son, 1934), pp. 180, 186.

was partially disabled due to a hip operation she had undergone as a teenager. Believing herself unable to do work requiring physical strength, she took up an apprenticeship with a dressmaker and stayed living with her parents until she was about seventeen years old. One day her stepmother flew into a rage, complaining that she was sick of acting as 'servant' and insisting that Jermy scrub out her own bedroom. Surprising both her stepmother and herself, Jermy managed to overcome her disability (which prevented her from kneeling without support) and scrubbed the floor by lying on her side. Her first experience of hard domestic labour was therefore associated with physical autonomy and empowerment. '[I]t was extraordinary how pleased I felt', she recalled, 'I began to see a way out now, I found I was not so helpless.' Jermy quickly translated her new-found capabilities into economic independence, and sought work as a domestic servant. In her first post she found that the manual labour actually improved her health and she relished the solitude made possible by her move away from the family home. She started work as a general in the Muirhead household at the age of eighteen. Her mistress, Mary Muirhead (c. 1862–1922), was a supporter of the suffrage cause and married to the philosopher John Henry Muirhead, a professor at Royal Holloway College and Bedford College in London.[74] Two years later, in 1897, Jermy moved with them to Birmingham where Professor Muirhead took up a position at Mason College. After five years in what Jermy remembered as a rewarding and stimulating job, she began to find it too great a strain on both her physical and mental health: 'I felt I wanted to get away and rest, and so at last, I'm sorry to say in a burst of temper, I left.'[75]

Louise Jermy's autobiography shows how mistresses could loom large in a servant's life. Her description of Muirhead is much more extensive than in the opposite view of the mistress–maid relationship given in the autobiographies of middle-class suffragists. Florence Lockwood and Helena Swanwick, for example, do not give over nearly as much space to remembering their treasured and long-standing maids.[76] Such a disparity may be further proof of inequality, affirming what subjugated peoples have long known – that the dominated must know their oppressor while the employer need barely notice the one upon whose

[74] Jermy, *The Memories of a Working Woman*, pp. 71–83; Jane McDermid, 'Jermy, Louise Jane (1877–1952)', in *Oxford Dictionary of National Biography*; C. G. Robertson, 'Muirhead, John Henry (1855–1940)', revised by Peter P. Nicholson, in *Oxford Dictionary of National Biography*; England and Wales Census (1911), Clarens, Alpine Road, Isle of Wight.
[75] Jermy, *The Memories of a Working Woman*, pp. 100–101.
[76] H. M. Swanwick, *I Have Been Young* (London: Victor Gollancz, 1935); Florence Lockwood, *An Ordinary Life 1861–1924* (London: Mrs Josiah Lockwood, 1932).

labour her comfort depends. Such close observation of and interest in an authority figure, however, could indicate rebellion as well as subservience, the assertion of a certain kind of power.[77] 'Do not the mistresses think that the maids study them many times?' one domestic threatened in a letter the *Glasgow Herald*, reminding the employer class that servants were not the only ones under surveillance.[78]

At seventeen years old, Jermy was also slightly older than the many girls who entered service upon leaving school at age fourteen. Despite her positive attitude towards her new career, she encountered very hard conditions. Her first mistress paid her only £7 a year, which was raised to £8 after her stepmother pressed her to ask for a raise. Her next post entailed such heavy work that her health broke down entirely and she had to return home for three months' recuperation. It was after this that Louise Jermy found employment with the Muirheads. A superficial reading of Jermy's memoirs might tempt readers to dismiss her as the stereotypical deferential servant, enamoured by her employers' sophisticated lifestyles, as one who devoted her energies to becoming a part of their world (and a subordinate one at that), rather than asking why she had been excluded from it in the first place. Jermy did at times enthusiastically rearticulate this well-worn trope, and it is worth noting that she was encouraged to write her memoirs by patrons in the Women's Institute who would themselves have been from the employer class.[79] Louise Jermy recalled the deep impression made when, on her first weekend working for the Muirheads, they entertained Professor Caird from Balliol College, Oxford. 'I had always admired educated and clever people', she wrote. 'I may say that my reverence grew as time went on, and I certainly made idols of some of them.' Above all, Jermy devoted herself to Mary Muirhead: 'I'll say at once that I loved this lady, I thought her wonderful and she was too' (though this effusive comment is immediately preceded by a reference to a pay rise Jermy had received in the first month of her employment).

Louise Jermy's comparative lack of interest in Mary Muirhead's husband is also striking. Her memoirs devote a couple of pages to describing Mary Muirhead and her household before even mentioning the existence of Professor Muirhead. John Henry Muirhead was in fact a renowned philosopher, but Jermy introduces him merely as 'in some College,

[77] Steedman, *An Everyday Life of the English Working Class*, pp. 16–17.
[78] *Glasgow Herald* 26 Sept. 1913, p. 5.
[79] Jane McDermid, 'The Making of a "Domestic" Life: Memories of a Working Woman', *Labour History Review*, 73:3 (Dec. 2008), 253–268, pp. 253–254.

I don't know where'. His wife, by contrast, is described in detail as 'a mistress of languages, Latin, Greek, French, German, it seems she knew everything'. Throughout this book I too focus overwhelmingly on the *female* employer, which may appear unfair. It was, after all, the family patriarch who benefitted most of all from a smoothly run household, and it was around his needs and comfort that domestic labour was structured. Jermy, for example, recalled how, in the year Professor Muirhead was writing his book *Political Economy*, she was even more overwhelmed by work than usual. Not only did she knit his socks, but she also had to manage 'the whole of the housekeeping' and weekly dinner parties as Mary Muirhead was kept busy 'writing everything for him to get it ready for the publishers'.[80] It is to the female employer that we must look, however, if we are to understand how class relations were made manifest for most domestic servants.[81] Louise Jermy was simply much more interested in Mary Muirhead than she was in her husband. In the Blathwayt and Clark families too it was Emily rather than Linley, and Helen rather than William, who decided whom to appoint as servants, on what basis to terminate their contracts and what should be included in their characters, as well as supervising their day-to-day labour. It was common for female servants to blame their mistresses for their poor treatment while exempting their masters as a pleasant, if distant, gentlemen.[82] For Jermy it was, undoubtedly, *Mrs* Muirhead who defined the experience of her employment, and who came to embody the power and seeming dignity of the middle class.

Louise Jermy had left school at age eleven, but when she entered the Muirheads' employment, she found that '[t]here were hundreds of books and I was at liberty to read any I liked'. One day, Mary Muirhead came into the kitchen to find her servant reading a geography book:

[Muirhead] fetched an orange, and rapidly drew with her penknife places all over the world, drew lines for the equator, and told me the reason of different seasons in different places, the reason of light and darkness, and why times differed in places … I know I kept that orange as long as I ever could.

A mistress able to explain the workings of the universe did sometimes appear to Jermy as an almost God-like figure. However, it is possible to see Jermy's adulation as a quite sensible and appropriate response. She enjoyed receiving the attention that her father and stepmother had

[80] Jermy, *The Memories of a Working Woman*, pp. 84–68, 94.
[81] Delap, *Knowing Their Place*, p. 16.
[82] *Woman Worker* 29 Sept. 1909, p. 296; WCML, Stephen, 'Submission Is for Slaves', p. 32.

denied her, wondering at how a woman who seemed to 'know every-thing' should take 'great interest in me'. There were also more tangible benefits offered by the relationship, especially considering Jermy's powerful, and until now thwarted, thirst for education. To work for a professional and well-connected mistress was to gain access to resources that working women such as Jermy would have otherwise found very difficult to obtain. Muirhead not only lent her books, she also investigated the possibility of Jermy joining a girls' club and sent her to reading classes. When she progressed rapidly with her reading, Muirhead expressed amazement that her servant had achieved so much on such little schooling: 'she said that undoubtedly had I gone on [in school], life must have held something very different to what it did'.[83]

Yet this better life, at least in the manner in which Mary Muirhead meant it, never actually materialised. Jermy's economic prospects did somewhat improve during the time she spent working at the Muirheads, who increased her wages a number of times (once by as much as £2 per year). She also gained more responsibility when Muirhead employed a Mrs Ryall as char to help her with the housework. Nevertheless, Jermy was the only full-time servant employed in this comfortably-off household. Although there were no children to look after, the Muirheads did often entertain a large number of high-profile scientists and writers, and Louise Jermy's workload was considerable. As well as keeping the house running, she also made some of Mary Muirhead's clothes, 'saw to her evening gowns, darned and mended linen … [and] served the weekly dinners'. Her mistress's philanthropic commitments only increased Jermy's responsibilities, such as being in charge of supplies for the first Women's Settlement in Birmingham. Jermy's memoirs finish this account of her involvement with the Muirheads' thriving intellectual and political life in Birmingham with an abrupt statement: 'Of course it made a lot for me to do and at times was a great strain, until there came a time when it really became too much and I was obliged to leave her.' No other information is given here, and Jermy moves to a different narrative thread over the next six pages, before returning to an account of the termination of her employment. This renewed attempt at explanation suggests a slightly different story, with Jermy claiming that it was her recurring hip injury that was at the root of the problem. She informed Muirhead of the great deal of pain that she had begun to suffer every night, in response to which her mistress offered her a hot water bottle.

---

[83] Jermy, *The Memories of a Working Woman*, pp. 85–86, 92–93.

This was no use and Jermy's ill-health worsened: 'want of sleep meant headache, and that meant bad temper. I began to forget things.' Without any further detail, Jermy skips to the end of this account, closing with the tantalising but unexplained statement: 'I'm sorry to say in a burst of temper, I left. Yet was I so much to blame after all? There is no doubt that it was a great strain on me and nobody realised it until it was too late.'[84]

How to interpret Louise Jermy's combination of professed adulation and more implicit intimations of resentment? What might be deduced from the disjointed way in which she narrates her experience? On the one hand, Mrs Muirhead represented Jermy's salvation. She provided her with the opportunity to leave an unhappy home, and later to escape the influence of her family by leaving London for Birmingham. Jermy also improved her literacy, general education and her skill at housekeeping through her employment at the Muirheads'. As a result, she felt grateful to her mistress, looked to her as a model of educated and self-realised womanhood and was excited by the new world that she opened up. Yet in this overwhelmingly positive account, there are suggestions that Jermy began to find Mary Muirhead's attentions inadequate. For example, Jermy described how, after keeping her disability a secret for so long, she eventually confided in her mistress: 'She was the only one I ever told of all the changes I made.' At the same time, Jermy's memoirs let us know that Muirhead had, up until that point, been entirely oblivious to the considerable physical pain that Jermy endured: 'She said she had never had such a surprise in her life ... that she had at times noticed a slight limp, she just put it down perhaps to a tight shoe.'[85] How could Muirhead have been so ignorant of her servant's state of health? Or, at the very least, how could she have been so unconcerned as to fail to enquire into the cause of Jermy's limp? And why, when Jermy's hip pain returned, did Mary Muirhead offer her a hot water bottle rather than paying for her to receive medical treatment? The reader (or at any rate this one) becomes indignant on Jermy's behalf, and perhaps this was Jermy's intention. The cultural narratives available to her (oppressed servant of tyrannical employer versus grateful recipient of maternal benevolence) left no space for the articulation of ambivalence. This is ultimately what Jermy's memoirs convey, an ambivalence implied through contradictory statements and fragmentary accounts of conversations between herself and her mistress. It thus becomes clear that a relationship which Jermy began describing as one of idolatry did in fact contain many tensions.

---

[84] Ibid., pp. 87–88, 94, 100–101.   [85] Ibid., p. 92.

In this way, Jermy and Muirhead's relationship was not exceptional. '[S]ervants through the ages' have experienced feelings of both resentment and appreciation and these are 'two sides of the same coin'.[86] The mistress's hot and cold treatment of her servant, and the servant's contradictory feelings towards her mistress, become much more intelligible when we understand that this relationship was structured at a day-to-day level not around abstract emotions and personal interactions but primarily by work. It was in the *doing* of domestic labour that Jermy and Muirhead most often encountered each other. The conversations with Muirhead that Jermy described all took place in the kitchen, when Muirhead came to lend a hand with the washing-up after a particularly late dinner, or when Jermy was helping her mistress undress and brush her hair.[87] We must not lose sight of the actual labour that formed not only the backdrop but also the purpose of the mistress and maid's encounters. Muirhead and Jermy may well have liked each other, but their relationship depended upon Jermy's ability to labour and Muirhead's ability to pay her. Kind Mary Muirhead may have been, but this did not prevent her from working Jermy beyond her physical and mental capacity. Nor did she employ a second servant to help Jermy when the work evidently became too much for her. Jermy was not deluded about the nature of this relationship. That she remembered the wage rise Muirhead had given her when writing her memoir thirty years later suggests that she was fully aware of the economic exchange at its heart.

It was not a lack of kindness or sympathetic attention that eventually led Louise Jermy to sever her contract with Mary Muirhead, but, according to her account, simply an excess of work. Historian Selina Todd has argued that much of the historiography on domestic service has over-emphasised the personalised and emotional aspects of the mistress–maid relation, and suggested instead that many servants simply experienced a sense of 'detachment' with regard to their employers.[88] This can hardly be said to have been the case for Louise Jermy, yet Todd's insistence that we should not forget that, for many, service was merely a job and nothing more is helpful here. In highlighting the contradictions and ambiguities within the mistress–maid relationship in all three households discussed in this chapter, I have sought to avoid a tendency towards either melodrama (mistress as tyrant) or sentimentality (mistress as bosom friend or mother) that characterises many cultural narratives of

---

[86] Light, *Mrs Woolf and the Servants*, p. 157.
[87] Jermy, *The Memories of a Working Woman*, pp. 86–87.
[88] Selina Todd, 'Domestic Service and Class Relations in Britain 1900–1950', *Past and Present*, 203 (2009), 181–204.

domestic service. Yet I am also resistant to a liberal even-handedness which emphasises variation within domestic service (sometimes mistresses were nice, sometimes they were nasty) to the extent that it becomes difficult to draw any overall conclusions about the nature of this particular kind of employment. In this chapter I hope to have offered a more textured account of how competing class interests and economic exploitation manifested themselves in the workplace of the home and class relations between women.

2   Servants in the Suffrage Movement

On Saturday, 18 June 1910, the Women's Social and Political Union (WSPU) staged one of its largest and most spectacular demonstrations. The Great Procession through the streets of central London was carefully choreographed and divided into numerous different 'contingents', each representing a particular class or type of suffrage supporter. There was a special contingent for Irish suffragettes, one for 'foreign supporters' and one for women who had attended university. Many of the contingents were organised according to profession, demonstrating the vast array of work done by disenfranchised women. There were teachers, musicians, civil servants and stenographers, gymnastics teachers, 'women pharmacists', sanitary inspectors and health visitors. Even that most overworked of professions, nurses, reportedly 'snatched a few brief hours from their labours to take part in the demonstration, and had a hearty welcome all along the line of the route'. Although the achievements of professional women were emphasised and celebrated, the Great Procession also featured women working in more lowly forms of employment. *Votes for Women* recorded that 'There were also sweated workers in poor clothes and hats that knew no fashion. There were boot-machiners, box-makers, and shirt-makers, who fight daily with starvation.' Efforts to mobilise for the Great Procession included holding meetings for laundry workers in North London, and the canvassing of 'factory and laundry districts' in South London.[1] Yet domestic servants, the most common and most numerous type of woman worker, were starkly absent from descriptions of the Great Procession, a fact strangely at odds with its raison d'être to showcase every aspect of female labour and experience.

This chapter looks at the participation and representation of domestic servants in the suffrage movement. It seeks to account for their invisibility in much of the official propaganda and public spectacle of all the leading suffrage societies, while, at the same time, uncovering the hidden

---

[1] *Votes for Women* 20 May 1910, p. 552; 3 June 1910, pp. 582–584; 24 June 1910, pp. 628–629.

history of servants' contribution to the fight for the vote. Class was a contentious issue within the suffrage movement. The various suffrage organisations argued over the basis upon which the franchise should be granted to women, since to ask for votes on the same terms as men was to accept the existing property qualification for male voters and exclude large numbers of working-class women. This debate on the criteria for enfranchisement related to wider disagreements over the movement's political alignments and whether it should be independent of political parties or make common cause with the organised working class and the Labour Party. The question of how class and gender competed with and reinforced each other as key determinants of political, social and economic inequality had been a continuing, though not always consistent, thread within feminist politics since the Owenite socialists' calls for women's emancipation in the 1840s. The debate intensified in the early years of the twentieth century, crystallising around the issue of cross-class alliances between women. The question of class has also exercised historians of the suffrage movement. The first histories to be written by non-participants, and therefore by male historians, portrayed women's suffrage as a middle-class movement, though since the 1980s feminist historians have exposed the often-dubious motivations that lay behind such assumptions. Disagreement remains, however, over the degree to which the WSPU in particular severed ties with its working-class supporters after it formally split from the Labour Party, as well as over the politics of seeking to organise women as a 'sex class'.

A focus on the role of domestic workers in the campaign for women's enfranchisement offers a new perspective on these debates. It not only shines a light on the involvement of a different kind of working-class woman, but also raises questions about how the suffrage movement defined the 'woman worker'. Perhaps one of the reasons why suffrage-supporting servants have almost never appeared in histories of the struggle was because they so rarely featured in the propaganda and public spectacle produced at the time. The 1910 Great Procession is typical of many such events organised by both the National Union of Women's Suffrage Societies (NUWSS) and the WSPU, which, although occasionally providing a role for domestic servants, always gave a far more prominent position to industrial and/or 'sweated' workers. Such representations obscured the involvement of domestic servants, who tended to contribute in less visible but nevertheless crucial ways to the cycles of care that underpinned the movement's more public achievements. Servants' long working days and strict surveillance by employers made it difficult to participate in meetings and demonstrations, yet many servants found the feminist press a conducive forum in which to feel part of the fight for the vote. Magistrates' court records and newspaper reports also reveal a number of otherwise anonymous servants who participated in militant actions.

Domestic servants could not be easily incorporated into the dominant definitions of working-class womanhood that circulated within the suffrage movement. Class difference within the various suffrage societies was negotiated in a number of ways, but its foremost organisations – the NUWSS, the WSPU and the Women's Freedom League (WFL) – believed firmly in the possibility of building cross-class alliances towards a common cause. Middle-class suffrage campaigners could sympathise with the factory worker, the mill girl and the sweated labourer, without having, in the main, to feel directly responsible for her suffering. Domestic servants, by contrast, offered a discomforting reminder that exploitation also occurred within many suffrage activists' very own homes. Thus, domestic servants signalled not just class difference, but also class conflict between women – the directly competing interests of mistress and maid. This potential for antagonism became real at certain moments in the correspondence pages of feminist newspapers when suffragette mistresses, complaining about lazy and incompetent servants, were challenged by militant maids calling on the women's movement to end their hypocrisy and attend to the oppression of that largest group of women workers.

Class and the Suffrage Movement

The NUWSS, the WSPU and the WFL demanded the vote for women on the same terms as men, which, before 1918, would have meant the continued disenfranchisement of large numbers of working-class women unable to meet the property qualification that still excluded over 30 per cent of men.[2] A counterdemand for 'womanhood suffrage', including all women over the age of twenty-one, was put forward in the 1890s by the radical suffragists based mainly among Lancashire mill workers in the north of England. As the first organised group of working-class women in the British suffrage movement, many of whom were also active in trade unions, the radical suffragists intended that the demand for womanhood suffrage should imply the simultaneous enfranchisement of the small

---

[2] Pat Thane, 'Women in the Labour Party and Women's Suffrage', in Myriam Boussahba-Bravard (ed.), *Suffrage Outside Suffragism: Women's Vote in Britain, 1880–1914* (Basingstoke: Palgrave Macmillan, 2007), 35–51, p. 35; Jill Liddington, *Rebel Girls: Their Fight for the Vote* (London: Virago, 2006), p. 8.

numbers of men who still lacked the vote, since no government would ever grant the suffrage to working-class women without giving it to their male counterparts.[3] The radical suffragists also played an important role in convincing members of the Independent Labour Party (ILP) to campaign for votes for women. From 1895 onwards its leader, Keir Hardie, pushed for its National Administrative Council to support an 'equal franchise' and 'every proposal for extending electoral rights', which might include but was not limited to a measure of women's suffrage in advance of full adult suffrage. By the turn of the century, support for women's suffrage in the ILP was widespread but not unanimous. Some men in the ILP and the wider labour movement (the ILP joined the Trades Union Council to fight elections as the Labour Representation Committee in 1900, becoming the Labour Party in 1906) dismissed women's suffrage as a 'middle-class' issue, calling instead for adult suffrage.[4] Keir Hardie, along with other Labour Party MPs such as George Lansbury, remained committed to any measures that would extend women's suffrage, working alongside the WSPU in calling for the vote on equal terms with men.[5] The Labour Party did not explicitly commit itself to women's suffrage, as a component of full adult suffrage, until 1912.[6]

There was, therefore, no clear left/right divide determining whether individuals thought women's suffrage or adult suffrage was the best way to formulate the demand. While many socialists and trade unionists believed that focusing on women's suffrage was the most effective first step towards securing votes for working-class women, the same demand was campaigned for by Conservative Party and upper-class women who wanted votes only for women of the propertied classes. On the other hand, calls for adult suffrage could be used to justify lack of active support for women's rights, coupled with vague gestures towards female enfranchisement once the rights of male workers had been fully achieved. 'Adultists' succeeded in repeatedly defeating women's suffrage

---

[3] Jill Liddington and Jill Norris, *One Hand Tied behind Us: The Rise of the Women's Suffrage Movement* (London: Virago, 1984), pp. 25–26.

[4] Laura Ugolini, "'It's Only Justice to Grant Women's Suffrage": Independent Labour Party Men and Women's Suffrage, 1893–1905', in Claire Eustance, Joan Ryan and Laura Ugolini (eds.), *A Suffrage Reader: Charting Directions in British Suffrage History* (London: Leicester University Press, 2000), 126–144.

[5] Krista Cowman, "'Incipient Toryism": The Women's Social and Political Union and the Independent Labour Party, 1903–1914', *History Workshop Journal*, 53 (Spring 2002), 128–148, pp. 135–136.

[6] Thane, 'Women in the Labour Party and Women's Suffrage', p. 41.

resolutions at Labour Party conferences between 1904 and 1909.[7] The Adult Suffrage Society (est. 1904) was often criticised for spending more energy opposing those organisations that supported votes for women on the same terms as men than on its professed aim of suffrage for all. Yet it also attracted some socialist women genuinely committed to enfranchising their sex, who believed that a property qualification would be a betrayal of working-class women and that adult suffrage was the only truly democratic demand.[8] The People's Suffrage Federation was founded in 1909 by a number of leading female trade unionists and the Women's Co-operative Guild, with the intention of reinvigorating the campaign for adult suffrage while also retaining an emphasis on women's rights.[9]

The 1918 Representation of the People Act retained a property qualification for women while removing it for men. Women over the new voting age of thirty qualified for the franchise if they or their husbands were property owners or local government electors (rate-payers). This did not equate to a wholesale exclusion of working-class women, but it did leave most domestic servants without the vote, since they resided in the homes of their employers and did not, therefore, pay rates. In the lead-up to the passing of the Act many suffrage activists protested that it still denied women the franchise on equal terms with men. But the leaders of the NUWSS, including Millicent Garrett Fawcett and Ray Strachey, resigned themselves to it as a first step towards removing the disqualification on grounds of sex alone.[10] Historian Jo Vellacott has argued that a much wider franchise would have been possible had it not been for a dispute in the NUWSS in 1915 over whether to support the women's peace congress at the Hague. This prompted mass resignations from the more progressive and pacifist wing of the organisation, leaving the leadership in the hands of more conservative members.[11]

[7] Sandra Stanley Holton, *Feminism and Democracy: Women's Suffrage and Reform Politics in Britain 1900–1918* (Cambridge: Cambridge University Press, 1986), pp. 57–59.
[8] Karen Hunt, *Equivocal Feminists: The Social Democratic Federation and the Woman Question 1884–1911* (Cambridge: Cambridge University Press, 1996), chapter 6.
[9] Ibid., p. 179; Elizabeth Crawford, *The Women's Suffrage Movement: A Reference Guide* (London: University College London Press, 1999), p. 533.
[10] 'There were approximately 2,000,000 women over thirty who failed to qualify. They fell into the following categories: professional and business women with business premises or unfurnished rooms, shop assistants and domestic workers who "lived in", and daughters living at home.' Women university graduates could vote for MPs representing the universities; Cheryl Law, *Suffrage and Power: The Women's Movement 1918–1928* (London: I. B. Tauris, 1997), pp. 182–183.
[11] Jo Vellacott, 'Feminist Consciousness and the First World War', *History Workshop Journal*, 23 (1987), 81–101; Jo Vellacott, *Pacifists, Patriots and the Vote: The Erosion of Democratic Suffragism in Britain during the First World War* (Basingstoke: Palgrave, 2007).

I suggest that we also need to consider the limitations of the 1918 Act in light of the precarious position that domestic servants occupied in the pre-war suffrage movement, given that they were the largest group of working-class women who continued to be denied a vote.

Just as contemporaries argued over the class politics of the demand for the vote, so historians have argued over the class make-up of the movement as a whole. Feminist historians, since the 1970s, have begun to challenge and nuance the notion that the struggle for the suffrage was exclusively fought by and for middle-class women.[12] Jill Liddington and Jill Norris showed that working-class Lancashire women were crucial in the formation of a radical suffragist current from the 1890s onwards.[13] Liddington's later work argued that similarly strong working-class support for the suffrage, especially for the WSPU, also emerged in Yorkshire, among women working as machinists, weavers, needle women, milliners and in other manufacturing jobs related to the textile trade.[14] Leah Leneman refuted earlier characterisations of the Scottish suffrage movement as more middle-class than its English counterpart, revealing a number of working-class women active in the militant societies. The Glasgow WSPU branch, of which Jessie Stephen was a member, had particularly close links with local socialists and trade unionists.[15] Gillian Scott showed how the Women's Co-operative Guild, a large national organisation of working-class housewives, also made an important contribution to the struggle for the suffrage.[16] Sandra Stanley Holton located such initiatives within a longer-standing tradition of 'democratic suffragism', which sought votes for women in the broadest terms. In the years leading up to the First World War, this political current brought the women's suffrage movement into closer and more organised alliance

---

[12] Those who argued that women's suffrage was a middle-class movement include R. S. Neale, 'Working-Class Women and Women's Suffrage', *Labour History*, 12 (1967), 16–34; Jihang Park, 'The British Suffrage Activists of 1913: An Analysis', *Past and Present*, 120 (1988), 147–162. For a critique of the masculinist politics that lay behind such assumptions, see June Purvis, 'Emmeline Pankhurst: A Biographical Interpretation', *Women's History Review*, 12:1 (2003), 73–102, pp. 73–76.

[13] Liddington and Norris, *One Hand Tied behind Us*; Jill Liddington, *The Life and Times of a Respectable Rebel: Selina Cooper 1864–1946* (London: Virago, 1984).

[14] Liddington, *Rebel Girls*.

[15] Leah Leneman, *A Guid Cause: The Women's Suffrage Movement in Scotland* (Aberdeen: Aberdeen University Press, 1991), pp. 93–94, 42–43, 138, 166.

[16] Gillian Scott, *Feminism and the Politics of Working Women: The Women's Co-operative Guild, 1880s to the Second World War* (London: University College London Press, 1998). See also Kay Cook and Neil Evans, '"The Petty Antics of the Bell-Ringing Boisterous Band"? The Women's Suffrage Movement in Wales, 1890–1918', in Angela V. John (ed.), *Our Mothers' Land: Chapters in Welsh Women's History, 1830–1939* (Cardiff: University of Wales Press, 1991), 159–188, p. 177; Ryland Wallace, *The Women's Suffrage Movement in Wales, 1866–1928* (Cardiff: University of Wales Press, 2009), pp. 181–183.

with the labour movement, via organisations such as the United Suffragists, the East London Federation of the Suffragettes and the NUWSS's Election Fighting Fund, established in 1912 to support Labour Party candidates against the Liberals who were still delaying the introduction of an effective women's suffrage bill.[17] The WFL, despite remaining independent from all political parties, also maintained close links to the labour movement and the ILP and actively sought to recruit working-class women.[18]

The WSPU followed a somewhat different trajectory from the other main suffrage organisations, moving away from its originally close relationship with the labour movement. The Pankhursts and other founding members of the WSPU were all ILP women seeking a forum in which they could focus on issues specific to women within their wider socialist political activity. The militant tactics that the WSPU began to deploy in 1905 were already widely used in the labour movement, and some in the NUWSS initially sought to distance themselves from the WSPU not so much because of the disruptive nature of these tactics but because of their strong association with working-class political activism.[19] Up until 1906 the WSPU de facto campaigned for the ILP due to their policy of supporting whichever election candidate was most sympathetic to women's suffrage. In August of that year, however, Christabel Pankhurst changed tack, deciding that the WSPU would oppose the government candidate, regardless of party. In practice this meant mainly trying to unseat Liberal MPs, usually to the benefit of the Conservatives and the disadvantage of Labour. Following this, Emmeline and Christabel Pankhurst resigned from the Labour Party in April 1907, and the two organisations parted ways even more decisively when the WSPU began to actively oppose Labour as well as Liberal candidates after the Labour Party refused the WSPU's demand that they vote against the Liberals in every division in Parliament. The split between the Pankhursts and the ILP did not, however, end all ties between the wider WSPU membership and the labour movement. At a local level, cooperation between the WSPU and the ILP often continued, many individuals remained members of both organisations, and socialism and support for women's

---

[17] Holton, *Feminism and Democracy*; Harold L. Smith, *The British Women's Suffrage Campaign 1866–1928* (Harlow: Pearson Education, 2010), pp. 59, 65–67.

[18] Claire Eustance, '"Daring to Be Free": The Evolution of Women's Political Identities in the Women's Freedom League 1907–1930', PhD thesis, University of York (1993), chapter 1, pp. 122–127, 133.

[19] Holton, *Feminism and Democracy*, p. 35; Cowman, '"Incipient Toryism"?', pp. 136–137.

suffrage intertwined. A number of working-class women continue to be active in the WSPU well into the final stages of militancy.[20]

This chapter on suffrage-supporting servants therefore contributes to an ongoing historical project to recover the experiences of working-class women in the struggle for the vote. All the main suffrage organisations took an interest in the needs of working-class women, even if it is hard to establish precisely how large a proportion of their membership might count as working-class, with almost certainly a majority from middle- to upper-middle-class backgrounds.[21] But in noting an interest in, as well as the presence of, working-class women, I want to avoid uncritically replicating the optimistic language of female solidarity transcending class difference that appeared in much suffrage propaganda. Annie Kenney was one of the few working-class women to achieve national

---

[20] June Purvis, 'The Prison Experiences of the Suffragettes in Edwardian Britain', *Women's History Review*, 4:1 (1995), 103–133; Michelle Myall, '"No Surrender!": The Militancy of Mary Leigh, a Working-Class Suffragette', in Maroula Joannou and June Purvis (eds.), *The Women's Suffrage Movement: New Feminist Perspectives* (Manchester: Manchester University Press, 1998), 173–187; Cowman, '"Incipient Toryism"?'; Krista Cowman, *Mrs Brown Is a Man and a Brother: Women in Merseyside's Political Organisations, 1890–1920* (Liverpool: Liverpool University Press, 2004); Krista Cowman, *Women of the Right Spirit: Paid Organisers of the Women's Social and Political Union, 1904–1918* (Manchester: Manchester University Press, 2007); Liddington, *Rebel Girls*, p. 95, 107, p. 216, part 4.

Purvis and Cowman maintain that the degree to which the WSPU gave up on recruiting working-class women after it split with the Labour Party has been overdetermined in many historical accounts due to too great a reliance on the version of events given in Sylvia Pankhurst's *The Suffragette Movement* (1931), written in a period when the left-wing Pankhurst was both politically and personally estranged from her mother and sister. Purvis, Myall, and Cowman also blame the 'socialist feminism' of many feminist historians in the 1970s and 1980s for a lack of interest in the WSPU, an organisation that sought political autonomy from male-dominated political parties and emphasised patriarchy over capitalism as the key source of women's oppression; Purvis, 'The Prison Experiences of the Suffragettes', p. 105; Myall, '"No Surrender!"', pp. 173–174; Cowman, '"Incipient Toryism"?', pp. 132–133; Purvis, 'Emmeline Pankhurst', pp. 73–75. In 2015 it was argued that such socialist feminism continued to taint the view of historians, including myself; see Diane Atkinson and Krista Cowman, 'Suffragette: 100 Years on Women's Rights Still Prompt Shrill Hysteria', *Telegraph* 30 Oct. 2015, www.telegraph.co.uk; June Purvis, 'The Right Kind of Feminists', *Times Higher Education* 19 Nov. 2015, www.timeshighereducation.com.

[21] Angela V. John, 'Radical Reflections? Elizabeth Robins: The Making of Suffragette History and the Representation of Working-Class Women', in Owen Ashton, Robert Fyson and Stephen Roberts (eds.), *The Duty of Discontent: Essays for Dorothy Thompson* (London: Mansell Publishing, 1995), 191–211. One of the few attempts to quantitatively analyse the class backgrounds of suffrage activists was based on the data provided in the *Suffrage Annual and Women's Who's Who* (1913), which did not include many of those active in both the women's and the labour movement, or the People's Suffrage Federation; Park, 'The British Suffrage Activists of 1913'.

prominence and an important leadership position in the WSPU. Her autobiography, written in 1924, recalls the relationships between suffragettes of different classes thus:

Women of every profession and trade and occupation had thrown in their lots with ours. Science ... music ... literature ... medicine ... art ... sculpture ... stage ... teachers ... the nursing profession ... shop assistants ... the secretarial world ... factory women ... housewives ... social workers ... aristocracy ... poor democracy ... North, South, East, and West, rich and poor.[22]

Economic and educational inequality between suffrage women did not, however, evaporate quite as easily as such an account suggests. Middle-class enthusiasm for working-class women's involvement was not always a guarantee against their being marginalised, fetishised, objectified as victims or pressured to appear more 'presentable'.[23] Moreover, poverty had many ways of preventing women from participating in suffrage activities. Nellie Best, a servant registry keeper and member of both the ILP and the WFL in Middlesbrough, complained in two letters to the *Woman Worker* in 1908 of how the fashion for wearing evening dress at London suffragist societies' 'At Homes' excluded 'servants and laundresses'.[24] Annie Kenney claimed that the WSPU was sensitive to class difference, recalling how they had tried to make it easier for their supporters in the East End of London to attend meetings in Caxton Hall by paying for travel into the centre of the city and providing 'hot drink and food on their arrival'.[25] Hannah Mitchell was more ambivalent on the matter. She remembered 'a unity of purpose in the suffrage movement, which made social distinctions seem of little importance', but her autobiography also recalls how some of the 'lady' suffrage speakers that she

[22] Annie Kenney, *Memories of a Militant* (London: Edward Arnold, 1924), p. 135. Much suffrage fiction foregrounded similarly idealised cross-class alliances; Elizabeth Robins, *The Convert* (London: Macmillan, 1913 [first published 1907]); Rebecca West, *The Sentinel: An Incomplete Early Novel by Rebecca West*, ed. Kathryn Laing (Oxford: European Humanities Research Centre, 2002); Constance Elizabeth Maud, *No Surrender* (New York: John Lane, 1912).

[23] Eustance, '"Daring to Be Free"', pp. 17, 122–127; Sandra Stanley Holton, 'Silk Dresses and Lavender Kid Gloves: The Wayward Career of Jessie Craigen, Working Suffragist', *Women's History Review*, 5:1 (1996), 129–150; June Purvis, *Emmeline Pankhurst: A Biography* (London: Routledge, 2002), p. 111; Sue Thomas, 'Scenes in the Writing of "Constance Lytton and Jane Warton, Spinster": Contextualising a Cross-Class Dresser', *Women's History Review*, 12:1 (2003), 51–71; Lyndsey Jenkins, 'From Mills to Militants: The Kenney Sisters, Suffrage and Social Reform c. 1890 to 1970', PhD thesis, University of Oxford (2018).

[24] *Woman Worker* 25 Sept. 1908, p. 430; 16 Oct. 1908, p. 502; *Labour Leader* 14 Jan. 1910, p. 29; Eustance, '"Daring to Be Free"', p. 125.

[25] Kenney, *Memories of a Militant*, p. 69.

and her husband often hosted were unused to staying in a house without domestic staff and instead treated her as if she was their servant.[26]

By contrast, married working-class women with sole responsibility for their own domestic labour often found this to be the main obstacle to participating in the suffrage movement. 'No cause can be won between dinner and tea', wrote Hannah Mitchell, 'and most of us who were married had to work [for the suffrage] with one hand tied behind us.'[27] She was far from being the only working-class suffragette whose suffrage experiences were permanently overshadowed by a mountain of domestic labour awaiting her return from political meetings and even prison. Emma Sproson (1867–1936) had worked first as a domestic servant and then as a Sunday school teacher before marrying Frank Sproson, a postman and fellow Wolverhampton ILP member, with whom she had four children. She gained some prominence as a WSPU speaker in 1907 before joining the WFL and becoming a member of its national executive in 1908.[28] The letters she wrote to Frank during two periods of imprisonment for participating in WSPU marches on Parliament in the spring of 1907 are greatly taken up with instructions about how to undertake the housekeeping in her absence:

I hope you will be able to get the early potatoes. And you might get another half pint of daisy peas and sow with them. The broad beans are in kitchen table drawer by the French window but they will need well soaking ... and get 1 lb of the enclosed wool for knitting childrens' socks. It will be about 2/ [s.] post it to me immediately as I want it to get on with and time is so much longer with nothing to do.[29]

Sproson's prison experiences were therefore very different from those of wealthier suffragettes who, though they may have worried about their husbands and children at home, knew that at least their basic needs would be catered for by servants.[30] Emma Sproson was certainly aware of the disparity in power, wealth and education that existed between her and her middle-class sisters. In April 1912 she resigned from the National

---

[26] Hannah Mitchell, *The Hard Way Up: The Autobiography of Hannah Mitchell, Suffragette and Rebel* (London: Virago, 1977), pp. 159, 119. For Mitchell's more positive comments on the WSPU, see Cowman, *Women of the Right Spirit*, p. 21.

[27] Mitchell, *The Hard Way Up*, pp. 130, 162.

[28] Wolverhampton Archive (hereafter WA), Emma Sproson, 'Autobiography' (unpublished manuscript), DX-686:1; Susan Pauline Walters, 'Emma Sproson (1867–1936): A Black Country Suffragette', MA dissertation, University of Leicester (1993); Jane Martin, 'Sproson [née Lloyd], Emma (1867–1936), Suffragist and Local Politician', in *Oxford Dictionary of National Biography*, online edn. (Oxford University Press, 2004); Eustance, '"Daring to Be Free"', pp. 417–418.

[29] WA, Sproson Correspondence, Emma Sproson to Frank Sproson, 4 April 1907, DX-686/5,9.

[30] Purvis, 'The Prison Experiences of the Suffragettes'.

Executive Committee of the WFL in protest against Charlotte Despard's autocratic style of leadership, explaining in a speech how it was 'especially difficult for one who is so much younger and who feels the difference in her social position' to stand up to and disagree with middle-class leaders.[31] In drawing attention to such differences, I do not wish to deny the sense of solidarity that women from different class backgrounds could feel when sharing a prison yard or demonstrating alongside each other. The exceptional circumstances of the suffrage movement did sometimes erode class hierarchies. Upper-middle-class women found themselves engaged in unthinkable activities such as washing up the dinner plates on an NUWSS caravan tour or making their own beds in prison, while working-class women were welcomed as guests in grand houses where, under other circumstances, they might have been employed as servants.[32] I do, however, wish to interrogate that female solidarity further, looking at how it related to women's class positions, and at the difficulties of attempting to overcome what would normally have been an unbridgeable social divide. Although Annie Kenney referred specifically to domestic workers to invoke an image of cross-class solidarity in the WSPU, declaring that 'A Girton girl or a charwoman, it made no difference', relations between suffrage-supporting servants and mistresses were rather more complex than Kenney would have us believe.[33]

Servants in the Suffrage Movement

> The WSPU is having a big demonstration here today. I am a member but I cannot get to any meetings. While I sit here my spirit is with the women, wishing them success. My wings are beating hard against the bars of my cage to be free and to be able to help them.[34]

In 1908 an anonymous 'Domestic' wrote the above words in a letter to the socialist feminist newspaper the *Woman Worker*. It lamented her inability to join what was probably the WSPU 'Woman's Sunday', when about 30,000 women processed through London, most of them wearing white.[35]

---

[31] Walters, 'Emma Sproson', p. 71.
[32] Mitchell, *The Hard Way Up*, p. 159; Purvis, 'The Prison Experiences of the Suffragettes', pp. 110–113; Liddington, *Rebel Girls*, pp. 47, 211–214, 318.
[33] Kenney, *Memories of a Militant*, pp. 124–126.
[34] *Woman Worker* 31 July 1908, p. 238.
[35] The 'Woman's Sunday' took place on 21 June 1908 and was the only large-scale public demonstration organised by the WSPU that summer; Lisa Tickner, *The Spectacle of Women: Imagery of the Suffrage Campaign, 1907–1914* (London: Chatto & Windus, 1987), p. 94. It is also possible that this 'Domestic' was referring to a smaller local demonstration, but she did not identify her location.

Like her, many other servants found it difficult to participate in the suffrage movement's regular round of meetings and demonstrations, not to mention highly public and/or illegal actions. The feminist press thus became an especially important forum. Instead of marching through the streets with her comrades, 'Domestic' described herself as 'sat reading the *Woman Worker*', which offered an alternative way of demonstrating her solidarity. Such newspapers would have been relatively accessible to servants since, by the first decade of the twentieth century, they were often sold on the streets or left lying about in cafes and railway station waiting rooms with the hope of picking up a new audience.[36] Short or serialised articles offered an ideal format for servants who might only have five or ten minutes to spare between the incessant tasks that constituted their sixteen-hour working day. The feminist press was characterised by a culture of controversy and debate. The *Common Cause*, for example, had an explicitly open policy with regard to its correspondence columns, and this may have helped servants acquire the confidence to make their voices heard.[37] Letters could be published anonymously and frequently provoked responses from other servants, providing a rare opportunity to collectivise the grievances of an otherwise fragmented and isolated workforce.

Between 1906 and 1907 Clementina Black collected 26,261 signatures on a 'Declaration' from women stating their wish to receive the franchise on the same terms as men. The professions of 25,000 signatories were analysed, and 2,769 of them described their job as 'domestic'. This was the second largest occupational group after 'educational', and more than ten times the number of factory workers' signatures.[38] Some of these servants even participated in the most visible and dangerous forms of suffrage activism. The anonymous 'Domestic' quoted above, for

---

[36] Maria Dicenzo, Lucy Delap and Leila Ryan (eds.), *Feminist Media History: Suffrage, Periodicals and the Public Sphere* (Basingstoke: Palgrave Macmillan, 2011). It was also common for servants to have access to their employers' newspapers; Margaret Beetham, 'Domestic Servants as Poachers of Print: Reading Authority and Resistance in Late Victorian Britain', in Lucy Delap, Ben Griffin and Abigail Wills (eds.), *The Politics of Domestic Authority in Britain since 1800* (Basingstoke: Palgrave, 2009), 185–203.

A couple of mistresses even complained to the *Common Cause* that the paper's content was either too sexually explicit or too informative about workers' rights to leave it lying within reach of their domestics; *Common Cause* 26 June 1911, p. 682; 7 Dec. 1911, pp. 621–622.

[37] Maria Dicenzo, Lucy Delap and Leila Ryan, 'Introduction', in Dicenzo et al. (eds.), *Feminist Media History*, 1–20, p. 2; Maria Dicenzo, 'Unity and Dissent: Official Organs of the Suffrage Campaign', in Dicenzo et al. (eds.), *Feminist Media History*, 76–119, p. 111; Barbara Green, *Feminist Periodicals and Daily Life: Women and Modernity in British Culture* (Basingstoke: Palgrave Macmillan, 2017), pp. 149–150.

[38] *Women's Franchise* 2 July 1908, p. 3. There is a separate category of 'Married', so it is reasonable to assume that these are waged domestic workers.

example, may have been trapped inside on the day of a large demonstration, but her letter also describes how she had, in the past, participated in militant activity and even gone to prison for it.[39] Likewise, twenty-six-year-old domestic servant Eliza Simmons was sentenced to fourteen days' imprisonment on 23 November 1910 for 'wilfully breaking three windows' at Winston Churchill's residence in Eccleston Square.[40] It is possible to catch only a brief glimpse of such women, since just their names and occupations were recorded in newspaper reports of suffragette arrests and the registers of magistrates' courts where they were sentenced. And these sources obviously do not capture servants who supported the 'law-abiding' wing of the movement.[41] Moreover, the prominence and wealth of their employer tends to determine whether suffrage-supporting servants turn up in the historical record.

Charlotte Griffiths of Rochdale was fifty years old when, on the evening of 11 February 1908, she joined hundreds of other suffragettes in a raid on the Houses of Parliament. Earlier in the day she had been participating in the Women's Parliament, which had been organised by the WSPU to discuss the injustice of women's continued disenfranchisement and the government's repressive action towards militant suffrage campaigners. Initially, St Stephen's Hall (part of the Houses of Parliament) was the target of a surprise attack by twenty-one suffragettes who arrived disguised inside a furniture removal van. Charlotte Griffiths joined the second wave of demonstrators attempting to enter the House in the evening, braving not only a 'solid phalanx of police', but also a 'mob of boys' who assaulted some of her party with 'stones and sticks'.[42] Griffiths was one of the fifty arrested and tried at Bow Street Magistrates Court where, refusing to find two sureties of £20, she was served a six-week prison sentence.[43] She spent only a week in Holloway Prison, however, accepting an offer of sureties to enable her to return home to nurse her ailing mother. These were paid for by John Albert Bright

---

[39] *Woman Worker* 31 July 1908, p. 238.
[40] London Metropolitan Archive (hereafter LMA), London, 'Register of the Court of Summary Jurisdiction Sitting at Bow Street', part 1, 1910, 23 Nov. 1910, PS/BOW/A/01/040; *Votes for Women*, 2 Dec. 1910, p. 143. Note that the report in *Votes for Women* spells Eliza's surname 'Simmins', and incorrectly states that she was sentenced on 24 November. Numerous variations on the spelling of this name make it impossible to determine for sure whether the Elizabeth Symmons arrested for militant activity the following year is the same person; *Daily Express* 22 Nov. 1911, p. 3.
[41] For brief references to other suffrage-supporting servants, see Purvis, 'The Prison Experiences of Suffragettes', p. 120; Liddington, *Rebel Girls*, pp. 113, 193–194, 276–280.
[42] *Manchester Guardian* 12 Feb. 1908, p. 7.
[43] *Rochdale Observer*, 19 Feb. 1908, p. 5; LMA, 'Register of the Court of Summary Jurisdiction at Westminster', part 1, 12 Feb. 1908, PS/WES/A/01/052.

(Liberal MP for Oldham), and Gordon Harvey (Liberal MP for Rochdale). It was in her capacity as a domestic servant rather than as suffragette that Charlotte Griffiths drew the attention of Members of Parliament, for since at least 1901 she had been employed as a 'nurse domestic' in the house of John Albert Bright.[44] Bright, son of the famous radical MP John Bright and cousin to Helen Clark, was, in his own words, 'rather weak-kneed' about the question of women's parliamentary franchise. Although he supported women's election to town councils and other public bodies, John Albert Bright claimed that he remained unconvinced that the majority of the female population wanted the parliamentary vote. Moreover, he felt that the Liberal government had more pressing legislation to pass, such as old age pensions. He nevertheless travelled to London to aid Charlotte Griffiths' release, and, shocked to find her clothed in 'hideous prison dress' normally reserved for criminals rather than prisoners of conscience, he moved a protest in the House of Commons about the treatment of suffragette prisoners.[45]

Charlotte Griffiths was fortunate to be employed by a family with a long tradition of supporting radical causes, and militant action did not cost her her job. The anonymous 'Domestic' writing to the *Woman Worker* in 1908 was not so lucky: 'I had a hard fight to get a situation after my imprisonment. I am afraid that if my present mistress were to know that I was an ex-convict she would not want me anymore.'[46] Mistresses frequently advertised for servants in *Votes for Women* and the *Common Cause*, occasionally promising that they would be free to attend suffrage meetings.[47] Servants also sometimes placed advertisements seeking politically amenable employers, such as one anonymous lady's maid 'out of place through her sympathies for votes for women'.[48] In

[44] England and Wales Census (1901), Manora, Hollington Park, Hollington St. John, Sussex; England and Wales Census (1911), One Ash, Rochdale, Lancashire. John Albert Bright claimed that he had known her for twenty years, although he did not state in exactly what capacity; 'The Imprisoned Woman Suffragists', House of Commons debate, *Hansard* 13 Feb. 1908, 184, cc. 284–288, www.hansard.millbanksystems.com.
[45] *Rochdale Observer*, 19 Feb. 1908, p. 5; 'The Imprisoned Woman Suffragists', House of Commons debate, *Hansard* 13 Feb. 1908, 184, cc. 284–288, www.hansard.millbanksystems.com. John Bright was rather mealy mouthed in his comments, describing Charlotte Griffiths as 'a very worthy woman, however mistaken', and the suffragettes in general as 'high-minded' 'whatever they [the House] might think of their actions'.
[46] *Woman Worker* 31 July 1908, p. 239.
[47] The Blathwayts also signed up for a servants' registry they saw advertised in *Votes for Women*; GA, E. M. Blathwayt, 'Diary', 3 Nov. 1908, p. 122, D2659/24/11; 17 July 1911, pp. 141–142, D2659/24/12; *Votes for Women*, 29 Oct. 1908, p. 85; *Common Cause* 24 Aug. 1911, p. 349.
[48] *Votes for Women* 23 Sept. 1910, p. 836. See also 16 Dec. 1910, p. 191.

1910 the North West London branch of the WSPU helped a house-maid 'who lost her berth [post] through going on the last Deputation' and a cook general 'who wishes to be free to volunteer for the next'.[49] There is some evidence to suggest that a few mistresses saw the political conversion of their maids as merely an extension of their responsibilities and authority as employers, rather than viewing such women as their equals in a common struggle for emancipation. A friend of the mother of aristocratic suffragette Constance Lytton once suggested that it would have been better if Lytton, instead of risking her life by imprisonment and force-feeding, had instead focused her energies on setting up a branch of the WSPU among the servants at her family estate in Knebworth.[50]

'Antis' certainly accused suffrage-supporting servants of mindlessly aping the politics of their betters or, worse, of being manipulated and exploited by their radical employers. Soon after the suffragettes' raid on St Stephen's Hall, the General Committee of the National Liberal Federation debated the question of votes for women, during which Maurice Levy MP denounced a 'band of women paid organisers ... bringing young girls from their employment, placing them on the streets of London amid horrible temptation'. He referred directly to Charlotte Griffiths' arrest, claiming that John Albert Bright's wife, Edith, 'afraid to go out into the streets herself, allowed and induced' her servant to 'go and take part in the rowdyism'.[51] Charlotte Griffiths, however, refused to be portrayed as her mistress' political puppet. The following week she wrote to the *Manchester Guardian* (the newspaper that had printed Levy's slander) insisting that 'I went entirely of my own free will, without any pressure or persuasion, but because I believed the cause was just and right, and that every woman who was able to do so should give her help.'[52] Rather than simply enacting the political enthusiasms of her employers, it is possible that, to the contrary, Griffiths might have helped spur the Brights towards more active support for women's suffrage. Certainly, it was her arrest that prompted John Albert Bright to make his protest in the House of Commons, and also to address female enfranchisement in a speech the following week on the occasion of the election of a woman to Rochdale Town Council. His wife, Edith Bright, became president of the Rochdale branch of the North of England Society for Women's Suffrage, and their daughter, Hester Bright, later became its secretary – but this branch was not founded until September

---

[49] *Votes for Women* 23 Dec. 1910, p. 204.   [50] Cowman, *Women of the Right Spirit*, p. 22.
[51] *Manchester Guardian* 22 Feb. 1908, p. 10.
[52] *Manchester Guardian* 3 March 1908, p. 5.

1908, a number of months after Charlotte Griffiths had served a week in Holloway prison.[53]

The servants employed at Eagle House also showed themselves to be independent political agents. Parlour-maid Ellen Morgan accompanied Mary Blathwayt to her first WSPU meeting. There is no suggestion that Morgan attended only in the capacity of chaperone (two other female friends also joined them), and since they did not return home until 2 a. m., leaving Morgan only four hours before her working day began, it is reasonable to speculate that she attended out of her own interest rather than solely to please her mistress.[54] In the coming months Ellen Morgan attended further suffrage meetings in Bath and Bristol, along with the cook, Elsie Harris, and the char, Ellen Martha Rawlings.[55] Did the Blathwayts put pressure on their domestics to support a cause which was not theirs? Emily Blathwayt, Mary's mother, occasionally bought her maids tickets for suffrage events, which no doubt provided extra motivation to attend.[56] Yet she also recorded in her diary how, during the WSPU 'week of self denial' in February 1908, Ellen Morgan, Elsie Harris and Moses Rawlings, the chauffeur, had all approached Mary 'spontaneously' to add their sixpence donations to her collection card.[57] Ellen Morgan and Elsie Harris not only attended suffrage meetings, but also helped to distribute WSPU propaganda. At one event Ellen Morgan had to dodge an attack by a group of 'hooligans' and 'very low men' who came to disrupt the meeting, possibly under orders from the local Liberal Party, but she still managed to sell 'a large number' of copies of a book entitled *Trial of the Prisoner*.[58]

After Ellen Morgan and Elsie Harris left the Blathwayt household, new servants May Woodham and Ellen (Nelly) Durnford also showed an interest in the suffrage movement, purchasing postcards featuring a prominent local suffragette, Mrs Morgan, posed in a rickshaw outside the Bath suffrage shop.[59] Working for a family involved in the movement

---

[53] Hester Bright became secretary in 1909–1910; Elizabeth Crawford, *The Women's Suffrage Movement in Britain and Ireland: A Regional Survey* (London: Routledge, 2008), p. 11.

[54] Gloucester Archive (hereafter GA), Mary Blathwayt, 'Diary', 8 Nov. 1907, n.p., D2659/27/12.

[55] GA, Mary Blathwayt, 'Diary', 11 March 1908, n.p.; 1 April 1908, n.p., D2659/27/13; E. M. Blathwayt, 'Diary', 2 March 1908, n.p.; 9 March 1908, n.p.; 11 March 1908, n.p., D2659/24/11.

[56] GA, E. M. Blathwayt, 'Diary', 2 March 1908, n.p.; 9 March 1908, n.p.; 1 April 1908, p. 39, D2659/24/11.

[57] GA, E. M. Blathwayt, 'Diary', 20 Feb. 1908, n.p., D2659/24/11.

[58] GA, Mary Blathwayt, 'Diary', 11 March 1908, n.p., D2659/24/11; E. M. Blathwayt, 'Diary', 18 Nov. 1908, p. 129, D2659/24/11.

[59] GA, Mary Blathwayt, 'Diary', 9 Nov. 1910, p. 313; 21 Dec. 1910, p. 355, D2659/27/15.

undoubtedly made it easier for servants to participate. Possibly, employment at Eagle House served as an introduction to the suffrage movement
and encouraged some servants to become involved in a campaign which
otherwise might have passed them by. And yet the political exchange was
not always entirely one way. Emily and Mary Blathwayt's diaries record
conversations with their servants that suggest a sense of shared struggle.
They describe, for example, Ellen Morgan looking in on her way to a
suffrage meeting to let the Blathwayts know how that day's 'At Home'
had gone. On other occasions Ellen Morgan and Elsie Harris found that
their knowledge of local and national suffrage events was superior to that
of their mistresses' because they subscribed to newspapers such as the
Mirror, which provided more in-depth and sympathetic coverage than the
Blathwayts' copies of *The Times*.[60]

Kathlyn Oliver did not write much about her relationship with her
mistress, Mary Sheepshanks, beyond expressing gratitude for allowing
her evenings off to attend political meetings and classes at Morley College. Oliver and Sheepshanks moved in similar activist circles, both were
socialists and pacifists as well as feminists and became members of the
People's Suffrage Federation.[61] Sheepshanks had far more power and
prominence in the suffrage movement than her servant, becoming secretary of the International Woman Suffrage Alliance in 1913 and editor of
its journal *Ius Suffragii*. Kathlyn Oliver's frequent letters to the press,
however, allowed her to contribute to a number of key feminist debates.
She is perhaps best known for taking on the free love feminist and birth
control campaigner Stella Browne in the correspondence columns of the
Freewoman in 1912. Whereas Browne initially published under the
pseudonym 'A New Subscriber', Oliver wrote under her own name in
defence of 'the spinster', explaining how she had always practised chas-
tity and that, contrary to what some of the new sexologists were claiming,

---

[60] GA, E. M. Blathwayt, 'Diary', 13 Oct. 1908, p. 109; 14 Oct. 1908, p. 109; 30 Oct. 1908,
      p. 119; 3 March 1908, n.p., D2659/24/11.
[61] For Oliver, *Woman Worker* 25 Aug. 1909, p. 182; 8 Dec. 1909, p. 522; 5 Jan. 1910, p. 606;
      4 May 1910, pp. 942–943; Kathlyn Oliver, *Domestic Servants and Citizenship* (London:
      People's Suffrage Federation, 1911); Sheffield Archives, Edward Carpenter Collection
      (hereafter SA), Kathlyn Oliver to Edward Carpenter, 25 Oct. 1915, MSS.386–362.
      For Sheepshanks, TWL, Mary Sheepshanks, 'Autobiography' (unpublished manuscript),
      7/MSH; TWL, The Women's Library Pamphlet Collection, Mary Sheepshanks, 'Women's
      Suffrage and Pacifism' (unpublished manuscript), 920; Sybil Oldfield, *Spinsters of This
      Parish: The Life and Times of F. M. Mayor and Mary Sheepshanks* (London: Virago, 1984);
      Sybil Oldfield, 'Mary Sheepshanks Edits an Internationalist Suffrage Monthly in Wartime:
      Ius Suffragii 1914–19', *Women's History Review*, 12:1 (2003), 115–127. Sheepshanks was
      active in the NUWSS and the International Women's Suffrage Alliance, but is also listed as
      a member of the General Council of the People's Suffrage Federation; TWL, 'People's
      Suffrage Federation Pamphlet' (c. 1909), p. 2, PC/06/396-11/11.

this had in no way damaged her health.[62] Oliver was also implicitly critical of the heterosexual bias of those who argued that sex with men was necessary to women's well-being. Although she did not mention her own sexual and romantic preferences in the *Freewoman*, she had already published a letter in the *Woman Worker* two years earlier in which she was open about the fact that 'I have been more in love with women than I have with any of the opposite sex'. This letter was both bold and hesitant, observing of her own proclivities that 'I cannot explain this (perhaps) unnatural state of things, but I know it is so.'[63] By 1915 Oliver had read *The Intermediate Sex* (1908), Edward Carpenter's defence of homosexual love, and was now even less apologetic about the 'physical desire' she felt for another woman. In a letter to Carpenter she declared that 'I ... should love above all things to be able to live with her and be as intimate as it is possible to be, and I don't feel that this desire is at all immoral or degrading.'[64]

In her contribution to feminist thinking on sexuality Kathlyn Oliver did not speak as somebody's maid, but as an independent woman confident enough to disclose personal details and assert the validity of her experience equal to that of women who had had 'educational opportunities' far greater than her own.[65] That these discussions of female love and desire were taking place in feminist newspapers alongside discussions of the 'servant problem' reminds us that the servants who participated in the latter would also have been exposed to the former, and were thus aware of a broad sweep of feminist issues. The question remains, however, of to what degree they were able to express their political interests in their day-to-day working lives. Kathlyn Oliver appears to have done so relatively freely. The suffragist Catherine Marshall's papers contain two letters from Oliver, who served Marshall when she was

---

[62] *Freewoman* 15 Feb. 1912, p. 252; 29 Feb. 1912, p. 290; Margaret Jackson, *The Real Facts of Life: Feminism and the Politics of Sexuality c. 1850–1940* (London: Taylor & Francis, 1994), pp. 91–93; Lucy Bland, *Banishing the Beast: English Feminism and Sexual Morality, 1885–1914* (London: Penguin, 1995), pp. 281–282; Lesley Hall, *The Life and Times of Stella Browne: Feminist and Free Spirit* (London: I. B. Tauris, 2011), pp. 28–30. Hall argues that it is likely that Oliver and Browne would have known each other since Browne was librarian at Morley College from 1907 to 1912. Oliver's assumption that 'A New Subscriber' was a man suggests she was not aware that the letters in the *Freewoman* were from Browne.

Oliver also called for sexual restraint in men, opposed legally binding marriage laws and believed that rape 'is a far worse evil than prostitution' and that the latter would be solved only by 'economic independence in women and self-restraint in sex matters for men'; *Freewoman* 11 July 1912, p. 156.

[63] *Woman Worker* 11 Aug. 1909, p. 126.

[64] SA, Kathlyn Oliver to Edward Carpenter, 25 Oct. 1915, MSS.386–362.

[65] *Freewoman* 14 March 1912, p. 332.

lodging with Sheepshanks in 1913. Both were written to inform Marshall of the various domestic arrangements Oliver was undertaking for her, yet the second letter combines this with a friendly and informal account of Oliver's meeting with an elderly servant who, she was shocked to find, supported the Conservative Party. 'I can quite understand the employing and parasitic classes being conservative', Oliver wrote to Marshall, '... but I simply can't understand Labour backing and sympathising [with] its exploiters.'[66] This short letter offers a glimpse into a relationship between a servant and a mistress that allowed for fairly open political discussion, including an acknowledgement of the potential for conflict between the servant class and the employer class. Another friend of Mary Sheepshanks, F. M. Mayor, featured a discussion about a domestic servants' union in her novel *The Third Miss Symons* (1913), suggesting that the mistresses who visited Sheepshanks' home paid attention to, or were at least aware of, Kathlyn Oliver's wider interests and activism.[67]

Kathlyn Oliver's relationship with her employers was not necessarily typical. Poverty following her father's death, combined with lack of professional qualifications, had compelled her to earn a living as a servant, but Oliver had been brought up as a civil servant's daughter and therefore probably exhibited manners and a style of speech that bore closer resemblance to those of her employers' than did most servants.[68] She was certainly an extremely articulate and fluent writer, and her letters to Marshall contrast with those written by another of Sheepshanks' servants by the name of Rose (surname unknown), who wrote in much plainer language and did not stray from the topic of domestic arrangements.[69] Perhaps the Eagle House servants were more representative in that shared suffrage activities appear to have opened up more space for an unusual degree and type of interaction between mistress and maid, without fundamentally challenging the power imbalance between them. Although the suffrage movement did at times encourage forging friendships across class boundaries, the direct employment relationship between mistress and maid limited this potential. For example, it is impossible to imagine Mary Blathwayt befriending her servants in the way she did the former mill worker and Annie Kenney.[70]

[66] Cumbria Archive (hereafter CA), Carlisle, Catherine Marshall Papers, Kathlyn Oliver to Catherine Marshall, 4 Sept. 1913, 13 Sept. 1913, DMAR/2/31.
[67] F. M. Mayor, *The Third Miss Symons* (London: Sidgwick & Jackson, 1913), pp. 129–132. With thanks to Sybil Oldfield for drawing my attention to this.
[68] SA, Oliver to Carpenter, 25 Oct. 1915, MSS.386–362.
[69] CA, Rose to Marshall, 12 Sept. 1913, DMAR/2/31.
[70] June Hannam, '"Suffragettes Are Splendid for Any Work": The Blathwayt Diaries as a Source for Suffrage History', in Eustance et al. (eds.), *A Suffrage Reader*, 53–69, p. 60.

The diaries of Emily and Mary Blathwayt also reveal the less visible ways in which the campaign for the vote was quietly yet consistently supported by women whose activity was confined to the home. Unlike Mary Blathwayt, Ellen Morgan, Elsie Harris and the Durnford sisters could not leave their work to accompany Annie Kenney on a speaker tour, nor even find much time in their sixteen-hour working day to attend suffrage demonstrations. Yet in their own way the Eagle House servants also made a crucial, if far less spectacular, contribution to the movement. They served tea and cakes at one of Annie Kenney's suffragette 'At Homes', and cooked, cleaned and cared for the leaders of the WSPU when they came to Eagle House to recuperate from their gruelling regimes of political activism.[71] In 1909, WSPU leader Emmeline Pethick-Lawrence published an appeal to daughters of wealthy families to devote a year of their lives to the Cause, naming Mary Blathwayt as a shining example.[72] Likewise, Annie Kenney's autobiography recalls how crucial the hospitality afforded by middle-class families such as the Blathwayts had been to the WSPU's network of itinerant organisers and speakers, saving a great deal of money that would otherwise have been spent on hotel bills.[73] What neither Pethick-Lawrence nor Kenney mentioned, however, is a fact so obvious that it did not need saying: that when affluent women such as Mary Blathwayt donated their free time and hospitality to the movement they also automatically offered up their domestic servants. Such suffrage work took place behind the scenes, as a contribution to a more public display of support for which their mistresses took the credit. It is likely, then, that many other servants in suffrage-supporting households played a similar role, which has gone entirely unrecorded. Mary Blathwayt's diary, for example, mentions other local suffragettes' servants attending meetings and joining the local WSPU. Domestics would have also cared for WSPU speakers when they stayed at other houses in the area including that of Mary's friends the Tollemaches.[74] Likewise, a number of prominent activists, including

Mary Blathwayt recorded in her diary how she washed Annie Kenney's hair and brought Kenney's dirty laundry back to Eagle House for her; GA, Mary Blathwayt, 'Diary', 12 March 1910, p. 71; 19 March 1910, p. 78; 6 April 1910, p. 96. For the women's movement and friendship, Ellen Ross, 'St Frances in Soho: Emmeline Pethick, Mary Neal, the West London Wesleyan Mission, and the Allure of "Simple Living" in the 1890s', *Church History* 83:4 (Dec. 2014), 843–883; Jenkins, 'From Mills to Militants'.

[71] GA, E. M. Blathwayt, 'Diary', 26 May 1908, p. 63; 21 Sept. 1908, pp. 100–101; 9 Dec. 1908, p. 137, D2659/24/11. Almost all the WSPU leaders stayed at Eagle House at some point; June Hannam, '"Suffragettes Are Splendid for Any Work"', p. 57.

[72] *Votes for Women* 11 Feb. 1909, p. 332.   [73] Kenney, *Memories of a Militant*, p. 120.

[74] GA, Mary Blathwayt, 'Diary', 29 March 1910, p. 96; 9 Dec. 1910, p. 343, D2659/27/15; Hannam, '"Suffragettes Are Splendid for Any Work"', p. 57.

Hilda Clark and Alice Clark as well as Catherine Marshall, lodged with Mary Sheepshanks at 1 Barton Street, London, where she lived between 1899 and 1919. Sheepshanks' autobiography recalls how this residence was renowned for its comforts and good food, although she did not mention that this was in large part thanks to her cook Kathlyn Oliver.[75]

The degree to which domestic labour and political activism overlapped could cause problems when the political views of domestic servants were at odds with those of their employers. Rhoda Churchill (née Reynolds, born c. 1874), the daughter of a stone mason, grew up in Street, Somerset and by 1901 was working as a parlour-maid for Helen Clark at Millfield House.[76] She and Clark corresponded for a number of years after Rhoda left her job at Millfield House and married Frank Churchill. Rhoda Churchill found it far more difficult to hold down charring jobs with employers who did not share what she described as her 'radical' politics. 'I am in disgrace with many places where I have been to work', she wrote to Helen Clark in 1910. 'The place before this one sent me going after being with them today because I refused to wear a blue [Conservative Party] rosette.' Her next post proved little better:

after I had been here four days, the lady asked me to go out for her and distribute Tariff R[eform] leaflets, I refused and she got very angry with me and said very nasty things about the Radical party, which I could not stand ... I have told them all, I refuse to be bought over. I go to them to work in their houses at household work, and have just as much right to my opinion as they.

Rhoda Churchill's account indicates that some mistresses expected their domestic servants to carry out the drudge work of political campaigning, viewing them as nothing more than proxy figures with no agency of their own.[77] Even when they shared similar political outlooks, the degree to which servants were working for the Cause or for their employers

[75] CA, Oliver to Marshall, 4 Sept. 1913, 13 Sept. 1913, DMAR/2/31; TWL, Mary Sheepshanks, 'Autobiography', p. 45. Kathlyn Oliver was working for Sheepshanks by 1909, and still in 1915; SA, Oliver to Carpenter, 25 Oct. 1915, MSS.386–362. Other suffragist lodgers included Gertrude Sandilands, Irene Cooper Willis and Emily Leaf; Oldfield, *Spinsters of This Parish*, p. 95.
[76] England and Wales Census (1881), Portway, Street, Somerset; England and Wales Census (1891), Portway, Street, Somerset; England and Wales Census (1901), Millfield House, Street, Somerset; England and Wales Census (1911), 18 Bury Road, Wood Green, London; Alfred Gillett Trust, Street, Millfield Papers (hereafter AGT), Helen Clark, 'Diary', 9 Aug. 1902, MIL/70/1. It appears that Emma J. Bennett knew Rhoda Churchill (possibly from having stayed at Millfield House) since she asked Helen to pass on her regards; AGT, Emma J. Bennett to Helen Clark, 21 July 1902, MIL/62/1.
[77] For the long-standing view of the servant's labour as an extension of the employer's capacity, see Carolyn Steedman, *Labours Lost: Domestic Service and the Making of Modern England* (Cambridge: Cambridge University Press, 2009), p. 19.

remained unclear, possibly even to themselves. At the same time, Rhoda Churchill's letter demonstrates that servants were able to assert some autonomy. Not only did she refuse to carry out certain tasks, she also retained her political selfhood while undertaking supposedly 'neutral' domestic chores such as 'waiting at Primrose functions'. These were tea parties organised for the women's section of the Conservative Party, during which Churchill kept her mouth shut, but her eyes and ears open, and 'saw and heard very queer things'. Sir Charles Hunter, the Conservative MP for Bath elected in January of that year, was 'advising very underhand methods just to get a hold on Votes' – information that Rhoda Churchill reported back to Helen Clark in the knowledge that her former mistress was an active Liberal Party supporter with important political connections in the local area.[78]

Representations of Domestic Servants in Pageantry and Propaganda

So servants were *there*: working in suffrage-supporting households, sitting in the audience at suffrage meetings, purchasing postcards from suffrage shops, writing letters to suffrage newspapers and, occasionally, smashing windows and breaking through police lines. But if 'real-life' servants were present at almost every level of the suffrage movement, they were very rarely represented in its political propaganda.[79] There were exceptions to this, but rather than simply recovering the odd glimpse of the servant as suffrage subject I want to ask why such depictions were so few and far between. Between about 1907 and 1914 the suffrage movement mass-produced postcards and posters, and organised seven national processions and pageants, which were carefully choreographed for maximum theatrical effect and involved beautifully crafted banners and costumes. The Artists' Suffrage League was founded by professional artists in 1907 to help with preparations for the NUWSS 'Mud March' (the first open-air public demonstration organised by the constitutionalists) and remained allied to them after that. The Suffrage Atelier (est. 1909), open

---

[78] AGT, Rhoda [Churchill] to Helen Clark, 20 Jan. 1910, MIL/64/2.
[79] Servants were more likely to be represented in suffrage fiction and theatre, most notably Gertrude Colmore's novel *Suffragette Sally* (1911) and Evelyn Glover's plays *A Chat with Mrs Chicky* (1912) and *Miss Appleyard's Awakening* (c. 1911); Laura Schwartz, 'Representations of Domestic Servants in Suffrage Literature' (unpublished conference paper presented at Women's Suffrage and Political Activism Conference, University of Cambridge, 2018).

to members who were not professionally trained, was non-affiliated but tended to work most frequently with the WFL. The WSPU did not have a dedicated artists' organisation but instead relied on a small group of individuals, including Sylvia Pankhurst, Marion Wallace Dunlop and Edith Downing.[80] The absence of domestic servants from their work is all the more striking given that the suffrage movement was particularly keen to represent women in their capacity as both professional and manual workers.

The 'Great Procession' of June 1910, organised by the WSPU and the WFL, was intended to symbolise suffragettes' aspirant journey 'from prison to citizenship'. It was typical of many of the large-scale suffrage demonstrations in organising marchers into blocks according to the type of work they did.[81] Such demonstrations were intended to prove to both the public and the government that women from all walks of life wanted the vote, and it was therefore important to ensure that working-class women were represented alongside more educated, wealthy and professional women. Although occupational banners of professional careers tended to be most numerous, many working-class women also attended these demonstrations.[82] In 1909 the NUWSS paid for silk workers, pottery workers, felt-hat makers, boot and shoe workers, hosiery workers and housewives (the last recruited by the Women's Co-operative Guild) to travel to London from the north of England for the Pageant of Women's Trades and Professions.[83] Cross-class solidarity was a key feature of many of these demonstrations, and a theme that was often remarked upon in the press. The *Daily News*, for example, reported that at the NUWSS demonstration of 13 June 1908 'one could see fair dames of Mayfair in costly lace and silk fraternising with working girls in shawls and feathers, while famous novelists and actresses walked side-by-side

---

[80] Tickner, *The Spectacle of Women*, chapter 2; Crawford, *The Women's Suffrage Movement*, pp. 16–18, 662–663; Tara Morton, 'Working Women, Activism and the Visual Propaganda of the Suffrage Atelier' (unpublished conference paper presented at Women's History Network, 15th Annual Conference, Women's Activism: History and Historical Perspectives, University of Wales); Tara Morton, 'Changing Spaces: Art, Politics, and Identity in the Home Studios of the Suffrage Atelier', *Women's History Review*, 21:4 (2012), 623–637. Tara Morton, '"An Arts and Crafts Society, Working for the Enfranchisement of Women"': Unpicking the Political Threads of the Suffrage Atelier, 1909–1914', in Zoe Thomas and Miranda Garrett (eds.), *Suffrage and the Arts: Visual Culture, Politics and Enterprise* (London: Bloomsbury, 2018).

[81] For pageants and processions, Tickner, *The Spectacle of Women*, chapter 3; Barbara Green, *Spectacular Confessions: Autobiography, Performative Activism, and the Sites of Suffrage, 1905–1938* (New York: St Martin's Press, 1997), chapters 1 and 2.

[82] *Votes for Women* 20 May 1910, p. 552; 3 June 1910, pp. 582–584; 24 June 1910, pp. 628–629; Tickner, *Spectacle of Suffrage*, pp. 55–59.

[83] TWL, Margaret Llewelyn Davies to Miss Strachey, n.d. [1909], ALC/2737.

with workers from the factory or the farm'.[84] Yet among the numerous and various working-class jobs on display, domestic service was rarely seen. Instead, suffrage postcards and posters, pageants and processions depicted working-class women in one of two ways: either as industrial workers – factory workers and Lancashire mill girls like Annie Kenney – or as sweated workers – seamstresses, piece workers and, occasionally, prostitutes.[85]

The difficulty of fitting the domestic servant into either one of these two 'types' of working-class womanhood is evident in the programme written to accompany the Pageant of Women's Trades and Professions organised by the NUWSS to mark the fifth congress of the International Woman Suffrage Alliance, which they hosted in London in April 1909. As the title of the pageant indicates, its primary aim was to showcase the great variety of women's work and to explain why each particular type of worker needed the vote. The pageant was divided into five blocks: one for doctors, nurses and teachers; another for writers, journalists, clerical workers and actresses; another for industrial workers; another for artists and craftswomen and also a block consisting of farmers, beekeepers, market and flower gardeners, jam and sweet makers, waitresses, cigar and cigarette makers, housewives and 'homemakers'. This last group incorporated all waged domestic workers.[86] The Artists' Suffrage League designed the banners, providing one for charwomen that featured a dustpan, a broom, an apron and a shield embroidered with a picture of a scrubbing brush and the slogan 'cleanliness is next to godliness' (see Figure 2).

Housemaids were also reported to have held a shield featuring caps and aprons and feather dusters, and the cooks carried golden gridirons with copper pans and bundles of herbs.[87] None of these groups of domestic workers, however, was given their own named section in the programme, which listed each of the ten other trades included in their

---

[84] Quoted in Tickner, *The Spectacle of Women*, p. 89.

[85] Ibid., pp. 50–51, 167–182; Morton, 'Working Women, Activism and the Visual Propaganda of the Suffrage Atelier'; Morag Shiach, *Modernism, Labour and Selfhood in British Literature and Culture, 1890–1930* (Cambridge: Cambridge University Press, 2004), chapter 3.

[86] TWL, International Woman Suffrage Alliance Quinquennial Congress, 'Programme, Women's Trades and Professions (April 27, 1909)', 9/08/47. This is similar to the organisation of servants on the NUWSS demonstration on 13 June 1908, which dedicated one of its eight blocks to the professions and another to working-class jobs, but invited 'the children's nurse, the cook and the parlourmaid' to march under the banner of 'Homemakers' alongside their 'lady' employers. Here also domestic servants marched in a separate block from industrial workers; *Times* 13 June 1908, p. 9; *Women's Franchise* 14 May 1908, p. 539; 4 June 1908, p. 581.

[87] *Common Cause* 6 May 1909, p. 60.

Figure 2 Postcard featuring charwomen's banners from the Pageant of Women's Trades and Professions (27 April 1909).
The Women's Library at the London School of Economics, London, TWL.2000. 40, Postcard Box 4 (reproduced by kind permission of The Women's Library at the LSE)

block and fifty-seven occupations in total. Each of these, including rather niche jobs such as 'artificial flower makers' and 'indexers', received a paragraph in the programme outlining their conditions of work and explaining why they, in particular, required the franchise. Not so for domestic servants, who were never named as an occupation but instead discussed rather obliquely under the heading of 'homemakers':

[I]t is not too much to say that the well-being of the whole social body rests on the efficiency of those who serve our households. Wholesome foods and domestic cleanliness, the two prime necessities of healthy human existence, committed to their charge, and the various and fatiguing duties involved in the efficient performance of their work, call for an amount of intelligence and training too often overlooked by those who profit by them.[88]

Here was an acknowledgement of the importance of the work undertaken by domestic servants, but the servants themselves were never referred to. Moreover, the programme made no mention of their working conditions,

[88] TWL, International Woman Suffrage Alliance Quinquennial Congress, 'Programme, Women's Trades and Professions (April 27, 1909)', 9/08/47, p. 6.

in contrast to the section on waitresses, who are described as suffering 'long hours and poor pay', often having to pay for their own uniforms and for accidental breakages. The working conditions of housewives were also related: '[t]he hours are unlimited, the work often carried on under over-crowded and insanitary conditions'.[89] In both cases exactly the same criticism could have been applied to the conditions of domestic workers, but they were not.

Perhaps, then, the silences produced by one of the few occasions when domestic servants *were* represented in suffrage propaganda can begin to explain why such sightings were so rare. The Pageant of Women's Trades and Professions positioned domestic servants in Block 1 alongside a seemingly miscellaneous array of workers who, if any coherency were intended, might have been perceived as pre-industrial workers (with the exception of the cigar and cigarette makers), or perhaps as workers who worked in the private sphere of the home (gardeners, housewives and sweated piecework). The pageant did not group domestic workers with the chain makers, pit brow women, cotton operatives, silk workers, tailoresses, machinists, boot and shoe workers, felt- and straw-hat makers, hosiery workers, artificial flower makers, furriers, machine and hand-lace workers, laundresses and shop assistants – who all appeared together in Block 3. The public/private divide appears to have been important in categorising types of women's work, meaning that industrial labourers could appear alongside shopworkers but not domestic servants.[90]

One of the main aims of the suffrage processions and pageants was to counter the claims of their opponents that women's place was in the home, and instead to demonstrate 'that women could, and did, and had to, operate successfully in the public sphere'. Industrial workers, portrayed as coarse but also independent, could be made to fit this narrative.[91] Domestic servants, labouring in the private sphere of the home, could not. The alternative model of working-class womanhood, that of the victimised sweated worker, was equally problematic in that to depict domestic servants in such a role might imply that their employers were to blame. The 'servant problem' was gestured towards

---

[89] Ibid., p. 6. The Women's Coronation Procession (17 June 1911) also included a contingent of 'Homemakers', although it is not clear whether this included domestic servants or only housewives; TWL, 'Postcard featuring "Homemakers" on the Women's Coronation Procession', 2000.40, Postcard Box 4.

[90] The distinction was not exact; many chain makers worked in their own homes rather than in factories despite performing heavy industrial labour; Cathy Hunt, *The National Federation of Women Workers* (Basingstoke: Palgrave Macmillan, 2014), p. 55.

[91] Tickner, *The Spectacle of Women*, pp. 67, 50–51.

in the Pageant's programme, when it noted that household work required 'intelligence and training too often overlooked by those who profit by them'. The organisers shied away from any more direct reference towards the potential for conflict between mistress and maid at an event that was intended to showcase women united in their demand for the vote.

A similar aversion to talking about domestic servants as exploited workers was apparent in the WSPU's working women's deputation to Lloyd George on 23 January 1913. This is in spite of the fact that one domestic servant, a Miss R. Perkins, about whom no other information was provided, was chosen to participate.[92] The deputation was organised to coincide with the passage of the Franchise Bill, to which women's suffrage amendments were attached.[93] Its leader, Flora Drummond, emphasised that the time had come for working-class women like herself to take action on their own behalf. Beyond the immediate aim of putting pressure on the government to commit to women's suffrage, the purpose of the deputation was twofold: to refute those critics who claimed that suffrage 'was a movement of rich women' and to shame the Labour Party for failing to fight for the interests of the women of the class they claimed to represent. From late November 1912, the WSPU dedicated considerable resources to organising the deputation, offering travel expenses and hospitality to as many working women as possible to come to London to participate in a week-long Women's Parliament. WSPU organisers were appointed to mobilise women in the industrial districts of London, especially the East End, as well as those engaged in the 'great industries' in the North. The WSPU's new newspaper, the *Suffragette*, claimed that the action would incorporate all women who had to work for a living, 'whether as wage earners outside the home or as working-men's wives inside the home' – a formulation that, technically, excluded domestic servants entirely.[94] The twenty women selected to meet Lloyd George, however, were all wage earners: four sweated workers from the East End of London, two nurses, one teacher, one shop assistant, one domestic servant, three Lancashire factory women, one woman from the Leicester

[92] *Suffragette* 24 Jan. 1913, p. 221.
[93] Sylvia Pankhurst claimed that the working women's deputation had originally been her idea, evolving out of her organising in the East End; Sylvia Pankhurst, 'The East London Federation of the Suffragettes', *Woman's Dreadnought*, 8 March 1914, in Jane Marcus (ed.), *Suffrage and the Pankhursts* (London: Routledge & Kegan Paul, 1987), 242–243; Sylvia Pankhurst, *The Suffragette Movement* (London: Virago, 1977 [first published 1932]), pp. 427–429.
[94] *Suffragette* 29 Nov. 1912, p. 95; 6 Dec. 1912, pp. 109–110, 115; 13 Dec. 1913, p. 129, 135; 27 Dec. 1913, p. 164; 3 Jan. 1913, pp. 174–175; 10 Jan. 1913, pp. 188–189; 17 Jan. 1913, pp. 197, 204–205.

boot and shoe trade, one laundress, one pit brow woman, two 'fisher-wives', and one tailoress. That a domestic worker was included in this select group possibly indicates that Miss R. Perkins' fellow servants were present in significant numbers on the larger demonstration.[95] But although the fisherwives, nurses and Lancashire mill girls were all encouraged to wear their work uniforms, none of the publicity photographs appearing in either the *Suffragette* and *Votes for Women* features anyone wearing a servant's cap and gown.[96] Nor was Perkins selected for one of the short life stories of five deputation members printed in *Suffragette*. Either Perkins did not give a speech or her speech was not reported in the suffrage periodicals which gave extensive coverage of speeches from representatives of every single one of the other trades on the deputation.[97]

One of the few times that servants became the subject of figurative representation in suffrage propaganda was in a series of three postcards and one cartoon produced by the Suffrage Atelier in protest against the 'servant tax' of 1911. This so-called tax, which I discuss in Chapter 5, was in fact a proposal to include servants in the new National Health Insurance. It provoked much opposition from mistresses and maids who resented having to make financial contributions, and from many women's suffrage and trade union organisations who felt that it was a poorly designed piece of legislation that discriminated against women. The series of images focusing on the 'servant tax' is revealingly anomalous when compared with much other suffrage propaganda. The cartoon,

[95] Two reports by Beatrice Harraden refer to the presence of 'charwomen'; *Suffragette* 31 Jan. 1913, p. 234; *Votes for Women* 31 Jan. 1913, p. 258.

In an interview shortly before her death, Jessie Stephen recalled her attendance on a working women's deputation in 'about' 1910, but given her uncertainty regarding the date, it is likely that this was the 1913 deputation. The photograph that appeared alongside another interview with Stephen in *Spare Rib*, with the caption 'Lloyd George received this delegation from the Glasgow WSPU in 1910', features delegates wearing badges that could be those produced for the 1913 working women's deputation and advertised in *Suffragette*, so it is possible that this image was misattributed, again due to Stephen's uncertainty of the date when interviewed so many years later; TWL, Harrison, interview with Jessie Stephen (1977), 8SUF/B/157, Disc 32–33; Susie Fleming and Gloden Dallas, 'Jessie', *Spare Rib*, 32 (Feb. 1975), 10–13. There is also some disparity in the secondary literature: Crawford writes that Stephen attended the working women's deputation in January 1912; Canning states that she was part of a group of Glasgow 'work-women' that lobbied Lloyd George and Edward Grey in March 1910; Elizabeth Crawford, *The Women's Suffrage Movement: A Reference Guide 1866–1928* (London: University College London Press, 1999), p. 653; Audrey Canning, 'Stephen, Jessie (1893–1979)', in *Oxford Dictionary of National Biography*.

[96] *Votes for Women* 31 Jan. 1913, p. 258; *Suffragette* 31 Jan. 1913, p. 235; TWL, Photograph of 'fisherwives and nurses admiring a portrait of Christabel Pankhurst', 2009.203.

[97] *Suffragette* 24 Jan. 1913, p. 221; 31 Jan. 1913, pp. 232–233; *Votes for Women* 31 Jan. 1913, p. 258.

Figure 3 Cartoon of servants and housewives protesting against the 'servant tax'.
Vote 6 July 1912, p. 185 (reproduced by kind permission of The Women's Library at the LSE)

published in the WFL's newspaper the *Vote*, depicts domestic workers on a protest march, wielding their brooms and dustpan brushes in a threatening manner at the suited men cowering in front of them (see Figure 3). A postcard with the headline 'What May Happen' shows a cook asking the delivery boy to tell Lloyd George to take away his unwanted present.[98] In both, servants are shown speaking for themselves and asserting their rights as workers – images that appear particularly arresting when considered in light of a general resistance within both suffrage and trade union propaganda to show any kind of woman worker engaged in the act of industrial militancy.[99] The reason it was possible on

[98] TWL, 'What May Happen', postcard produced by the Suffrage Atelier (c. 1911), 2002.267, Postcard Box 2. Other postcards in the series include TWL, 'Insurance Monday', postcard produced by the Suffrage Atelier (c. 1911), 2002.254, Postcard Box 2; TWL, 'The Closed Doors', postcard produced by the Suffrage Atelier (c. 1911), 2002.239, Postcard Box 2.

[99] Tickner, *The Spectacle of Women*, pp. 68, 180–181; Morton, 'Working Women, Activism and the Visual Propaganda of the Suffrage Atelier'.

this occasion, however, to depict domestic workers as political agents was because servants' opposition to the 'servant tax' was directed not towards their employers, but towards the government. The cartoon depicts servants protesting alongside 'housewives' rather than 'mistresses', implying that both groups of women laboured in the home on an equal footing. It emphasises their common cause without referring directly to the employment relationship's inherent conflicts and imbalance of power. Perhaps most importantly, it is the housewives in this image who have undertaken a 'national strike', rather than the domestic servants themselves.

Although visual propaganda tended to erase domestic servants, they were discussed in the suffrage press. This was not usually the result of direct editorial policy but tended to be prompted by letters from readers, often from servants themselves. Yet as soon as the suffrage movement's relationship to domestic servants was addressed, conflict broke out. In August 1911 an article in the *Common Cause* opposing a legislative attempt to ban women from working at the pit brows mentioned domestic service only incidentally, comparing the healthy working environment of the pit brow women to the far more insanitary conditions of domestic service.[100] The following issue published a letter from a Mrs C. H. M. Davidson, who protested that, to the contrary, most servants were treated with 'over-indulgence and misplaced consideration' yet were 'incapable of appreciating it'. She complained that the board school–educated girl had now come to think of service as 'derogatory', 'as she is only too pleased to have an excuse to be "independent"' – a quality that was apparently desirable only in middle-class suffragists such as herself.[101]

Davidson might have also noted that this new generation of independent-minded and literate servants could read suffrage newspapers and were capable of answering back, for this is what soon occurred. 'I see in your issue of August 24 that Mrs Davidson considers domestic service is well paid', wrote one (signing herself simply 'A Domestic Servant'); 'I wonder if she would feel she had been well paid when she had paid for two uniforms out of her wages?' This anonymous domestic worker understood her interests as directly counter to those of her employer. 'It is to the mistresses' advantage that things should remain as they are', she insisted, and she felt that the only way to improve the matter was for servants themselves to 'make a stir' and demand better wages and shorter hours.[102] Over the next six months, the letters pages of the *Common Cause* were taken up with, often extremely hostile, exchanges between mistresses and

[100] *Common Cause* 10 Aug. 1911, p. 313.   [101] *Common Cause* 24 Aug. 1911, p. 349.
[102] *Common Cause* 12 Oct. 1911, p. 466. See also 31 Aug. 1911, pp. 367–368; 28 Sept. 1911, p. 432.

maids. Rosamond Smith wrote towards the end of November, requesting that the discussion of domestic servants be dropped. It was a waste of precious column inches, she claimed, 'and I believe many of your readers would prefer to hear more about the conditions of employment in factories and in the sweated trades'.[103] Smith did not mention her own servants, but she did give her address as 12 Eaton Place, a large house in Belgravia, London. The 1911 census records Smith (age thirty-three) and her mother living there with a butler, a cook, a lady's maid, an upper house-maid, an under house-maid and a kitchen maid.[104] This mistress also seems to have found it easier to talk about the exploitation of women workers outside of suffragists' own homes. The hostility expressed by both sides in the correspondence pages gives some indication of why, in its more official propaganda, the movement avoided representations of domestic servants.

---

[103] *Common Cause* 30 Nov. 1911, pp. 600–602.
[104] England and Wales Census (1911), 12 Eaton Place, Belgravia, London. Rosamond Smith was a delegate to the International Woman Suffrage Alliance conference in Geneva in 1920; International Woman Suffrage Alliance, 'Report of Eighth Congress' (Manchester: Percy Brothers, 1920).

3   The Housework Problem

In the winter of 1908, and again in 1909, the *Woman Worker* printed a number of letters from women in professional employment who were struggling to juggle their domestic duties with work outside the home. One M. L. Hargreaves, who described herself as a 'business woman', explained how in addition to her paid employment she still had to help her mother with some of the housework and all of the cooking. She felt that, by comparison, her servant had an easy time of it. 'I often come home at 7 or 7:30 p.m., tired, cold, and famished', she wrote, 'to find ... [the maid] cosily seated by a big fire doing drawn thread work!' Another letter, this time from an anonymous mistress employed in her husband's medical practice, called for more sympathy for 'the often overworked professional wife and mother who has to keep servants that she may be free to do work other than housework'. She was aware of some of the contradictions of holding progressive political views while participating in 'the remains of our feudal system'. Yet she was also exasperated by the fact that her maids remained ungrateful and sloppy in their work in spite of her paying good wages, lending books from her library and even sending them to suffrage meetings. Alongside the snobbery of this writer's complaints about her servants' poor grammar and uneducated conversation was a note of poignant desperation. 'Please tell me whose fault it all is', she pleaded. 'Only it is no use saying I ought to take a flat and do all the work myself, as well as my other work and my mothering work. My husband's practice would disappear, for one thing, and then we could not live at all.'

When these mistresses complained about their servants they were undoubtedly expressing the prejudices of the employer class and contempt for those who laboured for them. They were also identifying a very real problem – the problem of housework and who should do it, especially once women had succeeded in their struggle to enter the male professions and develop an existence beyond the home. An article by Carra Lyle attempted to reframe the 'servant problem' as one that united rather than divided the *Woman Worker*'s readers, arguing that 'To me the servants' chains are the same chains that bind the mistress – the identical chains that fetter working-class women.' She insisted that the 'servant problem' rested upon an even more intractable 'problem of kitchen work', one that would persist even if all mistresses released their servants and did the work themselves.[1]

In this chapter, I argue that feminist responses to the 'servant problem' cannot be reduced to a narrative of selfish middle-class women refusing to share their new-found emancipation with their domestics. They must also be considered in relation to a wider problem of housework. Occasionally it was suggested that mistresses should stop wasting time lamenting the servant shortage and do the work themselves.[2] But in an age before modern housing and domestic appliances were widely available, no feminist saw this as a realistic solution. Whether performed by a servant or a housewife, the burden of housework during this period was immense. Keeping a house involved a great deal of heavy manual labour, carried out in unhealthy conditions. It was extremely difficult to run a middle-class household without the help of servants, and even full-time working-class housewives struggled under the work generated by their much smaller homes.[3] Feminists argued that the housework problem affected, and indeed united, women across the classes, whether they were single or married, professional women or mothers.

Housework was viewed not just as a practical problem, but also as a political issue. It was widely recognised that the all-absorbing and time-consuming character of housework prevented women from taking an interest in the world outside the home and especially from participating in movements for social and political change. Housework was also politicised by opponents of the suffrage movement, who fixated on domestic labour – or rather, women's failure to do it – as shorthand for feminism's destructive influence. Suffrage speakers were frequently heckled with taunts of 'Can any on ye bake a batch o' bread? Han yer mended the stockin's? Go whoam and mind yer babies', 'do the washing', 'get the dinner' or 'what about the old man's tea?'[4] The discussion of housework within the suffrage movement thus not only responded to an important reality in the lives of its activists and supporters, but also acted as a bearer of meaning within a broader conversation about what it meant to be an

[1] *Woman Worker* 7 July 1909, p. 6; 2 Dec. 1908, p. 670; 1 Nov. 1908, p. 591.
[2] *Woman Worker* 12 Jan. 1910, p. 626; Mrs J. G. Frazer, *First Aid to the Servantless* (Cambridge: W. Heffer & Sons, 1913).
[3] *Woman Worker* 16 Dec. 1908, p. 719; *New Age* 23 Oct. 1913, pp. 759–760.
[4] Hannah Mitchell, *The Hard Way Up: The Autobiography of Hannah Mitchell, Suffragette and Rebel* (London: Virago, 1977), p. 155; *Vote* 12 March 1910, p. 233; 19 March 1910, p. 245; 26 March 1910, p. 261; *Suffragette* 24 Jan. 1913, p. 220.

emancipated woman. This chapter focuses on the feminist press, and on
how housework featured not just as the subject of articles and correspondence but also in advertisements and lighter sections (advice
columns, short stories and competitions) of these newspapers. Here,
through the reiteration of images, descriptions and metaphors of domestic labour, various ways of assuming a feminist identity were formulated
and rehearsed. Readers across a range of feminist newspapers were
frequently assumed to be women who did not enjoy housework. This
in turn generated anxieties about the suffrage movement's supposed
renunciation of domesticity, and sat uneasily alongside the desire to
revalue the work of women in the home.

Suffrage and Housework

In arguing that housework occupied an important place in both the
political thought and identity of the suffrage movement, this chapter
contributes to wider historiographical efforts to show how the struggle
for the vote was not a single-issue campaign, nor concerned only with a
narrow definition of political rights, but also sought to transform women's
personal and home lives.[5] Recent work on consumer culture and the
feminist press has emphasised how the suffrage movement politicised
everyday practices such as shopping and fashion, using them as ways to
signify one's allegiance to the Cause.[6] By extending such an analysis to
think about the politicisation of housework, I argue that it was not just

[5] Susie Fleming and Gloden Dallas, 'Jessie', *Spare Rib*, 32 (Feb. 1975), 10–13; Claire
Eustance, '"Daring to Be Free": The Evolution of Women's Political Identities in the
Women's Freedom League 1907–1930', PhD thesis, University of York (1993), pp. 89,
118, 141–143, 216–222; Laura E. Nym Mayhall, 'Household and Market in Suffragette
Discourse, 1903–14', *The European Legacy: Toward New Paradigms*, 6:2 (2001), 189–199;
Susan Hamilton, '"A Crisis in Women's History": Frances Power Cobbe's Duties of
Women and the Practice of Everyday Feminism', *Women's History Review*, 11:4 (2002),
577–593; Maria Dicenzo, Lucy Delap and Leila Ryan, 'Publics, Social Movements and
Media History', in Maria Dicenzo, Lucy Delap and Leila Ryan (eds.), *Feminist Media
History: Suffrage, Periodicals and the Public Sphere* (Basingstoke: Palgrave Macmillan,
2011), 21–72, p. 33; Sheila Rowbotham, *Dreamers of a New Day: Women Who Invented
the Twentieth Century* (London: Verso, 2011); Barbara Green, *Feminist Periodicals and
Daily Life: Women and Modernity in British Culture* (Basingstoke: Palgrave
Macmillan, 2017).
[6] Katrina Rolley, 'Fashion, Femininity and the Fight for the Vote', *Art History*, 13:1 (1990),
47–71; John Mercer, 'Media and Militancy: Propaganda in the Women's Social and
Political Union Campaign', *Women's History Review*, 14:3–4 (2005), 471–486; Barbara
Green, 'Feminist Things', in Ann Ardis and Patrick Collier (eds.), *Transatlantic Print
Culture, 1880–1940: Emerging Media, Emerging Modernisms* (Basingstoke: Palgrave
Macmillan, 2008), 66–79; John Mercer, 'Shopping for Suffrage: The Campaign Shops
of the Women's Social and Political Union', *Women's History Review*, 18:2 (2009),
293–309.

consumption patterns that were constructed as a political act but also the *doing* of domestic labour, the *work* of housework. This chapter analyses the representation of housework in the official organs of the National Union of Women's Suffrage Societies (*Common Cause*, est. 1909), the Women's Social and Political Union (*Votes for Women*, est. 1907) and the Women's Freedom League (*Vote*, est. 1909).[7] Because this chapter explores one of the wider concerns of the suffrage movement, beyond the demand for the parliamentary vote, I also examine feminist newspapers with a wider remit. The *Englishwoman* (est. 1909) was both a suffrage newspaper and a more generalist monthly review devoted to politics and culture.[8] The *Woman Worker* (est. 1907) began life as the official newspaper of the National Federation of Women Workers, but committed itself to socialist feminism more generally after it went from a monthly to a weekly publication in June 1908. From then on it increased its coverage of the campaign for the suffrage, supporting votes for all women and men, while retaining a focus on women's workplace rights.[9] The distinction between specialist suffrage newspapers and those with a broader agenda is important, but not wholly clear-cut. For example, although the suffrage was the main focus of the *Common Cause* and the *Vote*, they also covered a range of issues relating to the wider question of women's emancipation.[10]

Combined, these newspapers attracted a significant readership, although the popularity of each paper varied considerably. *Votes for Women* (edited by Emmeline and Frederick Pethick-Lawrence both before and after their split with the WSPU in 1912) believed that a newspaper went from being of niche to national interest once it had surpassed a circulation of 30,000 – which they achieved between 1909 and 1912 with a peak of 40,000.[11] The *Common Cause* (edited by

[7] *Votes for Women* remained in the hands of Emmeline and Frederick Pethick-Lawrence after they split with the Pankhursts in 1912, becoming the organ of the Votes for Women Fellowship. They handed it over to the United Suffragists in August 1914; Elizabeth Crawford, *The Women's Suffrage Movement: A Reference Guide 1866–1928* (London: University College London Press, 1999), pp. 460–461.
[8] Leila Ryan and Maria Dicenzo, '*The Englishwoman*: "Twelve Years of a Brilliant Life"', in Dicenzo et al. (eds.), *Feminist Media History*, 120–158, p. 121.
[9] Cathy Hunt, 'Binding Women Together in Friendship and Unity? Mary Macarthur and *The Woman Worker*, September 1907 to May 1908', *Media History*, 19:2 (2013), 139–152; Green, *Feminist Periodicals and Daily Life*, chapter 4. The *Woman Worker* changed its name to *Women Folk* on 2 February 1910, but retained *Woman Worker* in its subtitle. For ease of reference, I refer to *Woman Worker* throughout.
[10] Maria Dicenzo, 'Unity and Dissent: Official Organs of the Suffrage Campaign', in Dicenzo et al. (eds.), *Feminist Media History*, 76–119, pp. 77, 109–110; Claire Eustance, '"Daring to Be Free"', p. 72.
[11] Maria Dicenzo, 'Militant Distribution: *Votes for Women* and the Public Sphere', Media History, 6:2 (2000), 115–120, pp. 115, 119–121.

Helena Swanwick until 1912 and later by Clementina Black and Maud Royden) was the other most influential suffrage organ, although members of the NUWSS, unlike the WSPU, were less inclined to volunteer to sell it on the street.[12] The *Vote* (initially edited by Marian Holmes and Mrs T. P. O'Connor, and after 1910 by Mary Olivia Kennedy, Charlotte Despard and Annie Smith) struggled with its sales. After 'strenuous appeals' it managed to sell 8,450 copies in December 1910.[13] In 1908, reports of sales in the *Woman Worker* (edited successively by Mary Macarthur, Julia Dawson and Winifred Blatchford), claimed figures between 20,000 and 40,000. Like the suffrage organs, it priced itself at 1d. and sought to appeal not just to activists but to working-class women more generally.[14] By contrast, the *Englishwoman* (edited by Elisina Grant Richards, and after 1910 by Maude Meredith) cost 1s. and was aimed at a 'cultured' middle- and upper-class audience.[15]

Reading these rather different newspapers alongside each other, identifying common themes and overlapping readerships, highlights the interconnections between the suffrage movement's politicisation of the home and debates taking place in working-class women's organisations.[16] Until 1909, the *Woman Worker* was also used for notes and communications for the Women's Labour League with which the National Federation of Women Workers had a close relationship. From June 1908 onwards it also developed editorial links with the *Clarion* newspaper and guild socialism.[17] This chapter therefore moves into the terrain of what has been termed termed 'suffrage outside suffragism', spheres of women's political activism that were 'not specifically suffrage organisations although suffragists belonged to them'.[18] The Women's

---

[12] Dicenzo 'Unity and Dissent', pp. 96–97; Crawford, *The Women's Suffrage Movement*, pp. 458–459.

[13] Eustance, '"Daring to Be Free"', pp. 73–74.

[14] *Woman Worker* 12 June 1908, p. 16; 26 June 1908, p. 138; Hunt, 'Binding Women Together in Friendship and Unity?', pp. 140–141. Macarthur was editor from 1907 to 1908, succeeded by Dawson in 1909; Blatchford became editor in February 1910 when the paper changed its name; Green, *Feminist Periodicals and Daily Life*, p. 158.

[15] Ryan and Dicenzo, '*The Englishwoman*', pp. 121, 123.

[16] Here I draw upon the new approaches to the feminist press suggested in Dicenzo et al., *Feminist Media History*.

The organ of the ILP, the *Labour Leader*, for example, took out a large advertisement in the *Common Cause* with the headline, 'The Labour Leader should be read by every person Interested in the Women's Movement'; *Common Cause* 30 Nov. 1911, p. 607.

[17] Cathy Hunt, *The National Federation of Women Workers, 1906–1921* (Basingstoke: Palgrave Macmillan, 2014), pp. 37–40; Green, *Feminist Periodicals and Daily Life*, p. 149.

[18] Myriam Boussahba-Bravard (ed.), *Suffrage Outside Suffragism: Women's Vote in Britain, 1880–1914* (Basingstoke: Palgrave Macmillan, 2007), 1–31.

Labour League was founded in 1906 and linked to, but autonomous from, the Labour Party, with about 5,000 members by 1913.[19] It supported women's enfranchisement, and although there was disagreement among its membership as to whether this demand ought to be formulated as women's or adult suffrage, many combined their activity in the League with membership of the WSPU or the NUWSS.[20] Another working-class women's organisation influential in the housework debates was the Women's Co-operative Guild, formed out of the co-operative movement in 1883 as a kind of trade union for housewives. By 1913 it had managed to organise 30,000 women into 600 branches across the country. It gave its formal support to female enfranchisement in 1904, set up a suffrage fund in 1905 and began collaborating with suffrage organisations thereafter. In 1909 its Congress passed a motion in favour of adult suffrage, while many of its members who wished to continue to promote votes for women joined the People's Suffrage Federation.[21]

Women's Common Burden of Housework

Turn-of-the-twentieth-century households generated an enormous amount of cooking, cleaning and caring work, at all times undertaken by women.[22] This applied across the classes, although the wealth of a household determined the nature of the work and whether and how it was divided between domestic servants and unwaged housewives. Most houses were still heated by coal fires, which required women to rise early to light them, to carry heavy buckets of fuel, and to blacklead or polish grates on a regular basis. Although gas and electricity began to enter middle-class homes from the 1880s onwards, access was limited to urban

---

[19] The Women's Labour League affiliated to the Labour Party in 1908, but did not receive financial assistance from it until 1911. It merged with the Labour Party in 1918; Christine Collette, *For Labour and for Women: The Women's Labour League, 1906–1918* (Manchester: Manchester University Press, 1989); Pat Thane, 'Women in the Labour Party and Women's Suffrage', in Boussahba-Bravard (ed.), *Suffrage Outside Suffragism*, 35–51.

[20] Thane, 'Women in the Labour Party and Women's Suffrage', pp. 37–38, 40–43.

[21] Gillian Scott, 'The Women's Co-operative Guild and Suffrage', in Boussahba-Bravard (ed.), *Suffrage Outside Suffragism*, 132–156, pp. 145–151.

[22] This overview is indebted to Davidson, *A Woman's Work Is Never Done: A History of Housework in the British Isles 1650–1950* (London: Chatto & Windus). Other histories of housework in this period include Jane Lewis (ed.), *Labour and Love: Women's Experience of Home and Family, 1850–1940* (Oxford: Basil Blackwell, 1986); Christina Hardyment, *From Mangle to Microwave: The Mechanisation of Household Work* (Cambridge: Polity Press, 1988); Joanna Bourke, *Husbandry to Housewifery: Women, Economic Change, and Housework in Ireland, 1890–1914* (Oxford: Clarendon Press, 1993); Joanna Bourke, *Working-Class Cultures in Britain 1890–1960: Gender, Class and Ethnicity* (London: Routledge, 1994).

and usually affluent areas. In 1901 only two-thirds of those households supplied with gas used it to cook with, while electric cookers did not become widespread until the late 1920s. Many middle-class homes continued to use closed ranges up until the First World War, consisting of various ovens and boilers heated by a coal fire that had to be carefully controlled by opening and closing front panels. Cooking on ranges required considerable skill, while maintaining, cleaning and blacking them was extremely arduous. Yet perhaps they were preferable to balancing a kettle or frying pan on an open grate as many city slum dwellers and countryside poor had to do. Coal fires and stoves also produced a great deal of soot, increasing the amount of dusting, sweeping and window cleaning. In turn-of-the-century industrial towns women had to wash windows once a week and their net curtains once a fortnight. The Victorian fashion for heavy furnishings and ornamental clutter continued to be embraced in most Edwardian homes, adding to the tasks of dusting, polishing and carpet-beating.

Cleaning was certainly made easier by the introduction of piped water into houses over the second half of the nineteenth century. By the 1870s about 80 per cent of Manchester's houses had internal water supplies and 28 per cent had baths, but although every street in a town such as Oxford had water laid on by 1912, in working-class neighbourhoods these taps were outside and had to be shared with a number of other houses. The modern flushing toilet began to appear in houses from the late nineteenth century onwards; but chamber pots still had to be emptied in working-class homes that shared outdoor toilets, and in wealthier households where residents were either slow to install indoor plumbing or unwilling to visit the bathroom in the middle of the night.[23] By the 1880s commercial soaps and soda (used to scrub flagstone floors on one's hands and knees) were widely available, but they would not have been very effective without hot water, which was piped only to more affluent neighbourhoods. Even by 1961, 22 per cent of the population remained without hot taps. Front doorsteps, especially, needed to be scrubbed and whitened in order to keep up appearances – most urban households had it done every morning, while those from the poorest of homes might manage it only on a Saturday. This reminds us how crucial keeping a clean and tidy home was to working-class respectability.

The technology for most modern household appliances – vacuum cleaners, gas and electric cookers and even a kind of dishwasher – had

[23] Lawrence Wright, *Clean and Decent: The Fascinating History of the Bathroom and the Water Closet* (London: Routledge & Kegan Paul, 1960), chapters 15 and 16; Alison Light, *Mrs Woolf and the Servants* (London: Penguin, 2007), pp. 120, 130, 136.

been developed by the early 1900s. Older, labour-intensive and time-consuming methods nevertheless persisted well into the twentieth century, due to the low status of housework and the relative cheapness of employing servants.[24] Advocates of 'servantless homes' failed to generate much enthusiasm from the majority of women living in older houses or more remote areas where, even if they could afford expensive household appliances, they had neither the space nor electricity to power them.[25] Moreover, although technological advances undoubtedly reduced the amount of time spent on individual domestic chores, they also raised standards and expectations.[26]

Once all this is taken into account, it is possible to see how the servant's excessively long working day was not only driven by employers' desire to extract the maximum amount of labour in return for wages, but also by the quantity of work necessary to keep a household going. The first survey recording how much time women spent on housework in Britain was carried out in 1934, based on 1,250 urban working-class wives. It showed that the majority got up at 6:30 a.m. and went to bed between 10 p.m. and 11 p.m., after spending twelve to fourteen hours per day engaged in household work. Even a propaganda exercise undertaken in 1935, intended to demonstrate how fully electrified homes could lighten the housewife's burden, found that women living in these supposedly ideal conditions still spent just over forty-nine hours per week on domestic labour, similar hours to full-time work outside the home.[27]

The housework problem was always viewed as a women's problem. Even feminists shied away from demanding that men take on their fair share of the work.[28] In middle-class homes it was mistresses and maids, rather than the male employers, who took responsibility for housework. There has been slightly more debate among historians over the degree to which working-class households also viewed domestic labour as women's sole responsibility. Most emphasise a total lack of male involvement or

[24] Hardyment, *From Mangle to Microwave*, p. 33; Lucy Delap, *Knowing Their Place: Domestic Service in Twentieth-Century Britain* (Oxford: Oxford University Press, 2011), p. 117.
[25] Mrs J. G. Frazer, *First Aid to the Servantless*; *Common Cause* 11 Aug. 1916, p. 229; Delap, *Knowing Their Place*, chapter 3.
[26] Davidson, *A Woman's Work Is Never Done*, p. 192. See also Ruth Schwartz Cowan, *More Work for Mother: The Ironies of Household Technology from the Open Hearth to the Microwave* (New York: Basic, 1983); Judy Giles, *The Parlour and the Suburb: Domestic Identities, Class, Femininity and Modernity* (Oxford: Berg, 2004), pp. 20–21.
[27] Davidson, *A Woman's Work Is Never Done*, p. 191.
[28] The most avant-garde circles occasionally considered the possibility of men undertaking childcare, but not cooking or cleaning; Lucy Delap, *The Feminist Avant-Garde: Transatlantic Encounters of the Early Twentieth Century* (Cambridge: Cambridge University Press), pp. 203–204.

argue that men contributed, at most, only to outdoor tasks such as fetching coal, chopping firewood or putting the rubbish out. Caroline Davidson suggested one of the reasons why refusal to do housework became such a point of pride for many working-class men was because, although they would sometimes be required to help around the house or care for children, this was most likely to occur in periods of male unemployment when women were compelled to seek work outside the home. Such principles had practical effects, and the shameful and emasculating connotations attached to men being seen performing domestic labour in public propped up the belief that it was women's work even when it was sometimes being done by men behind closed doors.[29] Joanna Bourke has questioned the prevailing historiographical view and argued that working-class autobiographies often featured fathers contributing to the work of the household. Yet she too acknowledged the important difference between tasks defined as 'manly' and those considered feminine, and the stigma attached to men who were seen to transgress this gendered division of labour.[30]

The feminist press often discussed how the problem of housework affected women across the classes, albeit in different ways. In the wealthiest households employing a large staff, mistresses might be expected only to manage the housekeeping, but many middle-class wives and mothers had to undertake at least some of the housework alongside their servants. In a household advice column in the *Woman Worker*, for example, Mrs D. J. M. Worrall described how, despite being able to afford to employ a 'young maid', her own domestic duties had got the 'upper hand' so that she was able to do or think about little else. Her readers wrote in to confirm that Worrall's experience was typical of many 'lower middle-class' married women who found themselves 'entirely absorbed by washing, cleaning and mending etc.'.[31] An article on 'The Burden of Housework' in *Votes for Women* complained that although women were now entering the professions in ever larger numbers, there had been no corresponding reduction in their responsibility for the household. The professional woman, on returning home from work, had thus to busy herself with housework while her husband settled down with a pipe and book.[32] In *A New Way of Housekeeping*, serialised in the *Common Cause* in 1916, Clementina Black pointed out that even single women employed

[29] Davidson, *A Woman's Work Is Never Done*, pp. 120, 185–188. See also Arthur J. McIvor, *A History of Work in Britain, 1880–1950* (Basingstoke: Palgrave, 2001), p. 182.
[30] Bourke, *Working-Class Cultures in Britain*, pp. 81–95.
[31] *Woman Worker* 12 June 1908, p. 23; 26 June 1908, p. 114. See also *Englishwoman* Feb. 1911, pp. 159–160.
[32] *Votes for Women* 7 April 1911, p. 442. See also *Englishwoman* Jan. 1910, p. 270.

in the new 'white blouse' occupations found it difficult to cater to their own domestic needs on top of full-time waged work, becoming 'worn out' by their 'double shift'.[33]

Married working-class women shouldered the heaviest burden and worked days of similar length and intensity to domestic servants. Many of them left service on marriage only to find themselves exchanging one gruelling regime for another.[34] Ada Nield Chew (1870–1945) wrote a number of articles and short stories in the *Englishwoman* and the *Common Cause*, documenting the enormous amount of domestic labour undertaken by the 'married working woman'. These writings drew in part on her first-hand experience. The daughter of a brick-maker, Chew had had to leave school at the age of eleven to help her mother with the housework and care for her eleven younger siblings. She began working in a clothing factory in her early twenties before becoming a paid organiser for the Independent Labour Party (ILP), then the Women's Trade Union League and in 1912 the NUWSS.[35] The prose style of Chew's semi-fictional account of working-class housewife 'Mrs Turpin' is typical of her rhetorical strategy in all her articles on domestic work. She depicted household labour in minute detail, task piled upon task, not only to convey the incessant and all-absorbing nature of the daily round, but also to force into public view a form of work that was usually hidden in the private sphere.

Her clothes thrown on with lightning speed, and three children have been wakened, the fire is lit and the kettle 'on'. Five minutes more suffices to 'wash the sleep out of her eyes' and 'straighten her hair'. By a quarter past, the bit of bacon for father and the boy who works is frizzling merrily in the Dutch oven before the fire; the children are downstairs, and she is buttoning on garments, and washing faces and combing hair, and putting out cups and saucers, making the tea, and turning the bacon ... there is ten minutes' rapid feeding, mother replenishing cups and plates with the baby under her arm. In the intervals she

---

[33] Clementina Black, *A New Way of Housekeeping* (London: W. Collins Sons, 1918), p. 8; *Common Cause* 11 Aug. 1916, p. 229; 18 Aug. 1916, p. 235; 25 Aug. 1916, p. 247; 1 Sept. 1916, pp. 263–264.

[34] Jill Liddington and Jill Norris, *One Hand Tied behind Us: The Rise of the Women's Suffrage Movement* (London: Virago, 1984), chapter 2; Dot Jones, 'Counting the Cost of Coal: Women's Lives in the Rhondda, 1881–1911', in Angela V. John (ed.), *Our Mothers' Land: Chapters in Welsh Women's History, 1830–1939* (Cardiff: University of Wales Press, 1991), 109–133; Ellen Ross, *Love and Toil: Motherhood in Outcast London, 1870–1918* (Oxford: Oxford University Press, 1993); McIvor, *History of Work in Britain*, pp. 178–182.

[35] Doris Nield Chew (ed.), *Ada Nield Chew: The Life and Writings of a Working Woman* (London: Virago, 1982); David Doughan, 'Chew, Ada Nield (1870–1945) Labour Organiser and Suffragist', in *Oxford Dictionary of National Biography*, online edn. (Oxford University Press, 2004). See also *Common Cause* 21 Sept. 1911, pp. 409–410; 12 Oct. 1911, pp. 457–458; 4 Jan. 1912, p. 674; *Labour Leader* 17 Feb. 1911, p. 109; *Englishwoman* July 1911, pp. 39–48.

keeps a sharp look-out for little coats, and is relieved to find they are in sight and will not need hunting for ... Half past nine. The baby is washed and dressed ... A quarter to ten. As much of the weekly wash as the little backyard will hold is pegged out, and the rest is hanging on the clotheshorse in front of the fire. Ten o'clock. The dirty pots are all in the little scullery, but there is no time to wash up now ... A quarter past ten. Mrs Turpin, baby in arms, is at the butchers purchasing half a pound of pork steak, a penn'orth of suet, and a penn'orth of bones. At the greengrocers next door she gets 5 pounds of potatoes, a penn'orth of onions, and a penn'orth of pot herbs ... What a long time it takes to make broth! Everything to be cut out, and washed, and bothered with ... Now there's the washing-up. And if it isn't raining! And the clothes not half dry![36]

Mrs Turpin's day continues, her multifarious labour recorded over nine pages of the *Englishwoman*, only ending after 11 p.m. when she falls into bed with the knowledge that 'she will be tired tomorrow morning when she rises, but she will gallantly face another day, much like today'. Ada Nield Chew wrote about both full-time housewives and women who combined housework with waged work such as the semi-fictional 'Mrs Bolt', up at dawn blackleading the kitchen range and laying the fire, making her husband and children breakfast before going to work in the weaving sheds. At the end of her ten-hour shift Mrs Bolt still has to make tea, shop for food, and put her children to bed.[37] Chew was also clear that it was not just mothers who suffered such excessive workloads, for the 'married woman who has no babies' was also 'slave to her pots and pans'.[38] Chew believed the 'average man' was horribly ignorant of the 'systematic, never-ceasing effort necessary to the keeping of an ordinary home clean by one pair of hands, even when bathroom and hot and cold water are all ready at hand'. Only such male ignorance could have prompted the sentencing, in 1911, of a mother of five to six weeks in prison for keeping a dirty house, and Chew commented that if women were allowed in the legislature they would never have passed such unjust laws.[39]

When Sylvia Pankhurst recalled her work in the East London Federation of the Suffragettes (ELFS) she too noted 'the too multifarious and often hugely conflicting labours of the home' as one of the main problems facing impoverished East End women.[40] ELFS was formed early in 1913, when Christabel Pankhurst decided to withdraw WSPU resources from organising in the area. Sylvia Pankhurst, whose commitment to

---

[36] *Englishwoman* July 1911, pp. 39–48.   [37] *Englishwoman*, July 1912, pp. 35–45.
[38] *Common Cause* 6 March 1914, pp. 933–934.
[39] *Labour Leader* 17 March 1911, p. 173.
[40] E. Sylvia Pankhurst, *The Home Front: A Mirror to Life in England during the First World War* (London: Cresset Library, 1987 [first published 1932]), p. 43.

socialism was creating an ever-greater breach with her mother and her sister, decided to stay, and ELFS declared itself independent of the WSPU in December of that year.[41] Concern about the grinding domestic labour necessary to keep working-class women's families alive played a central part in the political activism of ELFS women such as the former domestic servant Melvina Walker, and the suffragette militant and char-woman Mrs Pascoe.[42] In September 1914, shortly after war was declared in Britain, they made a deputation to the Minister of the Board of Trade to argue for the nationalisation of the food supply. One of their party 'produced the weekly budget of a mother who had eleven children to care for', while Melvina Walker 'expatiated on the cost of her every-Sunday knuckle of imported mutton, which had risen since the war from 4 ½d to 8 ½d per lb.'[43] Their insistence upon asserting every detail of their domestic labour is similar to the documentary style deployed by Ada Nield Chew.[44] The ELFS women focused on food prices to highlight not just their inadequate incomes, but also the time and labour it took to stretch household budgets, purchasing miniscule quantities of ingredi-ents in order to make just enough food to last their families for a week. Larger working-class women's organisations, such as the Women's Co-operative Guild and the Women's Labour League, also denounced the domestic 'drudgery' endured by women struggling to maintain clean and comfortable homes on their husband's low wages – leading them to campaign for better housing and some form of co-operative housekeeping.[45]

[41] Barbara Winslow, *Sylvia Pankhurst: Sexual Politics and Political Activism* (London: University College London Press, 1996), pp. 32, 38–39, 42, 66.

[42] Sylvia Pankhurst, *The Suffragette Movement* (London: Virago [first published 1931]), p. 524.

[43] Pankhurst, *The Home Front*, pp. 51–52.

[44] *Common Cause* 12 Oct. 1911, pp. 457–458.

[45] Collette, *For Labour and for Women*, pp. 20–22, 47; Alistair Thomson, "'Domestic Drudgery Will Be a Thing of the Past": Co-operative Women and the Reform of Housework', in Stephen Yeo (ed.), *New Views of Co-operation* (London: Routledge, 1988), 108–127; Pat Thane, 'Women in the British Labour Party and the Construction of State Welfare, 1906–1939', in Seth Koven and Sonya Michel (eds.), *Mothers of the New World: Maternalist Politics and the Origins of Welfare States* (New York: Routledge, 1993), 343–377, pp. 350, 356, 365; Gillian Scott, *Feminism and the Politics of Working Women: The Women's Co-operative Guild, 1880s to the Second World War* (London: University College London Press, 1998), pp. 73–74; Nicola Wilson, *Home in British Working-Class Fiction* (Farnham: Ashgate, 2015), pp. 66–67. As members of the Women's Co-operative Guild recorded in their own words, the poor health of working-class mothers was caused as much by the heavy burden of housework as successive pregnancies and inadequate medical care; Margaret Llewelyn Davies, *Maternity Letters from Working Women* (London: Virago, 1978 [first published 1915]). For socialist feminist critiques of household 'drudgery' in the *Clarion* and *Daily Herald*, Green, *Feminist Periodicals and Everyday Life*, chapter 3.

These feminist accounts present a very different picture to the argument put forward by Joanna Bourke that, rather than being unwilling household slaves, many working-class women in this period enthusiastically pursued the 'pleasures of housewifery'. She criticised those feminist historians who tended to emphasise the oppressive conditions of Victorian and Edwardian housewifery, for refusing to listen to the voices of their historical subjects. Instead, Bourke argued that working-class women had not been forced back into the home by domestic ideology or male-dominated trade unions, but made a positive choice to 'embrace this new identity'.[46] Were early twentieth-century feminists, in denouncing the time-consuming labours of the home, guilty of the same refusal to respect the decisions of 'ordinary' working-class women in choosing what might have been the best option available to them? I don't think so. When working-class women's organisations criticised the damaging effects of too much housework, they were drawing upon the experiences of their members. More middle-class suffrage activists also demonstrated an impressive knowledge of the working conditions and challenges that faced working-class wives in particular.[47] By the first decade of the twentieth century far fewer working-class women were engaged in paid employment outside the home than they had been half a century earlier, and far more of them were full-time housewives dependent upon their husband's wages. I agree with Bourke that this was often a rational choice on the part of individuals, and for many women preferable to the difficulties of combining childcare, domestic duties and waged labour. Women, moreover, may well have used this domestic identity strategically, to gain status and assert the value of their skills as wives and mothers, and even to derive pleasure from it, as Bourke argues.[48] But this should not mean we lose sight of the fact that housewifery was not just an identity, but also a form of labour that was invariably exhausting and frequently debilitating for the women who performed it. It

[46] Bourke, *Working-Class Cultures in Britain*, pp. 62–97, 64; Joanna Bourke, 'Housewifery in Working-Class England 1860–1914', in Pamela Sharpe (ed.), *Women's Work: The English Experience 1650–1914* (London: Arnold, 1998), 332–358.
[47] *Votes for Women* 27 Jan. 1911, p. 275; 24 Jan. 1913, p. 244; 11 July 1913, p. 606. Despite their limited experience, many middle-class feminists did educate themselves about the domestic predicament of working-class women; Carol Dyhouse, *Feminism and the Family in England 1880–1939* (Oxford: Basil Blackwell, 1989), p. 137; Ellen Ross, 'St Frances in Soho: Emmeline Pethick, Mary Neal, the West London Wesleyan Mission, and the Allure of "Simple Living" in the 1890s', *Church History*, 83:4 (Dec. 2014), 843–883, pp. 855–856. Nevertheless some of the semi-fictionalised accounts of their domestic lives, often written in first person with phonetic spelling denoting regional accents, objectified such women and sometimes made them appear ridiculous; Ross, *Love and Toil*, p. 20.
[48] Bourke, 'Housewifery in Working-Class England', pp. 333–335.

was against this that not only middle- but also working-class feminists spoke out.

The experiences of working-class housewives were not, therefore, erased in feminist condemnations of housework, nor was the suffrage movement afraid to acknowledge that its burdens fell heaviest on such women. What was obscured was the imbalance of power between women who worked in their own homes and women who worked in other women's homes. In 1911 Ada Nield Chew devoted three short stories in the *Common Cause* to writing about her own charwoman – a Mrs Worth whom Chew paid 4d per hour. Mrs Worth was typical of many wives and mothers who had to supplement their husband's earnings of around £1 per week with char work or taking in washing or sewing, thus adding to their own burden of domestic duties by undertaking them for other, better-off women. Although Ada Nield Chew paid tribute to Worth for her strength of spirit and skill at 'making it stretch', she ultimately conceptualised their relationship as a 'bond' of 'mutual help'. She saw them not as exploiter and exploited, employer and worker, but as women united by their common burden of housework.[49] Chew's working-class background probably made it easier for her to identify with her servant in this manner than mistresses of more secure middle-class status. Chew was also unusual in arguing that working-class women should bring in paid domestic help while they worked outside the home, asking, 'Why should it be so horrible for poor women to contemplate somebody else doing these jobs for them than it is for well-to-do women to have them done?' Here, Chew was once again railing against the injustice of sentencing working-class wives to a life of domestic drudgery, yet her analysis of the housework problem had little to say about how the women she proposed to employ as paid domestic help would be similarly liberated.[50]

Housework and the Politicisation of Everyday Life

Historical interest in the consumer culture of the British suffrage movement has grown in recent years, with particular attention paid to the role of suffrage-branded souvenirs and paraphernalia in generating collective identities and opportunities for more low-profile or 'everyday' forms of activism.[51] Here I want to explore a different aspect of this politicisation

---

[49] *Common Cause* 21 Sept. 1911, pp. 409–410; 5 Oct. 1911, pp. 441–442; 12 Oct. 1911, pp. 457–458; 25 Jan. 1912, p. 724.
[50] *Freewoman* 22 Aug. 1912, pp. 270–272.
[51] For socialist women's somewhat different politicisation of consumption, June Hannam and Karen Hunt, *Socialist Women: Britain, 1880s to 1920s* (London: Routledge, 2002), chapter 6.

of everyday life, focusing not so much on suffrage goods such as WSPU tea-sets and jewellery but on advertisements for household commodities, cleaning products in particular, which were produced for the mainstream market but advertised in feminist periodicals. Advertising was an important source of revenue for many of the newspapers discussed here, though editors differed over the degree to which they either saw it as a necessary evil or fully embraced its possibilities.[52] Of all the papers, *Votes for Women* was the least abashed about harnessing 'commercial tactics to a radical political agenda'. Within a year of initial publication it was managing to cover its own costs through sales and lavishly illustrated advertisements for products ranging from winter furs, cigarettes and suffrage-friendly grocers.[53] By comparison, the *Woman Worker* had a far less commercial aesthetic, but it, too, frequently contained advertisements for cleaning products and 'wonder working cookers'.[54] The placement of commercial goods in feminist periodicals was not simply a capitulation to conventional femininity, but also an attempt to negotiate negative representations of suffrage-supporting women elsewhere in the media and carve out new ways of being female and feminist.[55] Because advertisers simultaneously seek to appeal to a pre-existing market and to expand it via aspirational representations of the consumer, these advertisements can be used to shed light on both the everyday lives of a feminist readership and the process by which reading the feminist press helped to construct new female identities.

In 1908 a series of advertisements for Fels-Naptha multipurpose laundry soap appeared in both *Votes for Women* and the *Woman Worker*. Each told a story in which the character of 'Anty Drudge' (a comfortable 'auntie' of an older woman dressed in apron and old-fashioned bonnet) offered advice on housework to a rotating cast consisting of 'Mrs Young Mother', 'Mrs Hardwork', a 'Mistress' and her servant 'Bridget', 'Mrs Housemother', 'Mrs Careless', two flatmates 'Jenny' and 'Mary', and a 'Typist'.[56] The advertisements were illustrated in *Votes for Women*,

---

[52] Maria Dicenzo, 'Militant Distribution', pp. 122, 127; Lucy Delap, Maria Dicenzo and Leila Ryan (eds.), *Feminism and the Periodical Press, 1900–1980*, 3 vols. (Abingdon: Routledge, 2006), vol. I, p. xl.

[53] Dicenzo, 'Militant Distribution', pp. 116, 119–120.

[54] *Woman Worker* 5 June 1908, p. 15.

[55] Dicenzo, 'Militant Distribution', pp. 121–122.

[56] *Votes for Women* 1 Oct. 1908, p. 14; 8 Oct. 1908, p. 30; 15 Oct. 1908, p. 46; 22 Oct. 1908, p. 62; 29 Oct. 1908, p. 86; 12 Nov. 1908, p. 118; 26 Nov. 1908, p. 158; 17 Dec. 1908, p. 206; 31 Dec. 1908, p. 237; *Woman Worker* 11 Sept. 1908, p. 380; 18 Sept. 1908, p. 404; 25 Sept. 1908, p. 428; 2 Oct. 1908, p. 452; 9 Oct. 1908, p. 476; 16 Oct. 1908, p. 500; 23 Oct. 1908, p. 524; 28 Oct. 1908, p. 548; 4 Nov. 1908, p. 572; 11 Nov. 1908, p. 596.

whereas in the *Woman Worker* they appeared only in written form. In each, the processes of domestic labour are discussed in great detail, as are the day-to-day challenges of combining housework with childcare and waged labour. For example, the Typist who smears her shirt with ink complains that yet again she will have to spend an hour scrubbing it out when she gets home from work (see Figure 4).[57] Such young professional women appear in another advertisement in which Mary and Jenny discuss the difficulty of doing laundry when living alone in flats catering for working ladies.[58] A harassed Mrs Careless, who is trying to do the family wash at the same time as minding her baby, complains that the steam from the boiling water has upset his stomach, while Mrs Young Mother is delighted to receive assistance from Anty Drudge after her attempts at laundry have flooded the kitchen and put out the fire.[59] The minutiae of domestic work recounted in the Fels-Naptha series week after week is in stark contrast to the formal content of *Votes for Women*, which was mainly concerned with reporting on parliamentary manoeuvrings on the vote, WSPU militancy and branch activities. These advertisements thus provide a glimpse into the more mundane aspects of existence for suffrage-supporting women, those which were not always represented in the movement's official propaganda. They also reveal what historian Barbara Green has termed 'a shared interest in the everyday' that connects a WSPU readership with the more working-class, or at least labour movement–orientated, readers of the *Woman Worker*.[60]

The Fels-Naphtha advertisements give an indication of who the advertisers expected the readership of these feminist newspapers to consist of. In the *Woman Worker* they tend to feature more housewives and mothers struggling to stay on top of their overwhelming burden of domestic labour. In *Votes for Women* there are slightly more professional women in the advertisements, such as the Typist and other young, single 'working ladies', types to whom suffrage organisations explicitly sought to appeal.[61] There was nonetheless a significant overlap between the characters in each publication, suggesting a similar target demographic. The social class of such women is not immediately evident, given that even lower-middle- and middle-class women who employed servants

---

[57] *Votes for Women* 31 Dec. 1908, p. 237.
[58] *Votes for Women* 17 Dec. 1908, p. 206; *Woman Worker* 11 Nov. 1908, p. 596.
[59] *Votes for Women* 12 Nov. 1908, p. 118; 1 Oct. 1908, p. 14; *Woman Worker* 4 Nov. 1908, p. 572.
[60] Green, *Feminist Periodicals and Daily Life*, chapter 4.
[61] *Votes for Women* 15 Oct. 1908, p. 46; 31 Dec. 1908, p. 237; Gillian Sutherland, *In Search of the New Woman: Middle-Class Women and Work in Britain 1870–1914* (Cambridge: Cambridge University Press, 2015), pp. 100–103.

Giving the Typist a Bit of Advice.

Typist—"There! I knew I'd do it! Every time I clean this machine or change the ribbon I spoil a clean blouse. It'll take me an hour to scrub the smear out."

Anty Drudge—"Tut, tut! Don't be so foolish. Don't you know the easy way of washing? Get a cake of Fels-Naptha and follow directions, and after thirty minutes' soaking and a few rubs on the washboard, your blouse will be white as snow."

When you see the Fels-Naptha green-and-red wrapper at your grocers, don't pass it with the thought that it simply contains a cake of laundry soap, but remember it also contains a better and easier way of washing—a way that makes the clothes cleaner and whiter and saves them. Buy it —and try it. If it is your first experience with Fels-Naptha soap you will hardly believe that a washing can be done so easily.

But it can be done—is done by more than a million women every week.

Why not let Fels-Naptha do it?

Fels-Naptha

will do it.   Isn't it worth trying?

Figure 4 Fels-Naphtha advertisement.
Votes for Women 31 Dec. 1908, p. 237 (reproduced by kind permission of The Women's Library at the LSE)

would often have to undertake some housework themselves. Heavy work such as laundry, however, was more likely to be left to the servants or to a daily char, so in depicting wives and mothers engaged in such tasks Fels-Naptha was also targeting working-class women and presumably considered both *Votes for Women* and the *Woman Worker* as appropriate places in which to do so.[62] Mrs Housemother, for example, is certainly codified as a working woman with her heavy boots and working-class idiom.[63]

The Fels-Naptha advertisements convey the significance and ubiquity of housework, suggesting that women's burden of housework was a concern not just for the writers and activists discussed in the first section of this chapter, but also for a much larger readership whose experiences it is not always possible to access from the newspapers' more overtly political content. The advertisements also emphasise the hard physical toil that housework entailed – all the more so for the offhand way in which it is referred to. For example, in one advertisement appearing in the *Woman Worker*, Anty Drudge scolds a housewife for not using Fels-Naptha for her general cleaning since the traditional methods she used instead were so labour-intensive they have left the housewife 'bed-ridden' and in need of a doctor. Another depicts a mistress complaining of how her table linen always comes out 'yellowish' because her maid has to scrub so hard that her knuckles bleed and discolour the water.[64] Anty Drudge teaches these women an important lesson over and over again: housework need not and should not be so hard and time-consuming if only women would embrace the modern methods and technologies embodied by Fels-Naptha.

These advertisements illustrate a convergence of consumer capitalist modernity with the advancing feminist cause, with both, in this instance, seeking to appeal to similar 'types' of women.[65] There is also, however, some dissonance between the advertisements and the journalistic content of the newspapers, in that at least two episodes in the Fels-Naptha series feature domestic servants whose presence disrupts the prevailing feminist discourse of housework as women's common burden. The advertisement referring to the maid with bleeding knuckles is an uncomfortable reminder of how, even when mistress and maid shared in the housework, the servant's tasks were always rougher and harder. Another depicts a servant named Bridget who threatens to resign unless her mistress

---

[62] Delap, *Knowing Their Place*, p. 101.   [63] *Votes for Women* 22 Nov. 1908, p. 62.
[64] *Woman Worker* 18 Nov. 1908, p. 404; 11 Sept. 1908, p. 380.
[65] For the role of the housewife in consumer-orientated modernity in the interwar period, Giles, *The Parlour and the Suburb*, chapter 3.

purchases Fels-Naptha. Whereas other advertisements in the series clearly invite the reader to identify with the overworked and sometimes inexperienced housewife, 'Bridget's Ultimatum' is less clear as to where our sympathies should lie. The Mistress is the younger and the more attractive of the two women; her polite enquiry as to how her servant fares that morning receives only the gruffest of replies from Bridget. Invoking the 'servant problem' and the supposed travails of managing 'difficult' servants was an obvious tactic for gaining the empathy of middle-class audiences. Yet Anty Drudge takes Bridget's side in this particular case of conflict between mistress and maid, referring to the latter as 'a good sensible girl'. This endorsement is emphasised in the illustration which places the servant at the centre of the image and renders her with the same delicacy of line as her mistress. Bridget is right, says Anty Drudge, to insist upon Fels Naptha, and the servant is therefore applauded, not only for being good and sensible but also having 'a mind of her own'.[66]

While the Fels-Naptha advertisements exposed some of the contradictions of the feminist analysis of the housework problem, they can nevertheless be located within a wider conversation taking place in progressive circles. The company head, Joseph Fels, sat on the General Committee of the People's Suffrage Federation and was friend of the socialist and suffrage-supporting George Lansbury MP.[67] The advertisements' detailed representation of housework had much in common with Ada Nield Chew's short stories and the ELFS women's household budgets. Mrs D. J. M. Worrall's household advice column in the *Woman Worker*, entitled 'Home Notes', also honed in on the step-by-step mechanics of housework:

If you have any standing to do after you get home – perhaps after a long day's standing – provide yourself with an old cushion for your feet, thick enough to be restful. If you do your own washing and ironing, save yourself over the latter by not ironing woollen underwear or tea towels. Smooth these out as they dry.[68]

---

[66] *Votes for Women* 15 Oct. 1908, p. 46; 31 Dec. 1908, p. 237.

[67] The Women's Library at the London School of Economics (hereafter TWL), London, 'People's Suffrage Federation Pamphlet' (c. 1909), p. 1, PC/06/396-11/11; Arthur P. Dudden, 'Joseph Fels of Philadelphia and London', *The Pennsylvania Magazine of History and Biography*, 79:2 (April 1955), 143–166, pp. 147–148, 155–157; Evelyn Bodek Rosen, *The Philadelphia Fels, 1880–1920: A Social Portrait* (Madison: Fairleigh Dickinson University Press, 2000), chapter 8. Fels-Naptha was a US-based company, and its trademark character Anty Drudge also featured in its North American advertising campaign, yet the idiom of some of the women featured in this series of advertisements suggests that the dialogue at least was adapted for a specifically British audience. Fels moved to London in 1901.

[68] *Woman Worker* 5 June 1908, p. 18.

In these feminist newspapers, housework was politicised not simply as an idea, but also as a set of day-to-day material practices. The need to minimise its burdens was taken seriously, and the domestic labour process – the messy, tedious, nitty-gritty of how to wash clothes, clean the grate and mend stockings – was carefully considered as an object of feminist reform and transformation. In the same way that the Fels-Naphtha advertisements exhorted women to reject drudgery, the main purpose of Worrall's 'Home Notes' was to offer advice on how to reduce the amount of time spent on housework. 'Don't polish every grate by which you cook everyday,' counselled Worrall. 'Crumple up a slightly dampened piece of newspaper, and rub any spots off with this.'[69] Worrall's hints evidently struck a chord with her readers, and the following month the *Woman Worker* invited them to send their own 'labour saving hints'. The numerous suggestions received included allowing daughters to have bare legs in the summer in order to save on mending stockings, adopting a vegetarian diet and getting rid of decorative knickknacks that required constant dusting.[70] Understood in a wider context of concern about the heavy physical toll that domestic labour took on women's bodies and health, it is evident that such tips were not simply a way of filling up space but were an attempt to find a solution to a very real problem.

Housework and the Feminist Woman

Housework was conceived of not only as an objective problem but also as a subjective form of political practice. How one performed housework, how one felt about it and whether or not one did it at all became important in debates about the formation of feminists as political subjects. Mrs D. J. M. Worrall's household tips, for example, had a strong didactic element. She was keen to reassure her readers that scrimping on household tasks did not make them bad wives and mothers: 'Remember the art of making home homey is not to be eternally rubbing and scrubbing. It is to be comfortable and restful.' She was also gently critical of the way in which so many women rarely took 'an interest in anything outside domestic and nursery work', and thus neglected 'politics ... [and] social questions'. A similar message was communicated far more forcefully elsewhere in the *Woman Worker*. In the same issue in which Worrall regretted having previously allowed domestic duties to dominate her life, Monica Poulboise called upon her readers to take an interest in 'affairs

---

[69] *Woman Worker* 5 June 1908, p. 18.   [70] *Woman Worker* 31 July 1908, p. 238.

that range beyond washing, cooking, mending and nursing … We must not be content to perform only menial tasks. Let us rather lift our heads and learn the nature and purpose of our existence.' A column introduced in February 1909, entitled 'Domestic Dodges', began its series by proudly declaring that it was *not* for women who liked housework. Its pseudonymous author, Margery Daw (Mary Macpherson, one of the founders of the Women's Labour League), dismissed housework as 'such a waste of time … When there are so many books to read, friends to meet, and arts and handicrafts to study.' The rest of her column was devoted to yet more labour-saving tips.[71] The politicisation of housework thus extended beyond the simple desire to make women's lives easier; it was also about the best way to live and labour as a modern emancipated woman.

Housework was seen as a key obstacle to women expanding their mental capacities, becoming involved in politics and acting as the kinds of citizens the suffrage movement wanted and needed them to become. In 1909, the *Englishwoman* published an article by Madeleine Onslow that equated freeing women from housework with their emancipation more generally: 'The liberation of women from the position of a wife-servant is a matter of immense and world-wide significance. It means nothing less than the setting free of women to live the full life of the human being.'[72] Perhaps the most obvious problem that housework presented to women's development into 'full human beings' was that it robbed them of time they could have devoted to political action. When Ada Nield Chew was trying to organise women workers in rural areas of the West Riding, she reported how 'it is almost impossible to get a meeting anywhere in these parts on a Friday night (cleaning night)'.[73] This should not be misunderstood as implying that women were free on other nights of the week. Lavena Saltonstall, a tailoress and WSPU militant from Hebden Bridge, explained how 'In my native place the women, as a general rule, wash every Monday, iron on Tuesdays, court on Wednesdays, bake on Thursdays, clean on Fridays, go to market or go courting again on Saturdays, and to church on Sundays.'[74] A report of a meeting of the Women's Labour League in Sunderland in 1910 provides

[71] *Woman Worker* 5 June 1908, p. 18; 26 June 1911, p. 114; 12 June 1908, p. 20; 24 Feb. 1909, p. 172. McPherson also wrote a column entitled 'Woman's Corner' under this pen name in the *Railway Review*, organ of the Amalgamated Society of Railway Servants; Collette, *For Labour and for Women*, p. 31.
[72] *Englishwoman* Oct. 1909, p. 263.
[73] Quoted in Liddington and Norris, *One Hand Tied behind Us*, pp. 24–25.
[74] Quoted in Jill Liddington, *Rebel Girls: Their Fight for the Vote* (London: Virago, 2006), pp. 87–88.

an insight into the kinds of difficulties that the women Chew and Saltonstall were seeking to recruit might have faced, noting how 'one mother
of six was baking the weekly batch of bread at 5am in order to get away by
noon to attend our Conference'.[75] The Women's Co-operative Guild
also found that housework prevented many potential members from
active involvement, and had to steer a difficult course between asserting
the value of women's domestic labour while also arguing that 'as citizens
they had rights and responsibilities beyond the confines of the home'.[76]
The Guild's first paid organiser, the Lancashire mill worker Sarah Red-
dish, argued particularly forcefully for women's right to spend less time
doing housework and more time engaged in political activity.[77] Even
Margaret McDonald, president of the Women's Labour League, who
believed that 'the home will always be women's first care', recognised the
inherent tension between their domestic duties and 'an intelligent interest in the world outside'.[78]

Various theories were put forward as to how women's enslavement to
housework affected the formation of feminist consciousness. The
anonymous author of the 1911 article in *Votes for Women* on 'The Burden
of Housework' was not alone in lamenting the waste of so many housewives' 'born talents', and the denial of any opportunity for 'self-culture ...
[or] self-development'.[79] Katharine Bruce Glasier, a prominent member
of the Women's Labour League, wrote a regular women's page in the
ILP newspaper the *Labour Leader* which often noted the 'drudgery' of
housework for both working and middle-class women.[80] In 1910 she
recalled how, after finishing her studies at Newnham College, Cambridge, 'the moral meanness and essential vulgarity of a conventional
villa existence ... shatter[ed] once and for all my carefully established
sense of the right of intellectual womanhood to hold herself high above
the pots and pans, dusters and mops of life'. She asked her readers to
consider 'what miracles might not those same hours of monotonous
labour, now worse than wasted, on "Curtains" and the 1000 other fol-
lies', have achieved, especially if they had been dedicated to social and
political reform. Yet this politicisation of housework was not straightforward, and sometimes generated apparently contradictory statements.

---

[75] *Labour Leader* 16 Sept. 1910, p. 589.
[76] Scott, *Feminism and the Politics of Working Women*, pp. 69, 72, chapter 3. See also Jane
Lewis, 'Introduction: Reconstructing Women's Experience of Home and Family', in
Jane Lewis (ed.), *Labour and Love: Women's Experience of Home and Family, 1850–1940*
(Oxford: Basil Blackwell, 1986).
[77] Thomson, '"Domestic Drudgery Will Be a Thing of the Past"', p. 112.
[78] *Labour Leader* 1 July 1910, p. 412; 16 Sept. 1910, p. 589.
[79] *Votes for Women* 7 April 1911, p. 442.   [80] Collette, *For Labour and for Women*, p. 20.

Only a month after the publication of Katharine Bruce Glasier's denunciation of domestic labour, an article in that same paper announced the birth of her son and declared: 'Notwithstanding her enthusiasm as a propagandist, Mrs Glasier is a typical woman of the home, and takes as much delight in her household duties as in her public work.'[81] Glasier herself always insisted that homemaking was women's most important task.[82]

Such contradictions become more intelligible when located as a response to anti-suffrage propaganda, which frequently argued that the campaign for votes for women was a direct attack on the home.[83] The problem of housework was addressed not only by the suffrage movement, but also by its opponents.[84] A number of anti-suffrage postcards, for example, depicted the downtrodden husbands of suffragettes in the ridiculous and humiliating pose of washing clothes or polishing the grate, and in doing so they were not simply catastrophising about a dystopian future but also pointing towards what was already a reality for some men, and one greatly feared by others (see Figures 5 and 6). Hannah Mitchell claimed that many husbands of suffragettes turned 'anti' when their wives' suffrage activity led to skimping on domestic tasks.[85] Such concerns were not peculiar to working-class husbands.[86] The spectre of women's increasing freedom leading to the domestic servitude of their husbands was already a common trope in the response to middle-class women beginning to ride bicycles in the 1890s.[87] Anti-suffragist E. L. Somervell was praised in the *Anti-Suffrage Review* (and condemned in the *Englishwoman*) for her 1909 article in the *National Review* which prophesied the collapse of the home and family if women were tempted away from their domestic tasks towards the political sphere.[88] Just as the

---

[81] *Labour Leader* 18 March 1910, p. 173; 29 April 1910, p. 265.

[82] Collette, *For Labour and for Women*, p. 20.

[83] Opponents of socialism had long claimed that it would destroy the home. This was refuted by Katharine Bruce Glasier, 'Socialism and the Home' (London: Independent Labour Party, n.d.).

[84] Brian Harrison, *Separate Spheres: The Opposition to Women's Suffrage in Britain* (London: CroomHelm, 1978), p. 70; Julia Bush, *Women against the Vote: Female Anti-Suffragism in Britain* (Oxford: Oxford University Press, 2007), p. 233. Pro- and anti-suffrage arguments were often formed in dialogue; Lucy Delap, 'Feminist and Anti-Feminist Encounters in Edwardian Britain', *Historical Research*, 78:201 (Aug. 2005), 377–399; Bush, *Women against the Vote*.

[85] Mitchell, *The Hard Way Up*, p. 130.

[86] On this I disagree with Harrison; *Separate Spheres*, pp. 140–141.

[87] Sheila Hanlon, 'Is Your Wife a Suffragette or Scorcher?', www.sheilahanlon.com; Lena Wanggren, 'Dangerous Women on Bicycles', www.dangerouswomenproject.org.

[88] *National Review* March 1909, pp. 139–148; *Anti-Suffrage Review* April 1909, p. 3; *Englishwoman* Oct. 1909, p. 263.

Figure 5 Anti-suffrage postcard: 'My Wife's Joined the Suffrage Movement (I've Suffered Ever Since!)'.
The Women's Library at the London School of Economics, London, TWL.2004.1011.22, Postcard Box 2 (reproduced by kind permission of The Women's Library at the LSE)

Figure 6 Anti-suffrage postcard: 'Is Your Wife a Suffragette?'.
The Women's Library at the London School of Economics, London,
TWL2004.1011.18, Postcard Box 2 (reproduced by kind permission of The
Women's Library at the LSE)

suffrage movement recognised that the confinement of women to the domestic sphere was a material as well as an ideological problem, a question not just of feminine norms but of hard, time-consuming labour, anti-suffrage propaganda of this kind was not simply a way of telling women that they were not welcome in the public sphere but also can be understood on a more literal level – disciplining women for failing to carry out the necessary work of the home.

In March 1910 the *Vote* published a series of photographs entitled 'Suffragettes at Home', intended as a direct response to '[t]he man-in-the-street who, with hoarse reiterance, tells us to "go home and mind the baby", to "do the washing up", to "get the dinner"'.[89] The newspaper presented the series as a competition, inviting readers to send in photographs of themselves engaged in domestic labour in return for a cash prize. The first photograph depicted one of the newspaper's directors, Mrs J. E. Snow, making pastry. Subsequent entries showed other prominent figures in the Women's Freedom League (WFL) undertaking mundane household chores. Its president, Charlotte Despard, appeared, not addressing a crowd of supporters from a public platform, but at home 'knitting a comforter'. Alison Neilans, another well-known militant, was photographed cleaning a stove (see Figure 7). Over the next nine issues the photography competition represented a wide range of domestic tasks: cooking (pastry-making, jam-making and preparing a vegetarian dinner), sewing, cleaning, childcare and eldercare (see Figure 8). In an article accompanying the photography series, Edith How-Martyn, one of the founding members of the WFL, declared that 'Many of us, and I am not ashamed to be among the number, have a real liking for some domestic duties.'[90] The photography competition presented itself as a rebuke to those male opponents who denounced suffragettes as undomesticated. In depicting women whose public image more usually consisted of 'unwomanly' and sometimes violent confrontation with the state in highly traditional and feminine roles, 'Suffragettes at Home' ostensibly sought to prove that militant suffrage activism was indeed compatible with home duties.

The competition was evidently unpopular with readers since, despite being enthusiastically advertised over a number of issues, the only photographs featured were those of leading figures in the WFL. The cash prize of £1 1s. (donated by one of the newspaper's directors, Mrs Thompson Price) was excessively generous, amounting to more than some working-class families would have earned in a week.[91] Moreover, all the

---

[89] *Vote* 12 March 1910, p. 233.   [90] *Vote* 26 March 1910, p. 261.
[91] Maud Pember Reeves, *Round about a Pound a Week* (London: Persephone, 2008 [first published 1913]).

Figure 7 'Alison Neilans Cleans the Stove'.
Vote 2 April 1910, p. 273 (reproduced by kind permission of The Women's Library at the LSE)

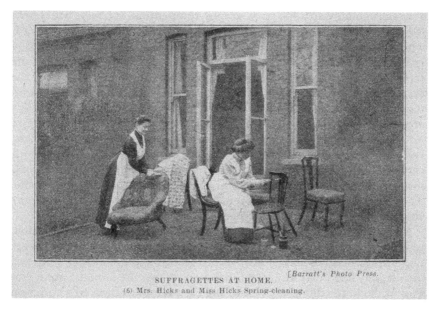

Figure 8 'Mrs Hicks and Miss Hicks Spring Cleaning'.
Vote 16 April 1910, p. 297 (reproduced by kind permission of The Women's Library at the LSE)

photographs were taken in the same studio – Barratts Photo Press in London – which also took more formal 'political' photographs for the suffrage movement.[92] All of this, when considered in the light of the wider politicisation of housework, strongly suggests that the 'Suffragettes at Home' series must ultimately be understood as ironic. Yet the irony is certainly not explicit. Edith How-Martyn's article entitled 'Suffragette Jam and Marmalade' illustrates the carefully balanced ambiguity that

---

[92] TWL, Photographs, 'Meeting of Women's Social & Political Union (WSPU) leaders' (c. 1906–c. 1907), 7JCC:O:02:109. The printed inscription on the reverse reads 'Barratt's Photo Press Agency, 8 Salisbury Ct, Fleet St, EC'; TWL, 'Demonstrations, Strikes, Marches, Processions: Suffrage March 1910', TWL.2004.315, photograph box E01. Crawford has also suggested that the series was a staged joke. She pointed out that one of the winning entries, 'Mrs Joseph McCabe weighing her baby', depicted the wife and offspring of an ex-Catholic priest who had abandoned his former faith for a militant brand of Secularism. The portrait would therefore have come across to contemporaries as rather more subversive than the 'homey' depiction of a suffragette it purports to be. The image of Alison Neilans cleaning her stove may have been a reference to her previous conviction during the 1909 Bermondsey by-election for pouring liquid into a ballot box as an act of protest against women's disenfranchisement; Elizabeth Crawford, 'Suffrage Stories: Alison Neilans Cleans the Stove', www.womanandhersphere.com.

Vote assumed towards the photography competition. It begins with How-Martyn recalling a recent meeting with a fellow member of the WFL who, on seeing the portrait of 'Mrs How-Martyn making jam', accused its president of 'fraud!', thus hinting at the tongue-in-cheek nature of the series. In response, How Martyn questioned the assumption that 'the duties and responsibilities of a [WFL] secretary are not compatible with those of a housewife'. Yet the rest of the article directly undermines this argument. Not only did How-Martyn acknowledge that she had to give up almost all domestic duties in order to concentrate on the fight for the vote, but the duties she listed ('making cakes and pastry … doing wood-carving, netting and embroidery') are far from being life's essentials and instead invoke the frivolous hobbies of the idle middle-class housewife. The idea that How-Martyn will return to a life of trivial pastimes once the vote has been won is made to appear ridiculous.[93]

Some historians have taken 'Suffragettes at Home' at face value, interpreting it as a refutation of accusations that suffragettes were undomesticated, and as indicative of the suffrage movement's interest in everyday life.[94] My argument, however, is that the feminist politicisation of the home did not generate any easy solutions or even a common analysis, but was rather characterised by debate and disagreement and fraught with contradiction. The 'Suffragettes at Home' series embodied one of these contradictions – the question of how to value women's work in the home while also ensuring that women were free to undertake political activity. 'Suffragettes at Home' can therefore be read as ironic in the sense of representing two contradictory truths. When the leaders of the WFL had themselves photographed in the hyper-feminine roles which make up the series, they were indeed refuting their critics' portrayals of them as unsexed harridans incapable of keeping comfortable homes. In depicting the actuality of women's daily tasks, such as spring cleaning or scrubbing the stove, which were never otherwise represented in what was still the relatively formalised genre of photography portraiture, the *Vote* also engaged in the subversive act of making domestic labour visible. The newspaper's editors were at the same time, however, mocking such work as utterly mundane when compared with the vital work of waging war against the government in the struggle for the vote.

---

[93] *Vote* 26 March 1910, p. 261.
[94] Mayhall, 'Household and Market', pp. 193–194; Hamilton, 'A Crisis in Women's History', p. 588; 'Maroula Joannou, 'The Angel of Freedom: Dora Marsden and the Transformation of the *Freewoman* into the *Egoist*', *Women's History Review*, 11:4 (2002), 595–611, pp. 597–598. None of these articles focuses on the 'Suffragettes at Home' series, but they merely refer to it as evidence in wider arguments.

'Suffragettes at Home' was far from a straightforward endorsement of female domesticity. Rather, it gestured towards the same difficulty that had worried the advice columnists at the *Woman Worker* – how to stop housework from distracting women from their more important social and political responsibilities without renouncing the domestic altogether or alienating the majority of their female readers who had little choice in the matter. Discussions of the housework problem, however, sidestepped the 'servant problem' and the potential for conflict between two types of women who were both, in their different ways, bound to the home. The 'servant problem' nevertheless persisted in interrupting and disrupting feminists' politicisation of the home, especially when they debated whether domestic labour ought to be included in campaigns for women's right to undertake useful, rewarding and well-remunerated work. Using a dislike of housework to signify one's feminist credentials, moreover, posed serious problems when it came to incorporating domestic servants into the suffrage movement.

4   Domestic Labour and the Feminist Work Ethic

'From the very beginning of the organised women's movement the "right to work" was recognised to be an essential part of real emancipation', wrote Ray Strachey, suffrage veteran and historian of the movement. In 1936 she recalled how, although the struggle for the suffrage had become the most 'fundamental' goal, 'the feminist ideal which was connected with the freedom to work remained unimpaired':

> [Feminists] thought of work as a satisfaction of personal needs, an outlet for gifts and powers, a fulfilment of personal individuality. If a woman could have an independent career, they felt, she would be safe in the certainty that she was justifying her existence.[1]

The right to professional employment, and the training and education that this necessitated, had been central demands of British feminism since the 1860s. Financial independence and the fulfilment of creative potential were counterposed to the enforced idleness and dependencies of the middle-class home. The association of emancipation with the public world of work retained a powerful hold over the feminist imagination into the twentieth century, and the suffrage movement often pointed to women's labour as the basis for their claim to citizenship. This rhetoric of work was seen to unite the interests of middle-class professional women and their working-class sisters: 'if a woman works, she has some claim to be called "respectable"; if she doesn't – well, she hasn't', Mrs D. J. M. Worrall insisted in the *Woman Worker*. Another of its leading journalists, Julia Dawson, further declared that 'To not work is a terrible state for a woman to be in.'[2]

There was much uncertainty, however, over whether domestic labour ought to be included in this vision of ennobling and liberating work. The desire to free women from the burden of housework was not simply

---

[1] Ray Strachey, 'Changes in Employment', in Ray Strachey (ed.), *Our Freedom and Its Results* (London: Hogarth Press, 1936), 117–172, pp. 122–124.

[2] *Woman Worker* 5 June 1908, p. 18; 18 Nov. 1908, p. 611.

about protecting them from overwork, or allowing them to do other work, but often articulated as the right to do *better* work. One of the main challenges faced by feminists was how to assert the value of women's labour in the home while at the same time fighting for their right to enter the public world of work on an equal basis with men. This chapter examines two debates in the suffrage movement that posed this question particularly sharply. First, those surrounding the proposal for the endowment of motherhood; second, the controversy over the course in Household and Social Science at Kings College for Women.

Whereas Chapter 3 examined feminist discussions of housework as a practical problem, here I extend this account to look at how domestic labour was constructed as a philosophical problem, especially within the context of what I term 'the feminist work ethic'. Once again, this chapter examines a broad range of feminist debates, taking place both within and outside, though always in dialogue with, the suffrage organisations. I therefore examine discussions on work occurring within not just suffrage publications, but also working-class women's organisations, and the more individualist and avant-garde form of feminism associated with the *Freewoman* newspaper.[3] These political and intellectual currents, and the various publications in which they gained a platform, were neither internally coherent nor entirely distinct. Readerships overlapped, suffrage activists published in more than one newspaper, and often the same debate took place across different periodicals, making reference to discussions in rival publications. I trace how these feminist constellations conceptualised 'work' and women's relationship to it, in order to delineate the feminist work ethic while identifying points of tension and disagreement. The final section of the chapter examines what all of this meant for women who worked as domestic servants and how it affected their ability to identify as feminists.

The Feminist Work Ethic

The right to gainful employment outside the home was one of the earliest and most enduring demands of 'first wave' feminism. It was certainly the central concern of the Langham Place Group and their *English Woman's Journal* (est. 1858), which is usually seen to mark the beginnings of an organised women's movement in Britain. One of their number, Jessie Boucherette, founded the Society for Promoting the Employment of Women in 1859, which helped train women for occupations in the

---

[3] Lucy Delap, *The Feminist Avant-Garde: Transatlantic Encounters of the Early Twentieth Century* (Cambridge: Cambridge University Press, 2007).

male-dominated spheres of trade and commerce. The Langham Place Group's firm belief that women should, at the very least, have the option of economic independence also informed their support for campaigns for women's education, especially the right to attend university.[4] Looking back in 1936, Ray Strachey was rather more circumspect about the zeal with which her own movement had promoted this vision of emancipation through work: 'Work, indeed, came to seem almost an end in itself to some of them, and they attached a value to the earning of their own livings which that somewhat dreary necessity does not in reality possess.'[5] Similarly, from the perspective of the twenty-first century, as feminists become ever more concerned about the neo-liberal compulsion to *over-work*, this 'first wave' feminist work ethic strikes one as a case of being careful what we wish for.[6] Yet in the nineteenth and early twentieth century, insisting that women should be usefully occupied and adequately remunerated was to challenge many of the founding tenets of their oppression. When conservatives proclaimed that women should remain unsullied by the world of work, feminists reminded them that a large number of women had little choice in the matter, having families that depended upon what meagre income they were able to bring in. It was necessary, therefore, that such women should have access to better-paid and more skilled forms of employment. Although the Victorian women's movement was cautious about advocating professional life as a positive alternative to marriage and motherhood, they did maintain that to marry purely in order to secure a roof over one's head and food on one's table discredited that sacred institution.[7]

The feminist work ethic was, however, about far more than economic necessity. As historian Joyce Senders Pedersen has argued, much

---

[4] Lee Holcombe, *Victorian Ladies at Work: Middle-Class Working Women in England and Wales 1850–1914* (Hamden, CT: Archon Books, 1973), pp. 1–15; Jane Rendall, '"A Moral Engine"? Feminism, Liberalism and the *English Woman's Journal*', in Jane Rendall (ed.), *Equal or Different: Women's Politics 1800–1914* (Oxford: Basil Blackwell, 1987), 112–138; R. Freuer, 'The Meaning of Sisterhood: The British Women's Movement and Protective Labor Legislation, 1870–1900', *Victorian Studies*, 31:2 (1988), 233–260, pp. 234–235; Ruth Livesey, 'The Politics of Work: Feminism, Professionalisation and Women Inspectors of Factories and Workshops', *Women's History Review*, 13:2 (2004), 233–262, pp. 239–240; Gerry Holloway, *Women and Work in Britain since 1840* (London: Routledge, 2005), chapter 3.

[5] Strachey, 'Changes in Employment', p. 124.

[6] For a critique of feminism's failure to fundamentally challenge the 'dominant legitimating discourse of work', see Kathi Weeks, *The Problem with Work: Feminism, Marxism, Antiwork Politics and Postwork Imaginaries* (Durham: Duke University Press, 2011), pp. 12–13.

[7] Jane Rendall, '"A Moral Engine"?', p. 124; Holcombe, *Victorian Ladies at Work*, p. 8.

Victorian feminism, influenced by both liberalism and Protestantism, 'invested work with existential hopes … with a sense of moral/spiritual agency' and with the belief that 'individual striving would ultimately promote the common good'.[8] The feminist work ethic thus had a dual imperative: to work was a woman's moral duty both to herself (in pursuit of self-actualisation) and to society (to work towards its betterment). Such a vision resonated across the women's movement's broad political spectrum. It informed the impulse towards 'social action' that drove so many late Victorian and Edwardian women to philanthropy and social work. This wish to live a 'useful' life conceptualised work (be this professional or voluntary) as a moral imperative (be this Christian or secular), which gave purpose to one's existence and complemented rather than competed with the duties of wives and mothers.[9] A very different current within early twentieth-century feminism centred on the *Freewoman* and its celebration of heterodox religious thinking, sexual experimentation and individualism. These avant-garde feminists were also deeply committed to a vision of work as a form of self-realisation and individual creativity, but one posited against the dependencies of marriage and motherhood.[10] In all of these various iterations, work was seen as central to forming women's characters and developing their sense of social and political responsibility. The idle, 'parasitic' woman of the upper classes was roundly condemned.[11] Olive Schreiner's widely read book *Woman and Labour* (1911), described by Vera Brittain as the 'Bible of the women's movement', devoted its first three chapters to the subject of 'parasitism'. This Schreiner saw as key to 'female degradation', describing feminist campaigns for women's right to enter the professions as 'an endeavour on the part of the section of the race to save itself from inactivity and degeneration'.[12]

The feminist work ethic was by no means a fixed or coherent ideology, but it was a capacious one, incorporating Protestantism and liberalism, eugenics and socialism, and related ideas of women as the symbol and drivers of modernity. *Woman and Labour* was intended as both refutation

---

[8] Joyce Senders Pedersen, 'Victorian Liberal Feminism and the "Idea" of Work', in Krista Cowman and Louise A. Jackson (eds.), *Women and Work Culture, Britain c. 1850–1950* (Aldershot: Ashgate, 2005), 27–47, p. 28. See also Alison Light, *Mrs Woolf and the Servants* (London: Penguin Books, 2008), p. 61.

[9] Jane Lewis, *Women and Social Action in Victorian and Edwardian England* (Aldershot: Edward Elgar, 1991), pp. 1–11.

[10] Delap, *The Feminist Avant-Garde*, pp. 230–232, 246.

[11] Holcombe, *Victorian Ladies at Work*, p. 8.

[12] Morag Shiach, *Modernism, Labour and Selfhood in British Literature and Culture, 1890–1930* (Cambridge: Cambridge University Press, 2004), p. 50; Olive Schreiner, *Woman and Labour* (London: Virago, 1978 [first published 1911]), p. 123.

and reappropriation of eugenicist thinking, especially the work of Karl Pearson. Schreiner rejected Pearson's belief that, in the ideal society, married middle-class women should not work but be financially supported by the state so that they could fill their ultimate duty of bearing healthy children. Schreiner subverted the eugenicist imperative to argue that reducing women to 'sex parasites' would in fact cause the 'degeneration' of the 'race'. Rather, modern civilisation would be secured only if women were free to pursue all the forms of work now available in technologically advanced societies on an equal basis with men.[13]

Olive Schreiner was not the only feminist thinker to concern herself with 'sex parasitism'. Her commitment to securing women a productive role in industrial society was also influenced by the socialist circles in which she moved. The Fabian Women's Group (est. 1908) likewise felt women's economic independence to be of central importance, though they focused more on working-class wives than on professional women.[14] The term 'parasitism' was not only applied to wealthy leisured women, but also described the enforced economic dependence of women of all classes who were denied dignified and remunerative work.[15] The rhetorical power of this term nevertheless derived from wider critiques within both Marxist and non-Marxist socialist thought of unearned wealth, landlordism and an increasingly 'leisured' bourgeoisie concerned more with 'conspicuous consumption' than production.[16] Socialism, therefore, had its own work ethic which sought to differentiate the working class from the idle rich, on the one hand, and so-called scroungers, malingerers or the 'lumpen proletariat', on the other.

By the early twentieth century, the feminist work ethic drew upon this multifaceted socialist tradition as much as upon the Protestantism and free-market liberalism that influenced the Victorian women's movement. Across Europe, working-class and socialist parties were emerging to demand that labour should have formal representation within the political system. Work was increasingly looked to 'as the source of ethical value and ... political legitimacy' as opposed to just economic worth.[17]

[13] Carolyn Burdett, *Olive Schreiner and the Progress of Feminism: Evolution, Gender, Empire* (Basingstoke: Palgrave, 2001), pp. 61–65.
[14] Sally Alexander (ed.), *Women's Fabian Tracts* (Abingdon: Routledge, 1988); Carol Dyhouse, *Feminism and the Family 1880–1939* (Oxford: Basil Blackwell, 1989), pp. 57–67.
[15] Liz Stanley, *Imperialism, Labour and the New Woman: Olive Schreiner's Social Theory* (Durham: Sociology Press, 2002), p. 152.
[16] For example, Henry George, *Progress and Poverty* (London: Hogarth Press, 1953 [first published 1879]); Thorstein Veblen, *The Theory of the Leisure Class* (Abingdon: Routledge, 2017 [first published 1899]), both of which were influential in Britain.
[17] Shiach, *Modernism, Labour and Selfhood*, pp. 16, 105.

The suffrage movement also appealed to women's labour and its contribution to the nation as the basis upon which to claim the right to full citizenship. But while the British Labour Party's main focus was on the male worker, suffrage activists emphasised the disenfranchisement of useful and productive women of all classes. In addition to arguing that women workers needed the vote to improve the 'sweated' conditions under which they laboured, the suffrage movement also highlighted the injustice of refusing women a say in laws which might have a direct effect on their ability to earn a living. A poster designed by Emily Ford of the Artists' Suffrage League in 1908, for example, depicted a Lancashire mill girl locked out of a factory bearing the notice 'Factory Acts regulations for women', to which she responds, 'They've a cheek I've never been asked.'[18]

The question of protective legislation for women workers was, however, extremely divisive. The Langham Place Group and the Society for Promoting the Employment of Women had opposed any laws which differentiated between male and female workers. This liberal faith in the egalitarian tendencies of the free market (so long as all individuals were free to participate in it) continued to find adherents into the twentieth century. At the same time, organisations such as the Women's Trade Union League, the Women's Industrial Council, the Women's Co-operative Guild and the Women's Labour League began to come out in support of protective legislation. Experience had taught them that 'free contract', even when countered by trade unionism, was not enough to protect women against the worst excesses of industrial brutality. Many of them favoured increased protections for all workers, but would accept female-specific legislation as a step in the right direction.[19] The early twentieth-century suffrage movement thus included both supporters and opponents of protective legislation. Helena Swanwick, a prominent member of the NUWSS, argued that excluding women from employment without considering where else they might earn a living was hardly motivated by a desire to 'protect' their interests. Clementina Black, however, who succeeded Swanwick as editor of the *Common Cause* in

---

[18] Lisa Tickner, *The Spectacle of Women: Imagery of the Suffrage Campaign, 1907–1914* (London: Chatto & Windus, 1987), pp. 50–51, 101–102.

[19] Holcombe, *Victorian Ladies at Work*, p. 9; Freuer, 'The Meaning of Sisterhood'; Pat Thane, 'The Women of the British Labour Party and Feminism, 1906–1945', in Harold Smith (ed.), *British Feminism in the Twentieth Century* (Aldershot: Edward Elgar, 1990), 124–143, pp. 138–139; Carolyn Malone, *Women's Bodies and Dangerous Trades in England 1880–1914* (Woodbridge: Boydell Press, 2003), chapter 7; Holloway, *Women and Work*, chapter 5.

1912 and was an active supporter of women's trade unions, campaigned for increased state regulation.[20]

How did a growing awareness of the terrible conditions under which much women's work took place affect the feminist work ethic? Some historians have suggested that, by the beginning of the twentieth century, feminists' celebration of the emancipatory potential of women's work came to focus only on professional careers.[21] I think, however, that the tendency to elide class distinctions and discuss manual women workers and professionals in the same breath remained common into the early 1900s.[22] It certainly informed the suffrage movement's arguments for political representation, the valorisation of the 'independent' woman factory worker discussed in Chapter 2 and the opposition to protective legislation that continued in some quarters. Moreover, the potential contradiction at the heart of the feminist work ethic – the tension between work as liberation and work as exploitation – was nothing new. As early as the 1860s Barbara Leigh Smith Bodichon had sought to distinguish 'work' from 'drudgery'.[23] What had changed by the beginning of the twentieth century was not so much a radical shift within feminist attitudes as a whole, but rather an increasing scrutiny of exactly what it was about various kinds of women's work that did or did not make them emancipatory. Without wishing to underplay the significance of class tensions within the suffrage movement, or the distinction that the whole of society drew between manual and professional work, I want to highlight another important dividing line within the feminist work ethic – that between labour in the public sphere and labour in the private home, between productive and reproductive work.

My argument that domestic labour was located uneasily within and sometimes against the feminist work ethic offers something of a corrective to a prevailing historiography that emphasises the ways in which much 'first wave' feminism sought to reappropriate and reconfigure domesticity rather than reject it outright. In the past few decades, historians have cautioned against defining feminism too narrowly and applying it only to those who argued for complete equality with men. They have highlighted aspects of women's movements across Europe that celebrated sexual

---

[20] Sandra Stanley Holton, *Feminism and Democracy: Women's Suffrage and Reform Politics in Britain 1900–1918* (Cambridge: Cambridge University Press, 1986), pp. 22–25.

[21] Pedersen, 'Victorian Liberal Feminism', pp. 28, 35; Lucy Delap, Maria Dicenzo and Leila Ryan (eds.), *Feminism and the Periodical Press, 1900–1980*, 3 vols. (Abingdon: Routledge, 2006), vol. I, p. xxxvi.

[22] See also Barbara Green, *Spectacular Confessions: Autobiography, Performative Activism, and the Sites of Suffrage, 1905–1938* (New York: St Martin's Press, 1997), pp. 35–36.

[23] Pedersen, 'Victorian Liberal Feminism', p. 35.

difference and mobilised around women's presumed nurturing capacities. These women too, it is argued, ought to be included in our historical understanding of feminism.[24] Working-class women's organisations, especially, have been associated with this current of what is often termed 'social feminism'.[25] Their growing support for protective legislation was, by the turn of the century, increasingly couched in terms of a more general questioning of whether married women and mothers ought to be working at all, and support instead for male workers to be paid a family wage so that women could afford stay at home.[26] Their belief that the home and women's domestic duties were an equally valid basis for citizenship claims is sometimes used contrast them to 'equality' or 'equity' feminists who promoted women's right to work outside the home.[27]

I argue that we need to be careful not to assume a too artificial distinction between 'social' and 'equality' feminism – terms that do not take us very far in an examination of broader early twentieth-century feminist debates on work. In fact, the Women's Labour League, the Women's Co-operative Guild and the Women's Industrial Council did not condemn outright mothers' participation in the paid labour market, but merely stressed that this ought to be a positive decision rather than one imposed by poverty.[28] Attention to such nuance needs to be paid when examining how domestic labour was understood in feminist debates on work. The various articulations of the feminist work ethic were always class-inflected, but we should not infer from this simply that

---

[24] Naomi Black, *Social Feminism* (Ithaca, NY: Cornell University Press, 1989); Karen Offen, 'Defining Feminism: A Comparative Historical Approach', in Gisela Bock and Susan James (eds.), *Beyond Equality and Difference: Citizenship, Feminist Politics and Female Subjectivity* (London: Routledge, 1992), 69–88, pp. 70, 75; Seth Koven and Sonya Michel, 'Introduction', in Seth Koven and Sonya Michel (eds.), *Mothers of the New World: Maternalist Politics and the Origins of Welfare States* (New York: Routledge, 1993), 1–42; Anne Summers, 'Public Functions, Private Premises: Female Professional Identity and the Domestic-Service Paradigm in Britain, c. 1850–1930', in Billie Melman (ed.), *Borderlines: Genders and Identities in War and Peace, 1870–1930* (London: Routledge, 1998), 353–376.

[25] Black, *Social Feminism*.

[26] Dyhouse, *Feminism and the Family*, pp. 90–91; Malone, *Women's Bodies and Dangerous Trades*, pp. 122–123.

[27] Black, *Social Feminism*.

[28] Thane, 'The Women of the British Labour Party', p. 127; Pat Thane, 'Women in the British Labour Party and the Construction of State Welfare, 1906–1939', in Koven and Michel (eds.), *Mothers of the New World*, 343–377, p. 349; Gillian Scott, *Feminism and the Politics of Working Women: The Women's Co-operative Guild, 1880s to the Second World War* (London: University College London Press, 1998), p. 72; Clementina Black (ed.), *Married Women's Work: Being the Report of Enquiry Undertaken by the Women's Industrial Council* (London:Virago, 1983 [first published 1915]), p. xxiii.

middle-class women valorised professional work in the public sphere and that working-class women defended their rights as unwaged housewives to remain in the home. Although the historiography makes a convincing case for the centrality of discourses of domesticity and maternalism to 'first wave' feminism, I am concerned that this should not drown out the ambivalence and sometimes outright hostility towards the *labour* of the home expressed (albeit often in different ways) by feminists of all classes. Even those feminists who wanted more value to be placed upon women's work in the domestic sphere understood that the home was a site of struggle. Like the waged workplace, it was a place in which women were both exploited and able to gain a sense of their power as (re)productive workers. Furthermore, feminists' attitudes towards domesticity, the *values* of the home, need to be distinguished from what they said about the actual work that took place within. When domestic labour was explicitly addressed, the question of whether housework should be incorporated into definitions of emancipatory work generated much ambivalence from women across the classes. This was as much the case when the endowment of motherhood was debated, a demand concerned primarily with the well-being of working-class housewives, as when a 'degree for housewives' was proposed for middle-class university students.

The Value of Housework and the Endowment of Motherhood

Many in the suffrage movement noted that the work of the housewife made an important contribution, not only to the well-being of her family, but also to society at large. It was recognised that keeping family members fed, clothed and comfortable was essential work done by women across the classes, but especially in working-class homes where the work of balancing a small budget and cooking food that was both cheap and nourishing ensured the family's economic survival.[29] Ada Nield Chew described married working women as 'carrying the nation's burden on their breaking backs', and declared that 'the whole fabric of

---

[29] Eleanor Rathbone, *How the Casual Labourer Lives. Report of the Liverpool Joint Research Committee on the Domestic Condition and Expenditure of the Families of Certain Liverpool Labourers. Read before and Published by the Liverpool Economic and Statistical Society* (Liverpool: Liverpool Economic and Statistical Society, 1909); Maud Pember Reeves, *Round about a Pound a Week* (London: Persephone, 2008 [first published 1913]); Black, *Married Women's Work*; Helena Swanwick, *The Future of the Women's Movement* (London: G. Bell & Sons, 1913), chapter 9; Ellen Ross, *Love and Toil: Motherhood in Outcast London, 1870–1918* (Oxford: Oxford University Press, 1993), pp. 21–22.

the State rests on the work she is doing'.[30] Emmeline Pethick-Lawrence, editor of *Votes for Women*, generated much discussion with her 1911 article 'Does a Man Support His Wife?', in which she condemned the 'present economic system ... built upon the unpaid and grossly exploited labour of married women'.[31] Many other feminists were also critical of how this labour was, moreover, unremunerated. Writers such Cicely Hamilton drew a connection between this and the low wages that women earned outside the home.[32]

Eleanor Rathbone, a member of the NUWSS executive committee, further theorised this belief as the basis for her arguments in favour of a much more controversial proposal for the 'endowment of motherhood'. Endowment was being discussed in many quarters at this time, on both the left and the right, and various different formulations were put forward. Rathbone and her fellow advocates in the suffrage movement framed their demand not as a payment for biological reproduction (having babies) but as remuneration for women's wider reproductive labour (all the housework entailed in raising children and keeping a family healthy).[33] In an article entitled 'The Economic Position of Married Women', published in the *Common Cause* in January 1912, Rathbone explained how '[s]ociety has to provide somehow for the continuance of its own existence by the bearing and rearing of fresh generations'. The work of the wife and mother was, therefore, of national importance, and under the present social system this was (inadequately and inefficiently) recognised by paying higher wages to men on the assumption that they had a family to support. Rathbone, however, preferred what was often 'crudely presented as the "payment of motherhood"' – the direct remuneration of women for their reproductive work.[34] She subsequently developed her demands for the 'payment of motherhood' in 'The Remuneration of Women's Services', published in the *Economic Journal* (1917) and *The Disinherited Family* (1924). The First World War prompted the partial introduction of the principle of the payment of mothers via the separation allowances given to the wives of soldiers and, subsequently, the introduction of widows' pensions. This lent renewed impetus to Rathbone's campaign, which continued into the

---

[30] *Labour Leader* 17 Feb. 1911, p. 109; *Englishwoman* July 1911, p. 48.
[31] *Votes for Women* 21 July 1911, p. 692. See also *Votes for Women* 16 June 1911, p. 608; 23 June 1911, p. 624; 28 July 1911, pp.702, 710.
[32] Cicely Hamilton, *Marriage as a Trade* (1909), cited in Laura E. Nym Mayhall, 'Household and Market in Suffragette Discourse, 1903–14', *The European Legacy: Toward New Paradigms*, 6:2 (2010), 189–199, p. 193.
[33] Delap, *The Feminist Avant-Garde*, p. 184.
[34] *Common Cause* 4 Jan. 1912, pp. 674–675.

interwar period supported by working-class women's organisations such as the Women's Co-operative Guild. Family allowances were finally introduced in 1945, although stripped of most of Rathbone's more radical vision and representing in reality only a small supplement to wage levels rather than full payment for reproductive labour.[35]

The demand for the endowment of motherhood was one of the most contentious issues facing the British women's movement. It provoked much disagreement within the suffrage organisations and wider feminist circles, both before and after the First World War.[36] In February 1912, a month after Rathbone had published her article in the *Common Cause*, the *Freewoman*'s editorial denounced as 'parasitic' the idea that a woman deserved to be paid for raising children and keeping house.[37] The *Freewoman* (est. 1911) was an independent and self-proclaimed 'feminist' publication, which was often critical of the main suffrage organisations and aimed to provide a forum for a discussion of women's rights that extended beyond the question of the vote. It was edited by Dora Marsden and, initially, by Mary Gawthorpe, both of whom previously had been paid organisers for the WSPU. Whereas Marsden was keen to distance herself from her former organisation, and to differentiate feminist politics from mere suffragism, Gawthorpe embraced many elements of the radicalism promoted by the *Freewoman* while maintaining links with the WSPU.[38] The readership of the *Freewoman* was tiny compared with the suffrage organs discussed in Chapter 3, no more than 2,500, but it gained notoriety within the suffrage movement and elicited both journalistic contributions and correspondence from many of its activists.[39] The *Freewoman*'s editors wrote that 'we do not believe state endowment of motherhood a workable proposition', although they did, somewhat vaguely, express a preference for 'a state insurance, contributory or

---

[35] Johanna Alberti, *Eleanor Rathbone* (London: Sage Publications, 1996); Susan Pedersen, *Eleanor Rathbone and the Politics of Conscience* (New Haven: Yale University Press, 2004).

[36] For debates on endowment before the First World War, Carol Dyhouse, *Feminism and the Family*, pp. 92–102; Hunt, *Equivocal Feminists*, pp. 137–142; Delap, *The Feminist Avant-Garde*, chapter 5.

[37] *Freewoman* 8 Feb 1912, p. 222.

[38] Krista Cowman, 'A Footnote in History? Mary Gawthorpe, Sylvia Pankhurst, *The Suffragette Movement* and the Writing of Suffragette History', *Women's History Review*, 14:3–4 (2005), 447–466. Cowman argues that Gawthorpe had never expected, and was upset by, Marsden's forthright attacks on the leadership of the WSPU, and that she only eventually conceded to Marsden's request to come on board as co-editor due to financial pressures.

[39] Lucy Delap, 'Individualism and Introspection: The Framing of Feminism in the *Freewoman*', in Maria Dicenzo, Lucy Delap and Leila Ryan (eds.), *Feminist Media History: Suffrage, Periodicals and the Public Sphere* (Basingstoke: Palgrave Macmillan, 2011), 159–200.

otherwise'. Expanding on this position in a subsequent editorial, entitled 'Woman: Endowed or Free?', they maintained that the remuneration of motherhood and/or the 'compulsory payment of wives' would constitute a 'repudiation of the human responsibilities of women', namely the 'freewoman's' duty to contribute to society via participation in the public sphere and 'in money-producing work', and to be entirely self-reliant upon 'the value and sales of their labour in the open market, and not in that special incalculable market where all sales are questionable – i.e. that of sentiment and passion'. Although the editorial acknowledged that there was a difference between the campaign for the state payment of mothers and the payment of wives by husbands, it saw both as problematic, reducing women to paid 'domestic servant[s]' or 'prostitutes'. The editors later clarified that childcare ought to be undertaken by trained professionals in a 'wholly free and efficient education system, from the crèche in kindergarten to the university'.[40]

The most robust defence of the endowment of motherhood came not from one of the *Freewoman*'s female readers but from the author H. G. Wells. He published two articles in its pages claiming that state support for 'motherhood' was very different from the payment of 'mothers': 'It is not human beings we want to buy and enslave, it is a social service, a collective need, we want to sustain.' Yet in his second article, Wells' argument that the endowment of motherhood would equalise the 'handicap' that childbearing placed upon women seeking to compete with men in the labour market led to his treating childcare responsibilities not as a form of work, but as an inherent function of womanhood. Wells wrote as if all women would inevitably be taken out of work for long periods of time by childbearing, child raising and possibly even by menstruation, and the only way to place women 'on an equal footing' with men was for the state to 'collective[ly] endow' them.[41]

Another correspondent, Russell Scott, protested that the *Freewoman*'s characterisation of housewives as 'idle and parasitic' was incorrectly based on the assumption that all women raised children 'in a house equipped with a nursery and a servant', whereas the reality for working-class women was that they were expected to raise their children 'without anyone to cook, wash or sew either for it or for you'. Working-class wives could not be expected, on top of all of this, to undertake waged work outside the home. Scott, however, also let slip a more ideological preference for women remaining in the home, and saw working-class motherhood as entirely preferable to '"earning your livelihood" as a lady's maid,

[40] *Freewoman* 15 Feb. 1912, p. 251; 29 Feb. 1912, pp. 281–283; 21 March 1912, p. 342.
[41] *Freewoman* 7 March 1912, pp. 301–302; 21 March 1912, pp. 341–342.

or as a vendor, or a maker of hats that cost 10 times your weekly wage'.
He also accused the editors of the *Freewoman* of secretly wishing for all
women to remain childless.[42] Dora Marsden and Mary Gawthorpe were
both from impoverished backgrounds, and had watched their mothers
burdened by the labour of raising children and keeping house on very
little money.[43] The next editorial responded to Scott's criticism, insisting
that the *Freewoman*'s model for economic independence was not the
middle-class professional woman but the Lancashire cotton operative
who continued in waged work after marriage and motherhood. It was
hoped that such women would be aided, not by being paid to remain in
the home, but by the provision of public childcare.[44]

Eleanor Rathbone also accused her opponents of being ignorant of the
realities of working-class women's lives. She denounced women in the
suffrage movement from wealthy and professional backgrounds who, she
felt, failed to understand why their working-class sisters so badly required
remuneration for their reproductive labour.[45] Yet this criticism could not
be levelled at everyone who disagreed with the endowment of motherhood. Ada Nield Chew had played a central role in making the burdens
of the 'married working woman' visible to readers of the suffrage press,
but she was a vocal critic of the state payment of mothers. In the early
spring of 1914 the *Common Cause* once again provided a forum for
debating the demand, when it published two articles by Chew warning
that endowment would treat 'motherhood (for poor women) as an occupation ... a trade'. She objected to it not in the manner of some conservative commentators, who held this sacred role above economic concerns,
but because she believed that it would 'rivet' women even more firmly to
'the chains that bind her' – 'her babies and her domestic jobs'. Instead,
Chew argued for childcare to become fully professionalised, undertaken
by 'trained mothers' in nursery schools rather than by unwaged women
trying to snatch a few minutes with their babies in between a mountain of
domestic chores. 'Slaves should break their chains', she declared, and
married women, rather than receiving payment from the state to continue slaving under such conditions, should instead 'insist on demanding

---

[42] *Freewoman* 8 Feb. 1912, pp. 221–223; 15 Feb. 1912, p. 251; 29 Feb. 1912, pp. 281–283; 14 March 1912, pp. 321–323; 21 March 1912, pp. 341–342; 4 April 1912, p. 396.
[43] Mary Gawthorpe, *Up Hill to Holloway* (Penobscot, ME: Traversity Press, 1962), pp. 54–55; Les Garner, 'Marsden, Dora (1882–1960)', in *Oxford Dictionary of National Biography*, online edn. (Oxford University Press, 2004); Delap, *The Feminist Avant-Garde*, pp. 208–209.
[44] *Freewoman* 4 April 1912, p. 396.   [45] Alberti, *Eleanor Rathbone*, pp. 50–51.

the right to paid work and to refuse to perform domestic jobs simply because they are wives'.[46]

Chew's sentiments here, and her insistence that domesticity was not a natural quality of womanhood but a form of skilled work, bear some similarities to those expressed in *Freewoman* editorials two years earlier. Chew had written to its editors around this time, professing herself an enthusiastic reader of their newspaper (although she felt that Marsden and Gawthorpe were in some respects naive). In July and August 1912 the *Freewoman* published three articles by Chew, which refuted Rathbone's belief that men were paid more than women because they needed a family wage, and asked its readers to 'attempt to consider women apart from their actual or possible husbands and children, and apart from their "domestic duties"'. Chew demanded instead that women be permitted to participate fully in the economic sphere alongside and equal to male workers. She linked the growing and, to her mind, laudable resistance of young working-class women to entering domestic service to the wider struggle to liberate all working-class women from incessant domestic labour under impoverished and technologically backward conditions.[47]

In many ways, the demand for endowment of motherhood was the closest that 'first wave' feminism came to insisting that domestic labour be treated on an equal basis with 'productive' work and should receive some kind of wage. Yet there were important caveats and elisions with regard to how the suffrage movement discussed this demand, which limited its wider implications. It is significant that endowment was framed as remuneration for motherhood rather than as 'wages for housework', as it was in the Women's Liberation Movement in the 1970s. This highlights the degree to which the 'drudgery' of housework was viewed as distinct from the supposedly more skilled and more creative job of looking after children. Although many in the suffrage movement were keen to acknowledge the importance of all kinds of labour undertaken by unwaged women in the home, most stopped short at demanding that the state should pay women for housework alone. Leading members of the Fabian Women's Group, such as Mabel Atkinson, for example, were in favour of endowment yet maintained that it should be paid only to mothers directly engaged in caring for young children, rather than to those struggling under the burden of housework more generally. [48]

---

[46] *Common Cause* 27 Feb. 1914, pp. 909–910; 6 March 1914, pp. 933–934.
[47] *Freewoman* 18 April 1912, pp. 434–436; 11 July 1912, pp. 149–152; 18 July 1912, pp. 167–169; 22 Aug. 1912, pp. 270–272.
[48] Dyhouse, *Feminism and the Family*, pp. 74–78.

Motherhood was the most legitimate basis upon which to claim state support for women's contribution to the nation. This was partly because the demand for the endowment of motherhood chimed with more socially conservative and widespread discourses on the need to improve mother and infant welfare and ensure the future of the 'race'.[49] It was also due to a hesitance over whether full-time housework, when not necessitated by motherhood, could be incorporated into feminist vision of useful and valuable work. In a letter to the *Freewoman*, one correspondent, writing in support of endowment, refuted the editor's claim that housewives were not 'productive' workers. 'How many men nowadays, in a civilised country, are "producers" in the real sense of the word?' Yet she had to resort to maternity rather than the other work of the household as evidence for this, asking, '[W]hat is the first "product" necessary to the nation if not healthy children?' Another correspondent, in the same issue, also placed motherhood above other forms of domestic labour. 'If the mother's work must be lightened, as it must be, let it be the cooking, and washing, and housework that are taken off us. These are mechanical tasks.' The *Freewoman* editorial also posited a similar distinction: the care of children was, it argued, better undertaken by 'an efficiently trained person educated for her profession'; while if the state and/ or a husband were to pay a woman merely for being a housewife, this would make her nothing more than 'a paid domestic servant' – hardly 'the ideal of the woman in the emancipation movement'.[50]

One of the reasons the proposal for the endowment of motherhood proved so controversial was that supporters and opponents alike often understood it as an alternative to the demand for equal pay for equal work. After the First World War, the National Union of Societies for Equal Citizenship (NUSEC, the successor to the NUWSS) eventually split over whether to support one or the other, but the two demands were already counterposed when endowment was debated in the *Common Cause* in 1912.[51] Eleanor Rathbone maintained that '[s]uffragists' ... advocacy of the doctrine of "equal wages for equal work"' was neither desirable nor possible until the endowment of motherhood had been achieved. She believed that without some financial provision for the inevitable disadvantages of having to take time off work for pregnancy and childbirth, all equal wages would mean was the ousting of women from male-dominated spheres of work, for why would an employer choose a woman over a more reliable male worker? This provoked

---

[49] Anna Davin, 'Imperialism and Motherhood', *History Workshop Journal*, 5 (1978), 9–65.
[50] *Freewoman* 15 Feb. 1912, pp. 251–252; 29 Feb. 1912, pp. 281–283.
[51] Alberti, *Eleanor Rathbone*, chapter 3.

number of people to write in defence of the demand for equal pay, including Ada Nield Chew, who argued that the best way to improve women's economic inequality in the labour market was to give them access to training, so that they could compete on an equal footing with men for better-paid 'skilled' work.[52] Thus we see how domestic labour so frequently came to function as the 'other' to those higher-status male spheres of work that suffragists were so keen for women to gain access to. This was the case not only in debates surrounding the endowment of motherhood but also over the so-called degree for housewives.

A Degree for Housewives?

In 1908, a three-year course in Household and Social Science opened at Kings College for Women. It became a fully fledged degree in 1920, and the Kings College of Household Science was established as one of the women's colleges within the University of London in 1928. In 1911 a fundraising campaign to endow the course provoked heated debates in the *Englishwoman*, the *Common Cause* and the *Freewoman*. The controversy was not over the teaching of domestic subjects per se, but their introduction into a university curriculum, and many opposed the idea of a 'degree for housewives' in principle. Working-class girls had, since the 1870 Education Act in England and Wales and the 1872 Act in Scotland, been taught cooking, sewing and other aspects of household labour in board-schools and training colleges preparing them for a future of domestic service and housewifery. Yet the prospect of middle-class women undertaking these studies at a higher education institution was, for many, extremely unsettling.[53] They felt that the course in Household and Social Science undermined the campaign for women to enter universities on an equal basis with men, by relegating them to so-called feminine and lower-status subjects.[54] Historian Nancy Blakestad has

---

[52] *Common Cause* 4 Jan. 1912, pp. 674–675; 11 Jan. 1912, pp. 688–689; 18 Jan. 1912, p. 710; 25 Jan. 1912, pp. 227–229.

[53] Carol Dyhouse, *Girls Growing Up in Late Victorian and Edwardian England* (Abingdon: Routledge, 2012 [first published 1981]), chapter 3; June Purvis, 'Domestic Subjects since 1870', in Ivor Goodson (ed.), *Social Histories of the Secondary Curriculum: Subjects for Study* (Lewes: Falmer Press, 1985), 145–176; Dena Attar, *Wasting Girls' Time: The History and Politics of Home Economics* (London: Virago, 1990); Helen Corr, '"Home-Rule" in Scotland: The Teaching of Housework in Schools 1872–1914', in Fiona M. S. Paterson and Judith Fewell (eds.), *Girls in Their Prime: Scottish Education Revisited* (Edinburgh: Scottish Academic Press, 1990), 38–53; Jane Martin, *Women and the Politics of Schooling in Victorian and Edwardian England* (London: Leicester University Press, 1999), pp. 81–82.

[54] *Common Cause* 14 March 1912, pp. 832–834.

argued, however, that the Kings College course should not be seen as a straightforwardly conservative or anti-feminist initiative. She noted that a number of its supporters, such as Mabel Atkinson, were advocates of women's rights and suffrage campaigners, and identified their interest in promoting household science as a form of 'social feminism'.[55] Since the beginning of campaigns for women's higher education in the 1860s, tensions had existed between those who insisted that women should have the right to study exactly the same curriculum as men, and those who allied with reformers seeking to modernise Britain's ancient universities more generally and establish entirely new degree subjects.[56] Supporters of the course in Household and Social Science situated themselves as part of these reforming endeavours, especially attempts to establish a place for the applied sciences within higher education. They argued that the universities needed to attend to the problems of the home and the wider social issues to which they pertained.[57]

The debate over the King's College course was not just about different approaches to women's higher education. Rather, it turned upon an interrogation of domestic labour and whether knowledge of the household could be considered as equal and equivalent to established academic subjects. The 1911 call for endowments quickly resulted in £100,000 being raised by early 1912. This sum compared extremely favourably to donations to other women's colleges where students were educated in less traditionally feminine subjects, prompting the *Common Cause* to suspect the motives of many donors:

We have nothing but approval for every effort to make domestic work better, more health-producing and more labour-saving. But we regard the notion that there can be a 'degree standard' for 'Home Science' as simply delusive.[58]

The following week, Hilda D. Oakeley, the Vice Principal and Warden of Kings College for Women, wrote a letter to the editor defending the course on the grounds that in the last century many new degrees, previously deemed beyond the university's remit, had been successfully established.[59] In the next issue of the *Common Cause*, Ida Freund, a chemistry lecturer at Newham College Cambridge, entered the debate. Freund was

---

[55] Nancy Blakestad, 'King's College of Household and Social Science and the Household Science Movement in English Higher Education c. 1908–1939', PhD thesis, University of Oxford (1994), pp. 8–17, 127–128.

[56] Laura Schwartz, 'Feminist Thinking on Education in Victorian England', *Oxford Review of Education*, 37 (2011), 669–682.

[57] Blakestad, 'King's College of Household and Social Science', pp. 127–128.

[58] *Common Cause* 15 Feb. 1912, pp. 761–762.

[59] *Common Cause* 22 Feb. 1912, pp. 788–789.

already a noted critic of the course in Household and Social Science, having previously published a paper in both *Education* and the *Englishwoman* in which she identified 'domestic science' as a threat to the teaching of 'pure' sciences in girls' secondary schools, which in turn obstructed their studying the sciences at university level.[60] In the *Common Cause*, Freund argued that the King's College course did not teach any kind of science – pure, applied or practical – in enough depth to achieve university standard. Moreover, 'domestic science' was not comparable to other newly established academic disciplines since it had no specialist journals and was not even a clearly defined body of knowledge. Rona Robinson, who had worked as an organiser for the WSPU in 1909–1910, also wrote to the paper explaining how she had resigned from her position as Gilchrist Postgraduate Scholar in Home Science and Economics at Kings College due to the superficial way in which the course merely touched upon chemistry, economics and biology. She now believed that it would not ever 'be possible to conceive of a degree in "domestic science"'.[61]

Nancy Blakestad has argued that this debate in fact reveals a considerable amount of common ground between opponents and supporters of the course in Household and Social Science, in that both sides agreed that women had important responsibilities in the home and that this work deserved respect and would benefit from some form of training.[62] Certainly Ida Freund began her critique of the course by attesting her '[r]eal pleasure at this magnificent recognition of women's activity in the home as a profession, which like any other profession, requires to be learned if real efficiency is to be attained'. Rona Robinson likewise affirmed her 'desire to aid every effort which may tend to the more efficient treatment of domestic work'. Yet Freund and Robinson made a crucial distinction between support for better training in 'practical house craft' and the serious study of science and other academic subjects worthy of a place in the university. They implied both a class distinction (Freund believed that the former should be directed towards raising 'the status and efficiency of the domestic worker') and, more fundamentally, that these two forms of knowledge were wholly different in nature. Rona Robinson

---

[60] *Education* 2 June 1911, pp. 335–337; 9 June 1911, pp. 350–352; *Englishwoman* May 1911, pp. 147–163; June 1911, pp. 279–296; Blakestad, 'King's College of Household and Social Science', pp. 151–159.

[61] Krista Cowman, *Women of the Right Spirit: Paid Organisers of the Women's Social and Political Union (WSPU), 1904–1918* (Manchester: Manchester University Press, 2007), p. 16; *Common Cause* 29 Feb. 1912, pp. 795–797.

[62] Blakestad, 'King's College of Household and Social Science', p. 163.

argued that legitimate university disciplines necessitated academic specialisation and 'detailed study', which it was impossible to apply to any kind of household work. She believed that future advancements in 'cookery, laundry-work and ... cleaning' would occur only once these activities were removed from the home to the public commercial sphere, 'but then they can no longer be termed "domestic"'.[63] Another correspondent, Mrs Ethel M. R. Shakespear, made an even more explicit distinction between the 'trivial and menial' work of 'house craft' and the 'more intellectual and therefore congenial' work for which students trained at university. Like Freund and Robinson, she claimed that she was not against instructing 'girls ... in the general principles and practice of housework', yet:

[i]t is no use disguising the fact that in the average household where one or two servants are kept, the expenditure of mental effort required in running the home ... is practically nil. All is routine ... Over and over again I have had friends, both university trained and otherwise, bemoan the fact that domestic work calls for so little mental activity that were their interest confined purely to domestic matters, their brains would be in danger of stagnating.[64]

This characterisation of domestic labour and household science as inherently less valuable and intellectually inferior had been made even more trenchantly in the *Freewoman* a few months previously, when it too debated what its editorial termed the 'degree for housewives'.[65] An article written by 'Educationalist' roundly attacked the course in Household and Social Sciences in the newspaper's very first issue, proclaiming it a 'tragedy'. This author was concerned that incorporating domestic subjects into the university curriculum would divert much-needed funds away from colleges seeking to educate women on an equal basis with men. They also believed that home science should remain in the domestic training schools, 'far removed from the precincts of the University'. They were much more explicit than the editor and correspondents of the *Common Cause* in their reasons for excluding household science from higher education:

---

[63] *Common Cause* 29 Feb. 1912, pp. 795–797.
[64] *Common Cause* 21 March 1912, p. 856.
[65] At least one correspondent noted that she was following the debates in both papers; *Common Cause* 21 March 1912, p. 856. Rona Robinson knew Dora Marsden, since they were both Manchester schoolteachers and then paid organisers for the WSPU; Cowman, *Women of the Right Spirit*, pp. 16, 24. Rebecca West later claimed Robinson as one of the initial group behind the *Freewoman*; Jane Marcus (ed.), *The Young Rebecca: Writings of Rebecca West 1911–1917* (Virago: London, 1983), p. 5.

Housework is a craft. Like a craft, it should be done deftly and accurately, either by those who have a natural leaning towards it or by those who are unfitted for work demanding a greater degree of intellectual endowment. *It is lower grade work*.[66]

No emancipated woman of any intelligence should waste her time on 'the mere removing of the mess of living and the arranging of the disorder of it'. Domestic labour 'should be done quickly and efficiently without anyone taking much note of it'. Even the servant paid to take on this task, as she became 'more highly evolved', would perform her work with an appropriate degree of distaste similar to 'a public executioner ... effective and swift'.[67]

In May 1912 the 'degree for housewives' returned once again to the pages of the *Freewoman* when Rebecca West, a young journalist recently moved to London after having been active in the Edinburgh WSPU, insisted that 'domestic work is the most elementary form of labour. It is suitable for those with the intelligence of rabbits.'[68] Not all readers of the *Freewoman* were opposed to the King's College course, nor did they agree that all housework was low-grade 'drudge' work. Adele Meyer wrote 'as a feminist and suffragist and one of those responsible for helping in the development of Home Science'. She argued that the aim of the course in Household and Social Science was to give due recognition to the important contribution to society that women made raising children and keeping house. Domestic work was therefore as deserving of the application of 'scientific principles and education' as the work which went into building naval battleships.[69]

This question of how housework compared to other forms of labour came up again in subsequent discussions of household 'drudgery' in the *Freewoman*, which scrutinised its practice to ask if there was something different about the *doing* of domestic labour. In June and July 1912, an article by Alice C. Burnett condemned 'cooking and drudgery' as suitable only for women of 'the primitive type of mind'.[70] One reader, a W. Gerrare, challenged Burnett to define exactly what it was about housework which made it thus. Granted, domestic labour was often tedious but what made it different from other types of repetitive labour? 'There is no more drudgery in washing up after a family feast ... than in

---

[66] *Freewoman* 23 Nov. 1911, pp. 16–18. My emphasis.
[67] *Freewoman* 23 Nov. 1911, pp. 16–18.
[68] Kathryn Laing (ed.), *The Sentinel: An Incomplete Early Novel by Rebecca West* (Oxford: European Humanities Research Centre, 2002), pp. xvi–xvii; Rebecca West, *Freewoman* 6 June 1912, in Marcus (ed.), *The Young Rebecca*, pp. 38–42.
[69] *Freewoman* 7 Dec. 1911, p. 54.
[70] *Freewoman* 27 June 1912, p. 119; 18 July 1912, p. 178.

cleaning up a laboratory after a debauch by an eminent or amateur scientist ... the home is still a more pleasant place to work than the office, the sales counter, or the daily round elsewhere'.[71] Those who argued that housework *was* somehow different from other forms of repetitive manual labour believed that the fundamental distinction derived from its location in the home, rather than the public sphere, and the fact that it was individualised and privatised rather than collectivised and industrialised. This analysis of domestic labour was not limited to the 'avant-garde feminists' at the *Freewoman*, but had currency in the wider suffrage movement. When the *Common Cause* had debated the King's College course in Household and Social Science, both Rona Robinson and the newspaper's editorial had argued that domestic labour needed to develop more in line with industrial forms of work, subject to 'organisation, specialisation and division of labour', which would necessarily entail its removal from the home.[72] Clementina Black made a similar argument in a series of articles in the *Common Cause* in the summer of 1916, later published as *A New Way of Housekeeping* in 1918. Black described domestic labour as a

primitive and undeveloped trade lacking the advantages of combined industry, machinery on a large scale, and the economy of production that depends on such developments. While other trades have passed from the dwelling house to the factory and into the workshop, and from the isolated worker to the group, gaining step-by-step the benefit of organisation, division of labour and socialisation of improvements, the domestic industry still remains in scattered homes.[73]

Here, Black was articulating a common view of housework as antithetical to modern, industrial, democratic society.[74] The idea that housework had failed to progress in line with other forms of work outside the home was rooted in a historical analysis that underpinned much thinking on the feminist work ethic. Victorian feminists had frequently contrasted the state of 'idleness' endured by the middle-class housewife of their own time to the busy and productive homemaker of the pre-industrial era.

[71] *Freewoman* 4 July 1912, p. 136.
[72] *Common Cause* 28 March 1912, pp. 863–864; 29 Feb. 1912, p. 797.
[73] Clementina Black, *A New Way of Housekeeping* (London: W. Collins Sons, 1918), pp. 15–16. See also *Common Cause* 12 Sept. 1919, pp. 393–394.
[74] Lucy Delap, *Knowing Their Place: Domestic Service in Twentieth-Century Britain* (Oxford: Oxford University Press, 2011), p. 2. See also Jane Hume Clapperton, *Scientific Meliorism and the Evolution of Happiness* (London: Kegan Paul, Trench, 1885), p. 289; Jane Hume Clapperton, *A Vision of the Future Based on the Application of Ethical Principles* (London: Swan Sonnenschein, 1904), p. 275; Charlotte Perkins Gilman, *The Home: Its Work and Influence* (Walnut Creek: AltaMira Press, 2002 [first published 1903]), pp. 106, 122, 109, 183; *Woman Worker* 30 Dec. 1908, p. 767.

Industrialisation, they argued, had removed tasks such as spinning and weaving, milk-churning and cheese-making from the home into the factory, depriving middle-class women of any socially useful occupation.[75] This analysis continued and was more thoroughly theorised in the work of a number of early twentieth-century historians and anthropologists around the Fabian Women's Group.[76] Olive Schreiner's *Woman and Labour*, for example, deplored the 'effete wife' that soon threatened to replace entirely the 'active labouring woman' of the past, as 'year by year, day by day, there is a silently working but determined tendency for the sphere of women's domestic labours to contract itself'. Such an argument might at first appear anomalous alongside the suffrage movement's concern about the overwhelming burden of housework on all working- and some middle-class women. In fact, Schreiner's book appears somewhat contradictory, at times claiming that in modern 'civilised' societies all the work of the household was now mechanised and commercialised, while at others denouncing the exploitation of 'washer women, cooks, and drudging labouring men's wives'.[77] Yet these two observations were not necessarily in opposition. For although it was widely argued that useful and productive domestic tasks had now been largely removed from the home, it was inferred that what remained was mere 'drudgery' – degraded, non-productive, monotonous work requiring little skill or creativity and untouched by the forces of modernity. Rebecca West repeated this argument on a number of occasions. Whereas once 'the housewife produced half the wealth of the country', grinding her own corn and baking her own bread, the coming of the Industrial Revolution 'snatched these occupations out of the hands of women and gave them to men, leaving women only the dish-washing and the floor-scrubbing', work which was nothing more than 'the merest tucking in of the untidy edges of an incomplete civilisation'.[78]

Even the strongest advocates of raising the status of domestic work struggled to incorporate everyday 'drudgery' into the feminist work ethic. In keeping with a belief in the importance of running a successful

---

[75] Holcombe, *Victorian Ladies at Work*, p. 4.

[76] Dyhouse, *Feminism and the Family*, pp. 63–68. See also Maxine Berg, 'The First Women Economic Historians', *The Economic History Review*, 45:2 (May 1992), 308–329.

[77] Schreiner, *Woman and Labour*, pp. 79–81, 22, 52, 114–115, 200. Schreiner's rhetoric obscured the degree to which she recognised that most women in the present day were still burdened with much domestic labour – 'parastisim' was as much a future threat as a present-day reality; Stanley, *Imperialism, Labour and the New Woman*, p. 85. Schreiner claimed that earlier drafts of *Woman and Labour* dedicated an entire chapter to the low pay and undervaluing of domestic labour; Burdett, *Olive Schreiner*, p. 61.

[78] Rebecca West, *Daily Herald* 22 June 1912 and *Manchester Daily Dispatch* 26 Nov. 1912, in Marcus, *The Young Rebecca*, pp. 360–362, 373–376.

household, the King's College course in Household and Social Science contained a practical element, and students were required to make their own beds and choose their own soft furnishings. They were never expected, however, to empty their own chamber pots, and by the 1930s domestic staff had taken over all aspects of the students' own housekeeping.[79] If, then, even these women felt that such work was beneath them, and unnecessary to an education in new scientific household management, the question of which women should undertake it remained unresolved.

Domestic Servants and the Feminist Woman

The feminist work ethic conjured up a particular image of the feminist woman – she to whom the women's movement both spoke and sought to bring into being. As we have seen, work was understood as central to self-expression and self-realisation. Earning one's own living and developing one's talents was one of the most important steps that women could take to gain greater control over their individual lives, and it was also seen as key to the collective transformation of womankind into fully engaged citizens. The direct causal relationship posited here between labour and selfhood, and labour and political consciousness, posed the question of what kinds of women and citizens housework produced. The debates over the endowment of motherhood and the 'degree for housewives' demonstrate how difficult it was to discuss that paradigmatically feminine form of work without immediately invoking its masculine counterpart, and contrasting domestic labour to higher-status and better-paid employment in the public sphere. Yet what of those women who did indeed leave their own homes to earn their own livings, but did so in the home of another? To what extent were domestic servants able to identify with the vision of emancipation offered by the feminist work ethic? And how were they to stake their claim to participate as feminists in a movement that felt so uneasy about, or at least could not agree upon, the character and value of the type of work they did?

It was certainly possible for servants to identify with the idea of gaining autonomy through work. Louise Jermy's memoirs narrate her entry into service as key to gaining economic independence from her unkind father and stepmother and overcoming her physical disability.[80] A powerful sense of agency is also asserted in Jessie Stephen's autobiography,

---

[79] Blakestad, 'King's College of Household and Social Science', pp. 355–356.
[80] Louise Jermy, *The Memories of a Working Woman* (Norwich: Goose & Son, 1934), pp. 76–77.

including its title, 'Submission Is for Slaves'. While offering an uncompromising critique of the conditions she encountered in her 'career as a
maid', Stephen also made it very clear that it was she, rather than her
employers, who decided when it was time to move onto a new post. Even
when Stephen was dismissed from various jobs, she recounted this as
having been prompted by her own deliberate acts of defiance rather than
the initiative of her mistress.[81]

Such narratives seldom featured, however, in the suffrage movement's
celebrations of healthy, happy independent women workers, and domestic servants were most likely to be mentioned only as a counter example.
Both the NUWSS and the WSPU were opposed to attempts in 1911 to
ban women from working at the pit heads.[82] The editor of the *Common
Cause* contrasted 'the work of the free, jolly, healthy, red-faced pit brow
girl' with the ill-health, 'interminable hours of confinement' and 'dread-
ful lack of freedom' suffered by the domestic servant.[83] Likewise, when
Sylvia Pankhurst published a series of articles and sketches on the subject
of working women in *Votes for Women* in 1907, she defended the health
and decency of one pit brow woman's work by contrasting it with her
former life in service. 'It brought me out so', this woman was quoted as
saying, which could be understood literally as meaning that open-air
work had made her feel and look better and stronger, but also that it
had brought her into the metaphorical openness of the public sphere in
contrast to the seclusion of her work as a servant.[84]

Some feminists even questioned the ability of women immersed in the
home to comprehend the significance and urgency of the struggle for the
vote. 'Of the girls who were at school with me nearly all, married and
single, have joined ... the suffrage movement', wrote Rebecca West, all

---

[81] Working Class Movement Library, Salford, Jessie Stephen, 'Submission Is for Slaves'
(unpublished manuscript), pp. 28–46. The only exception is when Stephen is fired from
Lady Chisholm's house after dislocating her ankle, p. 32. Winifred Foley and Margaret
Powell's autobiographies, recording their lives as politicised domestic workers in the
interwar period, also made use of picaresque narrative structures, whereby continual
moves from post to post became a way to narrate new stages in their own lives, with
employers' households serving as the background to stories of self-development;
Winifred Foley, *A Child in the Forest* (London: Ariel Books, 1974); Margaret Powell,
Below Stairs (London: Pan Books, 1968).
[82] Arthur Markham MP attempted this with an amendment to the 1910 Coal Mines Bill;
Malone, *Women's Bodies and Dangerous Trades*, pp. 132–134. For a similar attempt to
eliminate women from pit brow work in 1886–1887, Angela V. John, *By the Sweat of
Their Brow: Women Workers of Victorian Coal Mines* (London: Routledge & Kegan
Paul, 1984).
[83] *Common Cause* 10 Aug. 1911, p. 313.
[84] Quoted in Shiach, *Modernism, Labour and Selfhood*, p. 115. See also *Votes for Women* 11
Aug. 1911, p. 732.

except the 'dullest-witted pupils' who, rather than going on to become nurses, teachers or university students, remained 'in the isolated homes of their husbands or parents' and thus 'have taken nothing from life and given it nothing'.[85] In her novel *The Convert* (1907), WSPU activist Elizabeth Robins described her heroine, a glamorous aristocrat, attending a suffrage rally and finding herself in the first throes of her political awakening. She is accompanied by her lady's maid, known simply by her surname Gorringe, who, far from taking an interest in the speakers, is concerned only to stop her mistress' 'dainty wrap' from becoming dirty, and her skirt from getting trampled into the mud. While the rest of the crowd are swept up in the political debate, Gorringe is the only person who notices that it has started to rain and 'seemed to be the only one to think it mattered much'. She produces an umbrella anyway, holding it over the head of her mistress, who remains oblivious, enraptured by the rally.[86] The juxtaposition here between the high-minded upper-middle-class suffragette and the servant weighed down by the concerns of the everyday material world resonated with a common trope in the militant suffrage movement which frequently depicted its activists engaged in a spiritual battle, with little thought for the pain and deprivation inflicted upon their bodies by repeated police violence, imprisonment and hunger strikes.[87] This identity proved particularly difficult to reconcile with that of the domestic servant, whose job it was to attend to bodily needs and material comfort (including washing the muddy skirts of the overly enthusiastic suffrage devotee).

The emancipation that feminists believed waged labour was so central to achieving was not just 'freedom from' but also 'freedom to': freedom to think one's own thoughts, to pursue one's creative capacities to their full potential, to make one's mark on the world, to find pleasure in life and its activities, and to love out of desire rather than the need for security. The conditions of service were often seen as antithetical to achieving such an existence. Domestic servants were certainly excluded from the *Freewoman*'s vision of emancipated womanhood:

The Freewoman applauds the girl who prefers to work in a factory, for 10s per week, and live in her own independent squalid conditions, rather than earn 7s 6d

---

[85] Rebecca West, *Clarion* 4 April 1913, in Marcus, *The Young Rebecca*, pp. 170–174.

[86] Robins, *The Convert* (London: Macmillan, 1913 [first published 1907]), pp. 97–98, 113–114. For a very similar depiction of the modern mistress's frustration with a servant who cares only for dull domestic details, see Evelyn Sharp, 'The Servant Question', in Evelyn Sharp (ed.), *The War of All the Ages* (London: Sidgwick & Jackson, 1915), 139–152.

[87] Martha Vicinus, *Independent Women: Work and Community for Single Women 1850–1920* (London: Virago, 1985), pp. 268–280.

per week and live in better conditions in her employers' house ... We consider this attitude, with its resultant effects in a dearth of servants of the present order, one of the most hopeful signs in England today.[88]

The strong emphasis on individuality within avant-garde feminism fore-grounded women's need to access authentic experience as opposed to being protected or shut off from the real world by home and family. The importance placed upon acting on one's own behalf was contrasted to the traditional caring roles that celebrated self-sacrifice and encouraged women to live through their husbands and children.[89] The *Freewoman*'s opening editorial described the 'Bondswoman' (the opposite of the 'Freewoman') as one who 'By habit of thought, *by form of activity* ... round[s] off the personality of some other individual'. Although the servant was a wage-earning woman, the nature of her work undermined the emancipatory potential that this newspaper normally attributed to paid employment. Both practically and conceptually, the conditions and labour of the domestic servant mitigated against her aspiring to any of those qualities which this periodical believed to be such important indica-tors of the 'Freewoman'. The servant, like the servile wife, had exchanged freedom for 'security' and 'protection'. She was not the mistress of her own home, just as she was not the mistress of her own life, and although she earned a wage she did not do so on the 'free market', but in an economic terrain contaminated by emotions and dependencies. Worst of all, she laboured not for herself, but as proxy for another – and within the complex matrix of feminist debates on work and the importance placed upon it as a sign of spiritual independence, this was tantamount to becoming subsumed within another's personhood. [90]

Such beliefs were not limited to the *Freewoman*. Bessie Smallman, writing in the socialist feminist newspaper the *Woman Worker*, agreed that working as a domestic servant placed insurmountable obstacles to achieving the status of emancipated womanhood: 'no woman can hold the position of nurse or cook or lady's maid in ordinary households and be a free woman – that is, a woman free to think and express her thoughts'. Smallman described servants as 'women, who obey other women's minds, who must think other women's thoughts until they have nothing of their own left'.[91] This use of domestic service as a metaphor for the subjection of all women was common across the suffrage move-ment. Helena Swanwick's *The Future of the Women's Movement* railed

---

[88] *Freewoman* 7 Dec. 1911, p. 43.
[89] Delap, *The Feminist Avant-Garde*, pp. 151–152. See also Rebecca West, *Clarion* 12 Dec. 1913, in Marcus, *The Young Rebecca*, pp. 235–238.
[90] *Freewoman* 29 Feb. 1912, p. 281.   [91] *Woman Worker* 28 Oct. 1908, p. 555.

against the way in which women whose talents better suited them to professional work were often forced to give this up on marriage and motherhood, to become nothing more than 'a general servant'.[92] Christabel Pankhurst's *The Great Scourge and How to End It* derisively referred to the anti-suffragist man 'who expects women to act as unpaid domestic servant'.[93] The servant was imbued with a great many feelings and political aspirations: not only a symbol of victimhood, but also of the docility. Above all, she was an uncomfortable reminder of a form of feminine labour and domestic identity which remained an unresolved source of tension within the feminist movement.

[92] Helena Swanwick, *The Future of the Women's Movement*, p. 95.
[93] Christabel Pankhurst, *The Great Scourge*, p. 135, quoted in Mayhall, 'Household and Market', p. 193.

5 The Domestic Workers' Union of Great Britain and Ireland

In the 1970s, towards the end of her life, Jessie Stephen looked back upon a long and varied political career that combined feminism, trade unionism and Labour Party activism. She recalled how, at the centre of all of this, and '[r]ight from my teenage years and onwards':

> [T]here ran a continuous thread of resolve that I must never admit defeat in the campaign to improve the conditions of domestic workers. At every sort of meeting and conferences connected with women and their work, I raised the matter.[1]

Stephen had worked alongside Kathlyn Oliver, another suffragist, socialist and domestic servant, in the Domestic Workers' Union. Oliver, reflecting on her efforts to found this union, wrote of how:

> I think that I was for some time the best hated person in London. I received shoals of letters from indignant mistresses informing me of the iniquity of the proposed scheme ... that a union would make servants disloyal to their employers and oceans of similar rubbish ... [but] it will not deter me from writing and speaking whenever the opportunity occurs, against the unfair conditions of domestic labour which prevail.[2]

This chapter examines the 'servant problem' from the servant's point of view through a history of the Domestic Workers' Union of Great Britain and Ireland (est. 1909–1910). Although this union remained small and cannot in any way be viewed as representing domestic workers as a whole, many more servants contributed to the debates about the desirability or otherwise of servants joining a union. Some of these took place in the feminist press, especially the *Common Cause* and the *Woman Worker*. The history of the short-lived Domestic Workers' Union (DWU) thus provides an important new perspective on both class

---

[1] Working Class Movement Library (hereafter WCLM), Salford, Jessie Stephen, 'Submission Is for Slaves' (unpublished manuscript), p. 151.
[2] *Common Cause* 2 Nov. 1911, p. 521.

relations in the suffrage movement and the gender politics of labour organising in the years leading up to the First World War.

The DWU[3] was formed in September 1909 in response to letters written to the *Woman Worker*, the organ of the National Federation of Women Workers (NFWW) which subsequently agreed to bring the new union within its auspices. The official papers (minute books, membership lists etc.) of the NFWW do not survive, a factor which has contributed to historians' focus on its leaders, especially General Secretary Mary Macarthur and organiser Margaret Bondfield.[4] Cathy Hunt's important new history of the NFWW has gone a long way towards correcting this, but no history has ever before been written of the DWU.[5] My account relies upon the correspondence pages of the *Woman Worker* and the *Glasgow Herald*, and on press cuttings from the local and radical press in the Gertrude Tuckwell Collection held at the Trades Union Congress (TUC) Library. These frequently anonymous letters do not allow for a full-demographic portrait of union members, and over-represent more literate and politicised servants. They do provide, however, an unusual opportunity for the voices of rank-and-file domestic workers to be heard discussing working conditions and the possibility of self-organisation. In contrast to servants' societies with middle-class philanthropic backing, the DWU aimed to be a union run 'by servants for servants'. It sought to reconfigure the mistress–maid relationship as a formal employment contract, and did not shy away from the potential for class antagonism between these two groups of women.

The DWU occupied an uneasy position in the suffrage movement, troubling a widely held belief in the possibility of cross-class alliances between women. The union threatened to exacerbate class tensions by drawing attention to the domestic sphere as a workplace, and exposing the exploitation of working women that occurred within middle-class feminists' very own homes. Yet the DWU could not have formed without

---

[3] For short references to the Domestic Workers' Union, Barbara Drake, *Women in Trade Unions* (London: Virago, 1984 [first published 1920]), p. 180; Sheila Lewenhak, *Women and Trade Unions, Women and Trade Unions: An Outline History of Women in the British Trade Union Movement* (New York: St. Martin's Press, 1977), pp. 181–182; Pamela Horn, *The Rise and Fall of the Victorian Servant* (Stroud: Alan Sutton Publishing, 1990), pp. 179–180; Lucy Delap, *Knowing Their Place: Domestic Service in Twentieth-Century Britain* (Oxford: Oxford University Press, 2011), p. 26.

[4] For this argument, see Deborah Thom, 'The Bundle of Sticks: Women, Trade Unionists and Collective Organisations before 1918', in Angela V. John (ed.), *Unequal Opportunities: Women's Employment in England 1800–1918* (Oxford: Basil Blackwell, 1986), 261–289, pp. 262–264.

[5] Cathy Hunt, *The National Federation of Women Workers, 1906–1921* (Basingstoke: Palgrave Macmillan, 2014).

drawing strength from this movement. Although there was resistance among some suffrage-supporting mistresses to the idea of their own servants organising to improve pay, hours and conditions, the leaders of the DWU were politicised by the suffrage movement and used feminist arguments to support their cause. Supporters and opponents of the DWU also contributed to wider feminist debates on work. The question of whether domestic service was a job like any other, and if and how it compared to factory work in particular, was returned to again and again. Leaders of the DWU insisted that housework was real, useful and valuable work, and their critique at times overlapped with that strand of feminism which sought to reform the labour of the home. The Women's Industrial Council, for example, campaigned from the late 1890s onwards for improved training and qualifications for domestic servants as key to raising the standards, status and therefore conditions of this occupation. The inclusion of servants in the National Insurance Act of 1911 provoked further arguments as to whether mistresses ought to be treated as regular employers or the state had the right intervene in the workplace of the home. Yet despite a great deal of rhetoric regarding the need for service to be brought up to date and made more like other forms of work, there were always limits to feminists' willingness to treat it thus. Even the DWU contradicted themselves, when describing the nature of servants' exploitation as exceeding and inherently different from that of factory or shop work.

The Formation of the Domestic Workers' Union

From early in 1909 domestic servants wrote to the *Woman Worker* supporting the idea of a trade union and expressing their willingness to help organise fellow workers. Kathlyn Oliver, a London-based cook general of about twenty-four years of age, sent a particularly trenchant letter insisting that the servant 'should be encouraged to feel (what she really is) as important to the community as the worker in any other sphere' (see Figure 9). The paper's editors swiftly took her up on this, printing a response which asked 'Will Miss Oliver start a Domestic Union herself? The WOMAN WORKER will be happy to receive and forward names of those willing to join.' More letters appeared in favour of such a union, but the offer had to be put to Oliver again until, a full month later, she agreed to take on the organisation of 'A Domestic Servants' Trade Union', announcing a first meeting in October 1909 with the intention of forming a committee. Oliver advertised the prospective union as an organisation which would not only provide out-of-work benefits for its members, but also 'agitate for legislation to compel

Figure 9 Kathlyn Oliver, founder of the Domestic Workers' Union of
Great Britain and Ireland.
Mirror 1 Nov. 1909, p. 4 (reproduced by permission of the British Library)

employers to provide proper and healthy accommodation for servants,
and reasonable hours of labour and rest'. The *Woman Worker* summed
up the new development, declaring grandly (if incorrectly) that 'for the
first time in the United Kingdom ... a Servants' Trade Union has been
started'.[6]

Over the next few months, the *Woman Worker* reported frequently on
the hard work of Kathlyn Oliver, who was, she claimed, 'besieged on all
sides with letters from servants requiring information'. She announced
plans to organise 'park demonstrations' and a rally in Trafalgar Square,
appealed to readers for funds, and sent the union's existing supporters
knocking on back doors to recruit new members directly from London's
servant population. Following their first open meeting, the union printed
leaflets which were distributed among servants in the London suburbs
and elsewhere. The DWU was formally launched in the spring of 1910,
admitting both men and women members. Membership was to cost 2d.
per week, once an initial fee of 1s. had been paid, though for an extra 3d.
members would receive a weekly payment of 5s. after ten years of

[6] *Woman Worker*, 24 Feb. 1909, p. 189; 2 June 1909, p. 518; 28 July 1909, p. 78; 4
Aug. 1909, p. 102; 25 Aug. 1909, p. 182; 8 Sept. 1909, p. 230; 22 Sept. 1909, p. 275;
England and Wales Census (1911), 1 Barton Street, Westminster, London.

membership. The union also acquired its own banner, choosing the colours 'red (for Progress), green (for Hope), and gold (for the Dawn)'. Kathlyn Oliver remained in charge of funds, but passed her acting role of General Secretary over to a new member, Grace Neal.[7]

The new DWU acquired an office at 211 Belsize Road, London, and a dedicated group of working women on the executive committee. General Secretary Grace Neal gave up her job as a cook general to work full-time for the union on a wage of £1 a week. She took up residence in the back room of the union offices, equipped only 'with a little camp bed for night quarters'. Mrs Emmilia Cox soon joined her on the executive committee. Frances Dickinson, a housekeeper for a socialist family in the West End of London, was given the role of President, and Rose Black became Neal's Assistant Secretary. By January 1913, the union had acquired a regular subscribing membership of about 400 servants, while another 2,000 had been on its books at some point. Local branches were also established in Manchester and Oxford.[8] The executive opened their London office to 'ordinary members' every Sunday afternoon – the only time of the week when domestic servants were guaranteed any time off. Over tea and cakes they created a 'very pleasant and sociable environment' to share ideas and experiences. What they learnt from members regarding conditions of work and desire for change was translated into propaganda, which they distributed every week in Hyde Park and London's other open-air spaces.[9]

The objects of the union, first confirmed in 1910, were:

1. To raise the status of domestic work to the level of other industries, so that domestic workers shall cease to be a despised species, and to educate these workers to a proper sense of their own importance.

---

[7] *Woman Worker* 13 Oct. 1909, p. 345; 20 Oct. 1909, p. 382; 3 Nov. 1909, p. 426; 17 Nov. 1909, p. 451; 1 Dec. 1909, p. 494; 23 March 1910, p. 820; 27 April 1910, p. 920; 6 Oct. 1909, p. 321; 4 May 1910, pp. 942–943; 11 May 1910, p. 965.

[8] *Common Cause* 19 Oct. 1911, p. 486; *Mirror* 28 Nov. 1911, p. 5; *Manchester Guardian* 25 June 1912, p. 9; Stephen, 'Submission Is for Slaves', p. 56; London Metropolitan University: Trades Union Congress Library, Gertrude Tuckwell Collection (hereafter TUC), Press Cuttings, *Daily News and Leader* 16 Sept. 1913, Box 25, Reel 12, 609/38; *Weekly Dispatch* 5 Jan. 1913, Box 25, Reel 12, 609/21. Although the DWU was small, it should also be considered in relation to the relatively low overall percentage of women in trade unions at this time. There were only 357,956 female trade unionists in 1914, with the predominantly female shop assistants' union's 7,000 members constituting a large proportion of this; Pat Thane, 'Women in the Labour Party and Women's Suffrage', in Myriam Boussahba-Bravard (ed.), *Suffrage Outside Suffragism: Women's Vote in Britain, 1880–1914* (Basingstoke: Palgrave Macmillan, 2007), 35–51, p. 38.

[9] Stephen, 'Submission Is for Slaves', pp. 56–57.

2. To obtain better conditions for an overworked and often underpaid class of workers.
3. To agitate for legislation to compel employers to provide proper and healthy accommodation for servants.
4. To secure the inclusion of domestic servants in the operations of a Weekly Rest-Day Act.
5. To render it illegal for any servants to be on duty sixteen hours a day as many are at present.
6. To obtain a ten hours working day limit, after which servants shall be entirely free each day, and not kept in like prisoners or watch dogs.
7. To provide a free registry office.
8. To provide free legal advice.
9. Out of work pay to servants who shall have been members of the union for not less than twelve months.
10. Protection from bad and tyrannical employers.
11. To keep a black list of bad employers, as well as a black list of bad servants as we have at present.
12. To make it impossible or illegal for an employer to supply a servant with a bad or indifferent character for no better reason than that he or she wishes to leave their situations, or because an employer has for some petty reason taken a dislike to a servant.
13. Help for unfortunate girls.[10]

These objects reflected some of servants' most common complaints. The DWU constantly reiterated that room and board was not bestowed due to the kindness of employers but part of a servant's wage, and therefore inadequate food and uncomfortable sleeping arrangements constituted a breach of contract. Within a broad commitment to improving wages and conditions, the union focused particularly on definite hours of work and rest time when a servant would not be on call. The union also believed that the existing character system, whereby a servant was dependent upon an employer's reference to find a new position, needed to be radically overhauled. At present, it was felt that many mistresses withheld references or slandered their former employees simply because they were annoyed at their leaving. Servants were not permitted to see their references and had little legal recourse in the case of unfair treatment regarding this matter.[11] Object 13 – for the union to provide support for the unmarried mothers among their members – made oblique

[10] TUC, Press Cuttings, *Labour Leader* 20 May 1910, Box 25, Reel 12, 609/11.
[11] C. Violet Butler, *Domestic Service: An Enquiry by the Women's Industrial Council* (New York: Garland, 1980 [first published 1916]), p. 90; Delap, *Knowing Their Place*, p. 75.

reference to the workplace hazard of sexual harassment and the still common practice of firing servants if they were found to be pregnant.[12] "'It is a very sad and very difficult subject to talk about', Grace Neal told Rebecca West in an interview for the radical newspaper the *Daily Herald*: 'Wherever you go you are exposed to advances from your employers. If it isn't the husband, it's the sons or the visitors.'"[13] The union remained committed to these central demands throughout its lifetime, though its objects were extended and amended over the next few years, reflecting a responsiveness to feedback from members and an awareness of the everyday realities of servants' lives. For example, by 1913 the union's objects included the right to use the same bathrooms as their employers, and that 'no female servant be required to clean the outside of upstairs windows'.[14]

The DWU's aims were ambitious from the very start, when Kathlyn Oliver asked her new supporters 'to imagine a Union of, say, 5,000 servants, with 10,000 employers desiring these servants'.[15] Aware of industrial organising by other servants around the world, especially in Northern Europe, the United States, Australia and New Zealand, the DWU positioned itself as part of an international movement.[16] It was referred to by the *Woman Worker* as a 'national union' even before its first meeting.[17] By 1913 the DWU had linked up with a parallel organising effort in Glasgow, where Jessie Stephen, a twenty-year-old maid, had been organising fellow servants into the Scottish Federation of Domestic Workers since about 1911 (see Figure 10). Some years previously Stephen had been dismissed from her post as between maid in the house of Sir John Chisholm, when she dislocated her ankle and was unable to perform her duties to the standard required by her unsympathetic mistress. Yet Jessie Stephen's fury at this injustice was tempered by the knowledge that she had used her time in this post wisely, for she had

---

[12] *Common Cause* 10 Aug. 1911, p. 313; Suzie Fleming and Gloden Dallas, 'Jessie', *Spare Rib*, 32 (Feb. 1975), 10–13, p. 11.

[13] Rebecca West, *Daily Herald* 18 June 1912, in Jane Marcus (ed.), *The Young Rebecca: Writings of Rebecca West 1911–1917* (Virago: London, 1983), pp. 353–356.

[14] TUC, Press Cuttings, *Weekly Dispatch* 5 Jan. 1913, Box 25, Reel 12, 609/21.

[15] *Woman Worker* 3 Nov. 1909, p. 426.

[16] For reports of servants' unions internationally, *Woman Worker* 10 July 1908, p. 174; 10 March 1909, p. 227; 8 Sept. 1909, p. 222; 22 Sept. 1909, p. 275; 19 Jan. 1910, p. 646; 26 Jan. 1910, p. 666; *Woman's Dreadnought* 8 March 1914, p. 4. During the First World War the Domestic Workers' Union joined the International Labour Women and Socialist Committee, TUC, Press Cuttings, *Labour Leader* 11 Nov. 1915, Box 17, Reel 8, 353/8.

[17] *Woman Worker* 13 Oct. 1909, p. 345.

Figure 10 Jessie Stephen (back row, far left) with fellow Glasgow
WSPU members (c. 1910–1913).
Reprinted in *Spare Rib*, 32 (Feb. 1975), p. 12 (reproduced by permission of the
British Library)

spent the last few months meeting with other servants in the street with
the aim of organising a union.[18]

According to Stephen's autobiography, she had already, at this point
(and while working a sixteen-hour day) formed the Scottish Federation
of Domestic Workers to which she recruited her fellow maids. After
leaving the Chisholms, to work for the artist David Gould, she kept in
touch with her provisional committee. 'This was not at all a simple
matter because I only had one afternoon or evening free a week.' She
continued to enlist further support by visiting and writing to other
servants, helped by 'a labour man' named Bailie Alston who owned a
chain of teashops in Glasgow where the Scottish Federation of Domestic
Workers held many of their meetings. Stephen then took a new post as a

---

[18] Stephen, 'Submission Is for Slaves', pp. 30–33.

daily live-out maid, which left her evenings free to 'get around more of my members'. It was this agitation which, Stephen subsequently claimed, led to the flurry of correspondence from domestic servants in the *Glasgow Herald*.[19] Over the course of two and a half weeks, sixty-three letters were printed on the question of whether servants should be permitted a weekly half-day holiday (time off during the week in addition to the Sunday afternoon which was already the general rule).[20] More than half of these letters were from servants expressing support for some form of collective action or trade union to improve their working lives. Only eight were from servants who were content in their posts or believed the institution of service did not require reform. Employers also contributed their views, and the correspondence only ceased when an October editorial on 'Mistress and Maid' signalled the close of the debate.[21]

Jessie Stephen 'took advantage of this opportunity by writing ... [to the *Glasgow Herald*] and inviting girls to get together in a meeting'.[22] More than sixty years later Stephen still remembered how:

I and my colleagues arrived ... least half an hour before the meeting was due to start and we got the biggest surprise of our lives, it was already packed with girls who had come from all parts of the city and they were overflowing into the corridors outside.[23]

The newspaper men were also present and later reported that between 130 and 150 maids attended the meeting. 'After a general discussion of the grievances of domestic servants a series of demands was formulated and agreed by the meeting.' These amounted to thirteen points, including the weekly half-holiday, and it was agreed that '[t]he three things they should agitate for first were shorter hours, increased wages, and better food'.[24] Jessie later remembered that about 200 people joined the union that evening, but even if this was an overly optimistic recollection,

---

[19] Stephen, 'Submission Is for Slaves', pp. 33–35.
[20] The demand for the half holiday had been among some of the earliest made by London-based Domestic Workers' Union; TUC Press Cuttings, *Daily News* 2 Oct. 1909, Box 25, Reel 12, 609/8.
[21] *Glasgow Herald* 17 Sept.–4 Oct. 1913.
[22] *Glasgow Herald* 24 Sept. 1913, p. 5; 14 Oct. 1913, pp. 1, 3. Stephen's autobiography remembers the meeting taking place in the Christian Institute, Bothwell Street, though the notice in the *Glasgow Herald* advertised it at Alston's Tea Rooms which were in the same street; Stephen, 'Submission Is for Slaves', p. 35.
[23] Stephen, 'Submission Is for Slaves', p. 35.
[24] *Glasgow Herald* 16 Oct. 1913, p. 10; 17 Oct. 1913, p. 8. These demands were: weekly half holiday, two hours' daily (rest), specified meal hours, abolition of servants' registries, provision of uniform, graded scale of wages, recognition of union, twelve-hour day, fourteen days' annual holiday, public holidays, Sundays off at 2 till 10 o'clock, fortnightly payments, a week's notice instead of a fortnight's.

organising efforts certainly gained momentum with frequent meetings and social events held in Glasgow over the next few months.[25]

The *Glasgow Herald* reported at the time that Jessie Stephen's meeting had been held under the auspices the Glasgow branch of the DWU, which had been in existence for more than a year and of which Stephen was Secretary.[26] This is consistent with Stephen remembering elsewhere that the Scottish Federation of Domestic Workers merged with Grace Neal's London-based union in the early months of 1913, though her autobiography insists that the decision to affiliate did not occur until some time after the Scottish Federation of Domestic Workers had established itself following the *Glasgow Herald* correspondence and the subsequent public meetings.[27] Either way, the final months of 1913 were important ones for domestic worker militancy in Scotland. Stephen decided to take up temporary work as a servant so that 'I would be able to spread my trade union activities over a much wider field than was possible in a permanent position.' She began frequent trips to towns outside of Glasgow to agitate among the Scottish servant population.[28] Soon domestics in Glasgow's outlying areas of Falkirk, Milngravie, Rutherglen, as well as Edinburgh and Aberdeen and towns in Fifshire and Ayrshire, attempted to form branches.[29] Some concessions from employers were secured by these militant maids, including winning two hours' rest time each day. Such success, however, brought Jessie Stephen her own problems. The situation in Glasgow eventually became 'too hot', and she found herself blacklisted by mistresses and unable to secure a post. She decided to move to London, where the DWU Registry found her a job as maid with a union-friendly family in Purley, South London, and the union executive committee welcomed her with 'open arms'.[30]

[25] The Women's Library at the London School of Economics (hereafter TWL), London, 'Oral Evidence on the Suffragist and Suffragette Movements: The Brian Harrison Interviews' (1974–1981), interview with Jessie Stephen (1977), 8SUF/B/157, Disc 32–33. For reports and advertisements for subsequent meetings, *Glasgow Herald*, 23 Oct. 1913, p. 13; 3 Nov. 1913, p. 1; 7 Nov. 1913, p. 5.

[26] *Glasgow Herald* 16 Oct. 1913, p. 10.

[27] Stephen, 'Submission Is for Slaves', pp. 54–55. Stephen recalls that it was after returning from the Women's Social and Political Union's Working Women's delegation to London that she decided to look into affiliation with the Domestic Workers' Union of Great Britain and Ireland, but this occurred in January 1913, some months before the *Glasgow Herald* correspondence.

[28] Stephen, 'Submission Is for Slaves', pp. 40–46.   [29] *Glasgow Herald* 7 Nov. 1913, p. 5.

[30] TWL, Harrison, interview with Jessie Stephen; Stephen, 'Submission Is for Slaves', pp. 54–55.

The DWU did not survive the First World War, when thousands of women, including many of its members, left service for war work.[31] Only a few weeks after war was declared Grace Neal began looking for a new job, advertising in *Daily Herald* for 'clerical or organising work'.[32] Efforts were made to re-establish it in 1919, under the leadership of Jessie Stephen, as a branch of the NFWW, but after managing to recruit a few thousand members it fairly quickly petered out.[33] A parallel attempt that same year to organise domestic workers in Birmingham was supported by Julia Varley of the Workers' Union, although this tended towards a greater degree of employer–employee co-operation than Stephen was prepared to accept.[34] The Irish Women Workers' Union (IWWU) began organising servants towards the end of 1918. Its Domestic Workers Section managed to recruit an impressive 800 members in Dublin before being discontinued in 1919.[35] Although I have not been able to identify any direct links with the pre-war Domestic Workers' Union, Grace Neal spent almost six months in Dublin during the 1913 Lockout, assisting Dora Montefiore in her scheme for British labour movement families to take in the children of impoverished Irish strikers.[36] During this time she met a number of the activists who went on to organise the IWWU, possibly including some of the coordinators of the Domestic Workers' Section, Helena Molony and Margaret Buckley,

---

[31] Stephen, 'Submission Is for Slaves', p. 66.

[32] *Daily Herald*, 26 Aug. 1914, p. 7; 1 Sept. 1914, p. 7; 5 Sept. 1914, p. 7.

[33] TUC, 'The Annual Report and Balance Sheet of the National Federation of Women Workers: 10th Report for the Years 1918 and 1919'; TUC, Press Cuttings, *Daily News* 9 April 1919, Box 21, Reel 10, 504e/3. See also Hunt, *The National Federation of Women Workers*, pp. 101–102, 157.

[34] TUC, Press Cuttings, *Birmingham Post* 13 May 1919, Box 21, Reel 10, 504e/3; University of Warwick: Modern Records Centre, Trades Union Congress Archive (hereafter MRC), Trade Union Correspondence Regarding the Organisation of Domestic Workers (1926–1936), 'Association of Employers of Domestic Workers' (n. d.), MSS.292/54.76/4.

[35] Mary Jones, *These Obstreperous Lassies: A History of the IWWU* (Dublin: Gill & Macmillan, 1988), pp. 29–30; Mona Hearn, *Below Stairs: Domestic Service Remembered in Dublin and Beyond, 1880–1922* (Dublin: Lilliput Press, 1993), p. 87; Nell Regan, *Helena Molony: A Radical Life, 1883–1967* (Dublin: Arlen House, 2017), pp. 170–171.

[36] Dora Montefiore, *Our Fight to Save the Kiddies in Dublin: Smouldering Fires of the Inquisition* (London: Utopia Press, 1913); Padraig Yeates, *Lockout Dublin 1913: The Most Famous Labour Dispute in Irish History* (Dublin: Gill & Macmillan, 2001), pp. 248–249; Theresa Moriarty, '"Who Will Look after the Kiddies?": Households and Collective Action during the Dublin Lockout, 1913', in Jan Kok (ed.), *Rebellious Families: Household Strategies and Collective Action in the 19th and 20th Centuries* (New York; Oxford: Berghahn, 2002), 110–124, pp. 118–122; Karen Hunt, 'Women, Solidarity and the 1913 Dublin Lockout: Dora Montefiore and the "Save the Kiddies" Scheme', in Francis Devine (ed.), *A Capital in Conflict: Dublin City in the 1913 Lockout* (Dublin: Dublin City Council, 2013), 107–128.

the latter of whom had previously worked as an organiser for the Irish branch of the NFWW.[37]

Jessie Stephen sat on the Women's Advisory Committee on the Domestic Service Problem appointed by the Ministry of Reconstruction in December 1918, and tried to persuade it to adopt an eight-hour day and a national standard of wages for domestic workers in private homes. Most of the Committee (which included titled ladies as well as women's labour organisers such as Clementina Black and Marion Phillips of the Women's Labour League) rejected her 'radical proposal', and the resulting report focused mainly on the need to offer more training to domestic workers.[38] Stephen attempted to revive the DWU again in 1926 and, although this was abortive, a number of rank-and-file trade unionists continued to write to the Trades Union Congress (TUC) throughout the interwar period, inquiring about the possibility of forming another servants' union.[39] In 1930 moves were made by the Standing Joint Committee of Industrial Women's Organisations, again supported by Jessie Stephen, to establish a Domestic Workers' Charter, approved by the National Conference of Labour Women in 1931.[40] The two main general unions, the Transport and General Workers' Union and the National Union of General and Municipal Workers, were, however, unenthusiastic at the prospect of devoting their resources to another organising project.[41] In 1932 the TUC, the National Union of General and Municipal Workers and the Hampstead Trades Council supported the formation of a Domestic

---

[37] Jones, *These Obstreperous Lassies*, p. 29; Hearn, *Below Stairs*, p. 87; Hunt, 'Women, Solidarity and the 1913 Dublin Lockout'; Hunt, *The National Federation of Women Workers*, pp. 132–133; Regan, *Helena Molony*, pp. 170–171. Grace Neal arrived in Dublin on 18 October 1913, travelled back and forth between Dublin and Liverpool, but did not return to England definitively until March 1914; Dublin: National Library of Ireland (hereafter NLI), Francis Sheehy Skeffington to Grace Neal, 8 March 1914, MS 33,612 (15).

[38] 'Memorandum on Wages by Miss Stephen', in *Report of the Women's Advisory Committee on the Domestic Service Problem Together with Reports by Sub-Committees on Training, Machinery of Distribution, Organisation and Conditions* (London: Ministry of Reconstruction, 1919), pp. 35–36. Marion Phillips also refused to sign the main report because it failed 'to make any definite recommendations as to wages and hours'; 'Memorandum by Dr Marion Phillips', in *Report of the Women's Advisory Committee*, p. 6.

[39] MRC, Trade Union Correspondence Regarding the Organisation of Domestic Workers (1926–1936), H. V. Tewson to C. L. Norman, 27 Nov. 1926, MSS.292/54.76/4.

[40] MRC, Trade Union Correspondence Regarding the Organisation of Domestic Workers (1926–1936), 'Report of the Sub-Committee on Questionnaire for the Domestic Workers' Charter' (8 Sept. 1930), MSS.292/54.76/4. This charter was based upon a Labour Party document 'What's Wrong with Domestic Service?' (1929); Delap, *Knowing Their Place*, p. 89.

[41] MRC, Trade Union Correspondence Regarding the Organisation of Domestic Workers (1926–1936), Ernest Bevin to E. P. Harries, 2 Dec. 1931, 'Minute of Meeting of Advisory Committee' (17 Feb. 1932), MSS.292/54.76/4.

Workers' Guild in Hampstead, North West London, but this emphasised welfare and recreational provision over agitation around wages and conditions. [42] A new Domestic Workers' Union was not established until 1938, this time by the TUC, as a top-down project that pursued a conciliatory policy towards employers – a far cry from the rank and file militancy of its pre–First World War namesake.[43]

A Union Such as the Miners Have

The DWU, from the very start, identified themselves as 'a section of the nation's workers' operating within a broader labour movement – indicated by their decision to call themselves a 'Domestic Workers'' rather than 'Servants'' union.[44] Kathlyn Oliver wished to claim for servants the same rights for which factory and shop workers had fought and won, asking, 'Why should the domestic worker be the only one of all the nation's workers whose work is never done?'[45] The union demanded that servants be included in existing labour legislation, especially with regard to limited hours of work, and in 1914 it joined demonstrations in support of the Shop Hours Act.[46] The DWU leaders frequently spoke of servants in the same breath as industrial workers. Jessie Stephen, for example, argued for servants' entitlement to public holidays 'such as their brothers and sisters got in the workshop and factory'.[47] In 1914 Grace Neal made a proposal to the TUC asking that 'the private houses where they [servants] are employed should be inspected by officials' just as factories were.[48]

The union's members and supporters also expressed a desire to stand alongside the 'factory girl' in her ongoing fight for workplace rights.[49] 'It is surprising', wrote one anonymous servant to the *Glasgow Herald*, 'that

---

[42] MRC, Trade Union Correspondence Regarding the Organisation of Domestic Workers (1926–1936), E. P. Harries to C. E. Catford, 22 Feb. 1932, 'Domestic Workers' Guild Hampstead' (13 May 1932), MSS.292/54.76/4.

[43] Delap, *Knowing Their Place*, pp. 90–91.

[44] Kathlyn Oliver, *Domestic Servants and Citizenship* (London: People's Suffrage Federation, 1911). For the evolution of the union's name, *Woman Worker* 6 Oct. 1909, p. 321; 20 Oct. 1909, p. 382; 17 Nov. 1909, p. 451.

[45] *Woman Worker* 17 Nov. 1909, p. 451.

[46] *The Times* 14 Nov. 1914, p. 8. The Shop Hours Act of 1910 entitled workers to a half holiday a week and stated meal times. A subsequent Act in 1913 limited hours of work to sixty-five a week but this applied only to restaurant workers; Drake, *Women in Trade Unions*, p. 60.

[47] *Glasgow Herald* 16 Oct. 1913, p. 10.

[48] TUC, Press Cuttings, *Glasgow Herald* n.d., Box 21, Reel 10, 504c/32, *Daily Sketch* 21 July 1914, Box 25, Reel 12, 609/44.

[49] *Common Cause* 9 Nov. 1911, p. 543.

British girls have surrendered to this form of slavery for so long ... but the day is near at hand ... [when] they, *like other workers*, are beginning to realise that they not only have a right to work and exist, but also the right to live and enjoy life'. 'What we think is needed', wrote Sadie and Margie in the same paper, 'is a union of domestics such as the miners have'. Glasgow servants even advocated employing the tactics of local labour movement heroes, the Clydeside dock workers, in the knowledge that their labour too was 'indispensable to our employers'. 'Why don't all girls come out on strike?' implored one letter-writing servant; 'I for one would raise the banner [for] "Shorter Hours".' Although discussion of servants' unionisation initially made it into the *Glasgow Herald* through its correspondence pages, DWU meetings were eventually reported on alongside the efforts of other workers in the regular 'Labour Affairs' column.[50]

This wish to assert a working-class identity might also partly explain the silence around questions of race and Empire in debates over the 'servant problem'. While identification with the wider working class in Britain was fairly common, this was usually an implicitly 'white' identity and I have not found any examples of servants drawing comparisons between their situation and that of workers and/or indentured labourers in the colonised territories.[51] Historians continue to debate the degree to which British socialism, the labour movement and the working class critiqued, ignored or endorsed imperialism.[52] In the case of domestic workers, lack of engagement seems to have predominated. The one exception to this is Ireland, which was still a British colony, with the Irish still to some degree excluded from the category of 'whiteness'. The full title of the Domestic Workers' Union of Great Britain and Ireland

---

[50] *Glasgow Herald* 20 Sept. 1913, p. 3; 22 Sept. 1913, p. 3; 25 Sept. 1913, p. 3; 26 Sept. 1913, p. 5; 29 Sept. 1913, p. 5; 30 Sept. 1913, p. 3; 1 Oct. 1913, p. 5; 23 Oct. 1913, p. 13. My emphasis.

[51] Campaigns against indentured labour were growing in the years leading up to the First World War; Ron Ramadin, *The Making of the Black Working Class in Britain* (Aldershot: Gower Publishing, 1987), pp. 61–65; Shobna Nijhawan, 'Fallen through the Nationalist and Feminist Grids of Analysis: Political Campaigning of Indian Women against Indentured Labour', *Indian Journal of Gender Studies,* 21:1 (2014), 111–133.

[52] Partha Sarathi Gupta, *Imperialism and the British Labour Movement, 1914–1964* (London: Macmillan, 1975); Ramadin, *The Making of the Black Working Class*, chapter 4; John M. MacKenzie, *Propaganda and Empire: The Manipulation of British Public Opinion, 1880–1960* (Manchester: Manchester University Press, 1994); Catherine Hall and Sonya O. Rose (eds.), *At Home with the Empire: Metropolitan Culture and the Imperial World* (Cambridge: Cambridge University Press, 2006); Karen Hunt, 'Towards a Gendered and Raced Socialist Internationalism: Dora Montefiore Encounters South Africa (1912–14)', *African Studies,* 66:2–3 (2007), 321–341; Bernard Porter, *The Absent-Minded Imperialists: Empire, Society and Culture in Britain* (Oxford: Oxford University Press, 2007); Billy Frank, Craig Horner and David Stewart (eds.), *The British Labour Movement and Imperialism* (Newcastle: Cambridge Scholars, 2010).

could indicate an unreflective colonising tendency on the part of the union's founders, in that it was assumed that Ireland should be incorporated into a London-based union's sphere of organising without any particular effort being made to establish branches there. On the other hand, the fact that Ireland was acknowledged separately from 'Great Britain' might also have been intended to signal political sympathies with the Irish struggle for independence. Certainly Grace Neal built links with Irish nationalists during the time she spent in Dublin in 1913–1914.[53]

Service was sometimes described as 'slavery', and although it may have retained the emotional force of the abolitionist movements of the early nineteenth century, this metaphor was seldom explained or pursued any further.[54] Because 'slavey' was another common term for young put-upon maids of all work, the connotations were not necessarily those of African slavery or the British or North American slave trade.[55] When servants did describe themselves as slaves, it was often in the context of actively renouncing such a label. When the DWU organised a demonstration in 1913, which reportedly 'took possession of Trafalgar Square', one of the main mottos with which they decorated their plinth was 'We will be slaves no longer.'[56] Slavery was associated with passivity and abjection. Kathlyn Oliver lamented, and contrasted herself to, an older generation of servants who refused to complain about their conditions and who still possessed a 'slave soul'.[57] The title of Jessie Stephen's autobiography similarly declared that 'Submission Is for Slaves'.[58] The *Woman Worker* described African slavery as 'an anachronism' like the 'chattel slave and the serf of the soil', condemned to more primitive periods of history. Oliver likewise condemned the conditions of domestic service by comparing them to a form of slavery that had 'been abolished some time ago'. To claim, as the radical *Reynolds Newspaper* did, that 'The servant no longer sees herself as part of the "slave class"', was to invoke a teleological vision of servants' consciousness finally catching up

[53] NLI, Francis Sheehy Skeffington to Grace Neal, 8 March 1914, MS 33,612 (15).
[54] *Woman Worker* 31 July 1908, p. 239; 19 Jan. 1910, p. 646; *Common Cause* 10 Aug. 1910, p. 313.
[55] An exception is Bessie Smallman, who made a comparison between domestic servants and enslaved people in the United States in the early nineteenth century, but since she came from North America she would have been working with the different set of references and a somewhat more recent experience of slavery in that country; *Woman Worker* 28 Oct. 1908, p. 555.
[56] TUC, Press Cuttings, *Standard* 21 April 1913, Box 25, Reel 12, 609/23.
[57] Cumbria Archive, Carlisle, Catherine Marshall Papers, Kathlyn Oliver to Catherine Marshall, 13 Sept. 1913, DMAR/2/31.
[58] Stephen, 'Submission Is for Slaves'.

with the rest of the modern industrial working class.[59] Subjugated and/or indentured workers in the colonised territories were also, in contemporary discourse, associated with 'backwardness' of slavery, which politicised servants wished to leave behind.[60] The unlikelihood, therefore, of servants forming bonds of solidarity with such workers is summed up in the casual nationalism of a domestic servant's letter to the *Common Cause* in 1911, which condemned the miserable conditions of her industry, welcomed the formation of a servants' union and looked forward to 'the time when we can sing along with the free factory girl, "Britons never never shall be slaves!"'[61]

The DWU was not, as its champions in the *Woman Worker* claimed, the first union for domestic servants but it did offer a new and distinctive vision of organising. In 1872 attempts were made by the maidservants of Dundee and the manservants of Leamington to 'combine in order to improve their working conditions', though this lasted only for a 'short time'.[62] A London and Provincial Domestic Servants' Union, whose committee included a number of servants from the higher end of the industry, such as butlers, cooks and lady's maids, existed between 1891 and 1893. Like the DWU, this earlier union demanded higher wages and shorter hours, yet the preface to their rule book also insisted that its aim was to educate and improve servants so that the good feelings that had existed between them and their employers of old might be re-established. They were also opposed to strikes.[63] The DWU, by contrast, had little time for nostalgic musings on the 'the good old faithful servant' and the sentimental bond between mistress and maid. 'Ladies complain that servants today are not what they were years ago', wrote Kathlyn Oliver, '... and we rejoice to hear it'.[64] Such sentiments indicate some

---

[59] *Woman Worker* 30 Dec. 1908, p. 767; *Labour Leader* 2 Dec. 1910, p. 765; *Reynolds Newspaper*, 11 Oct. 1908; TUC Archive, London, Gertrude Tuckwell Papers, Press Cuttings Box 25, Reel 12, 609/3.

[60] For example, 'Home Life: English Dwellings', *Westminster Review*, 57 (Jan. 1875), 173–192, pp. 176–177.

[61] *Common Cause* 9 Nov. 1911, p. 543.

[62] Horn, *The Rise and Fall of the Victorian Servant*, p. 178; Jan Merchant, '"An Insurrection of Maids": Domestic Servants and the Agitation of 1872', in Louise Miskell, Christopher A. Whatley and Bob Harris (eds.), *Victorian Dundee: Image and Realities* (East Lothian: Tuckwell Press, 2000), 104–121; Fae Dussart, 'The Servant/Employer Relationship in 19th Century India and England', PhD thesis, University College London (2005), pp. 175–189.

[63] Horn, *The Rise and Fall of the Victorian Servant*, pp. 178–179. A branch was formed in South Wales in 1892; Carys Howell, 'Wales' Hidden Industry: Domestic Service in South Wales, 1871–1921', PhD thesis, University of Swansea (2014), pp. 172–175.

[64] Oliver, *Domestic Servants and Citizenship*, p. 11.

awareness among servants of how much attitudes within their industry had transformed over the previous two decades.

The DWU's intransigent tone also distinguished it from other organising efforts taking place at the time. In Scotland, the Glasgow branch of the DWU came into conflict with a rival Scottish Domestic Servants' Union. This competing organisation had previously confined itself to the work of a friendly society, providing benefits and financial assistance to its paying members. A representative from this organisation attended Jessie Stephen's first public meeting and argued that her society was far larger than the Glasgow branch of the DWU (having 5,000 members as opposed to the sixty maids who had already signed up to Stephen's union) and should therefore be in charge of organising servants in that city.[65] The following evening, the Scottish Domestic Servants' Union held another meeting in which they reiterated their more established position (15,000 members throughout Scotland) and determined to form themselves into a union proper with similar demands to those agreed upon by the DWU. It is possible that some of this conflict resulted from internal divisions within the Glasgow labour movement. Jessie Stephen denounced her rivals, claiming that 'she had attempted to speak at a meeting two years ago of the Scottish Union and she was howled down'. There were nevertheless important ideological differences between the two organisations. The *Glasgow Herald* reported how the Scottish Union's Secretary, Miss Elizabeth M'Lean, told her audience that she had attended a meeting of the DWU and 'been disgusted with the tone of the speaking; it seemed to be a wholesale slanging of mistresses'. She also reassured those present that 'it was important not to disturb existing good relations between employers and employed', while Mr J. C. M'Lean, Treasurer of the Scottish Domestic Servants' Union, said that 'he did not think a strike would be desirable even in the worst straits'.[66]

Another key difference between the DWU and their rivals was the former's emphasis on servants' self-organisation. The DWU was emphatically not a charitable association, nor even a top-down labour movement project concerned with the welfare of domestic workers. It wanted, instead, to be a grass-roots union. Jessie Stephen was insistent upon 'the fact that the Domestic Workers' Union worked entirely by servants for servants'.[67] The DWU was also clear that its success

---

[65] *Glasgow Herald* 16 Oct. 1913, p. 10.
[66] *Glasgow Herald* 16 Oct. 1913, p. 10; 17 Oct. 1913, pp. 8, 13.
[67] *Glasgow Herald* 23 Oct. 1913, p. 13. Elizabeth M'Lean attempted to defend her organisation against accusations that, by contrast, the Scottish Union 'was run entirely

depended, not on its leadership, but on the hard work of its members. Kathlyn Oliver explained in one of her early reports how:

Many of the letters sent to me have been written in a 'God bless you' strain. I appear to be regarded almost as another Messiah. This is very nice, and I appreciate it muchly; and reluctant as I am to disillusion these friends, I want to candidly tell them that if they are waiting for *me* to make better conditions for them, they will wait a long time ... *I* cannot insist that servants shall not be on duty sixteen hours a day ... but they can rise *en masse* and say it themselves.[68]

Having voiced sentiments which one Scottish housemaid believed were part and parcel of 'the awakening of the democratic spirit amongst the masses', the DWU called upon the rest of the labour movement to support them.[69] The response was mixed. Charles N. L. Shaw, a supporter of the DWU who lent his office on the Strand for early committee meeting, wrote in the *Woman Worker* of how:

Some time ago, when I mooted the idea to some friends in the trade union world, they laughed at it and said, 'You will never be able to get the domestic servants to join a union. The long hours of employment make it difficult for them to attend meetings – there is no trade to bind them together, as in the case of factory workers – the field is too nebulous.'[70]

Servants themselves admitted that 'the task of combination is a difficult one on account of the fact that we work in ones, twos, threes, and fives and not in fifties and hundreds as mill workers do'.[71] Some trade unionists also believed that servants were 'snobbish' (even Jessie Stephen suggested this) and unwilling to ally with other workers.[72] Worse still, a few labour movement activists reiterated the widespread belief that servants were stupid, 'ignorant of economics' and deferential to the values of their middle-class employers.[73] Such attitudes reflected a widespread resistance to acknowledging that the private home was in fact a workplace for millions of waged female workers. In 1913, the editor of the *Glasgow Herald* answered all the talk of unions, strikes, rights and struggles that maids had brought to its letters pages, with a wilful reiteration of the belief that 'The relation between mistress and maid is necessarily a personal one ... and cannot be likened to the relation

by ladies, and that domestic servants should not join... because it would not be a democratic society'. Domestic servants made up only two-thirds of the existing committee of the Scottish Union; *Glasgow Herald* 17 Oct. 1913, p. 13.
[68] *Woman Worker* 3 Nov. 1909, p. 426.
[69] *Glasgow Herald* 29 Sept. 1913, p. 5; 2 Oct. 1913, p. 3.
[70] *Woman Worker* 22 Sept. 1909, p. 275. See also 23 March 1910, p. 820.
[71] *Common Cause* 23 Nov. 1911, p. 579.   [72] *Glasgow Herald* 24 Sept. 1913, p. 5.
[73] TUC, Press Cuttings, *Labour Leader*, 9 Dec. 1910, Box 25, Reel 12, 609/12.

between a manufacturer and his women employees. The home and the factory are poles asunder.'[74]

The DWU did not, however, meet with the same level of resistance and disdain from the established labour movement as the TUC servants' union in the 1930s.[75] Male trade unionists writing in the *Woman Worker* expressed their pleasure at the idea of a union for 'a body of women workers who have been too long neglected'.[76] 'Representatives of the various trade unions' also spoke at the DWU's rally when, in 1913, it 'took possession of Trafalgar Square' to protest at their lack of employment rights.[77] That same year the DWU was affiliated to the Trades Union Congress.[78] The Glasgow branch was aided by the exceptional levels of labour unrest, involving many women workers, which dominated that city from 1910 onwards.[79] Jessie Stephen recalled that her union branch was 'greatly helped' by Labour councillors including Patrick Dolan and John Taylor. At the Glasgow union's second public meeting, Mr Thomas Hamilton of the Workers' Union enthused that 'it was going to be an easy matter to organise the domestic servants', and the branch subsequently affiliated to the local Trades Council.[80]

The Domestic Workers' Union and the Suffrage Movement

The DWU was as much the product of the suffrage movement as it was the trade unions. It was often noted how 'waves of suffrage agitation' had also opened the minds of servants to their own struggles as workers in the home.[81] Many of the union's leaders and members were active in the suffrage movement, convinced that the vote would improve the lot of domestic workers just as it would transform the lives of all women. Stephen was active in the Women's Social and Political Union, which

---

[74] *Glasgow Herald* 4 Oct. 1913, p. 6.   [75] Delap, *Knowing Their Place*, pp. 91–92.
[76] *Woman Worker* 18 Sept. 1908, p. 406.
[77] TUC, Press Cuttings, *Standard* 21 April 1913, Box 25, Reel 12, 609/23.
[78] MRC, 'Minutes of the Meetings of the Trades Union Congress Parliamentary Committee', MSS.292/20/2, p. 19, 33.
[79] Eleanor Gordon, *Women and the Labour Movement in Scotland, 1850–1914* (Oxford: Clarendon, 1991); William Kenefick and Arthur McIvor (eds.), *Roots of Red Clydeside 1910–1914? Labour Unrest and Industrial Relations in West Scotland* (Edinburgh: John Donald Publishers, 1996).
[80] *Glasgow Herald* 23 Oct. 1913, p. 13; Stephen, 'Submission Is for Slaves', p. 47.
[81] Butler, *Domestic Service*, p. 11. See also *Common Cause* 7 Dec. 1911, pp. 621–622; Oliver, *Domestic Servants and Citizenship*; TUC, Press Cuttings, *Labour Leader* 3 June 1910, Box 21, Reel 10, 504e/1; TUC, Press Cuttings *Manchester Guardian* 20 June 1913, Box 25, Reel 12, 609/23.

in Glasgow had close ties to the labour movement.[82] During the First World War Stephen worked for the East London Federation of the Suffragettes, and later for the Workers' Birth Control Movement. Frances Dickinson was also in the 'militant wing' of the suffrage movement, and was arrested in 1913, appearing on the Roll of Honour of Suffragette Prisoners. Kathlyn Oliver and Grace Neal supported universal suffrage for all men and women, and had associations with the People's Suffrage Federation and adult suffrage, respectively.[83]

The *Common Cause*, under the editorship of Helena Swanwick, was the only suffrage periodical to give its official support to the DWU.[84] In February 1911 its editorial declared that 'Nothing could be of greater advantage to the status of women than to raise domestic work to a skilled trade with proper conditions ... protected by unions.'[85] That summer, readers of the *Common Cause* began to use its correspondence columns to discuss the 'servant problem'. The debate continued into the autumn, when Grace Neal and Kathlyn Oliver wrote letters promoting the DWU, and raged on until January 1912.[86] The *Common Cause* published an editorial alongside Grace Neal's initial letter, which 'welcomed' the establishment of servants' unions and argued that if domestic workers' conditions and training were improved, there was no reason why, in the future, domestic service should not become a prestigious and popular occupation. The newspaper took a sympathetic editorial line towards the numerous letters from domestic servants complaining about their working conditions.[87]

By contrast, many of the letters from mistresses were very hostile, refusing to accept the first-hand testimonies of domestic workers from within their own suffrage ranks.[88] One anonymous mistress, responding to a letter from a servant who had complained about long hours, low pay

---

[82] Leah Leneman, *A Guid Cause: The Women's Suffrage Movement in Scotland* (Aberdeen: Aberdeen University Press, 1991), pp. 43, 50, 52, 138.

[83] TWL, Harrison, interview with Jessie Stephen; Fleming and Dallas, 'Jessie'; Stephen, 'Submission Is for Slaves', p. 56; National Archives, London, Home Office Records, 'Suffragettes: Amnesty of August 1914: Index of Women and Men' (1914–1935), HO 45/24665; TWL, 'Roll of Honour of Suffragette Prisoners', 7LAC/2; Oliver, *Domestic Servants and Citizenship*; *Daily Herald* 3 Jan. 1913, p. 6.

[84] The *Freewoman* applauded the increasing militancy of servants without mentioning the DWU explicitly, *Freewoman* 25 Jan. 1911, p. 187.

[85] *Common Cause* 9 Feb. 1911, p. 710.

[86] *Common Cause* 24 Aug. 1911, p. 349, to 4 Jan. 1912, pp. 672–673.

[87] *Common Cause* 19 Oct. 1911, p. 484; 26 Oct. 1911, pp. 503–504.

[88] Ten letters were published from mistresses either hostile to the union or dismissive of the complaints put forward by servants; only one letter from a mistress attempted to take a balanced view of the debate; fifteen letters were published from servants; and only one of those had anything good to say about her job.

and monotonous work, accused her of substituting 'half facts for facts ...
She speaks of "putting in 16 hours a day" as though she *worked* all those
hours.'[89] This correspondent, like many of the other mistresses who
wrote to the *Common Cause*, disputed the notion that service imposed
an excessively long working day on the basis that there were within it
many moments of respite. The DWU, which sought as one of its ten
'objects' 'to render it illegal for any servants to be on duty 16 hours a day
as many are at present', was accused of exaggeration.[90] C. C. Stopes
(probably the prominent suffragist and historian Charlotte Carmichael
Stopes, mother of Marie Stopes) wrote a particularly dismissive letter. 'I
am afraid', she declared imperiously, 'that much of the discontent among
servants of the present day lies in the fact that they expect to give too little
and get too much'. She claimed that servants had many opportunities for
'comparative leisure' between lunch and tea, and 'the chance of fresh air,
by going on errands'.[91]

The DWU was equally willing to enter into conflict with employers,
even when the mistresses with whom they clashed were also sisters in the
struggle for the suffrage. Although the union maintained that it did not
represent a threat to *good* employers, it also consistently made the case for
unionisation regardless of the sympathies or otherwise of individual
mistresses.[92] 'I rejoice in one of the best employers myself', Kathlyn
Oliver told two servants who had written to her, 'but I say most emphatically that servants want a union'.[93] The union's view of the home as a
workplace – note Oliver's reference to her 'employer' rather than her
'mistress' – made it necessary to recognise that mistresses and maids had
competing and sometimes opposing interests. In a sense, this was the one
point upon which mistresses and their militant servants appeared to
agree. C. C. Stopes, in her letter to the *Common Cause*, illustrated the
careful attention mistresses paid to every penny spent on housekeeping.
In addition to the £18 per year she paid her servants (not much for a
London household when compared with the £22–£26 per year that the

[89] *Common Cause* 26 Oct. 1911, pp. 503–504.
[90] TUC, Press Cuttings, *Labour Leader* 20 May 1910, Box 25, Reel 12, 609/11; *Common Cause* 9 Nov. 1911, pp. 542–543; 23 Nov. 1911, p. 578.
[91] *Common Cause* 30 Nov. 1911, p. 602. Only one other woman with the surname of Stopes and a first name beginning with C appears in the 1911 census. Charlotte Carmichael Stopes was a member of the NUWSS; Elizabeth Crawford, *The Women's Suffrage Movement: A Reference Guide, 1866–1928* (London: University College London Press, 1999), pp. 656–657.
[92] *Woman Worker* 20 Oct. 1909, p. 382; 13 April 1910, p. 880.
[93] *Woman Worker* 8 Dec. 1909, p. 522. See also Oliver, *Domestic Servants and Citizenship*, pp. 12–13. See also the demands for 'rights, not privileges' by Scottish servants; *Glasgow Herald*, 30 Sept. 1913, p. 3; 1 Oct. 1913, p. 5; 2 Oct. 1913, p. 3.

Blathwayt family in Bath, of a similar social standing, paid their house-
maids), she also calculated that she spent 1s. 6d. weekly on food, £10 a
year on accommodation, 1s. 6d. per week on washing, and then a further
sum on wear and tear, presents, breakages and holidays. Stopes was
typical of mistresses who, for all the talk of the personal bond between
mistress and maid, understood only too clearly the cold hard economics
of their employment relation.[94] If servants were successful in their
attempts to shorten their working days or gain more rest time, employers
would lose out on returns from such an investment. Jessie Stephen
acknowledged this, evenly stating that mistresses had their own 'business' to 'look after', 'and no one can ... blame them', yet the servant
likewise needed to 'become fully awake to her own interests'.[95] Although
the union had invited sympathetic mistresses to attend its early meetings,
Kathlyn Oliver was also clear that 'we have never attempted to deny the
fact that the Domestic Workers' Union is to benefit the *workers*. We think
employers are quite able to guard their own interests.'[96] Jessie Stephen
likewise told the audience at a founding meeting of the Scottish Federation of Domestic Workers, composed of both maids and mistresses, that
'she was out to preach the divine doctrine of discontent, and if there were
any there who were content to put up with the present conditions she
asked them to leave the meeting'. [97]

Servants were also quick to point out the hypocrisy of those claiming to
fight for women's emancipation while benefitting from the exploitation of
women workers in their own homes.[98] Despite the support offered by the
editor of the *Common Cause*, some of them still felt excluded from the
vision of emancipation promoted by the suffrage movement. One pseudonymous servant wrote to that paper of how: 'it is one thing to plead
equality in pamphlets and from the platform, but we want it in reality and
not as an idea only. We don't want mistresses, saying, "who is that man
you spoke to just now? Why have you had bacon for breakfast instead of
butter?" We want to be treated like free human beings and not as slavish
economic units.'[99] Grace Neal likewise subverted feminist rhetoric to
argue for greater attention to the rights of domestic workers. 'We so often

---

[94] *Common Cause* 30 Nov. 1911, p. 602. See also *Woman Worker* 24 Nov. 1909, p. 475.
[95] *Glasgow Herald* 24 Sept. 1913, p. 5.
[96] *Woman Worker* 13 April 1910, p. 880; 4 May 1910, pp. 942–943.
[97] *Glasgow Herald* 16 Oct. 1913, p. 10.
[98] *Common Cause* 9 Nov. 1911, p. 543. The editor of the *Common Cause*, surveying the
correspondence that took place in their paper during 1911, also commented how 'It is
curious to notice how many women who see the need for political enfranchisement do
not extend their sympathy to this deeper and more elementary need for social and
domestic enfranchisement'; *Common Cause* 4 Jan. 1912, pp. 672–673.
[99] *Common Cause* 9 Nov. 1911, p. 543.

hear it said', she wrote in the *Common Cause*, 'that women are anxious to leave the home but of equal importance to this movement are the conditions still imposed on domestics'.[100]

A Job like Any Other?

An insistence upon household labour as real work was at the centre of the DWU's strategy to be taken seriously. Kathlyn Oliver's 1911 pamphlet *Domestic Service and Citizenship* drew upon a suffrage discourse of women's work as the basis for enfranchisement, while at the same time arguing against those feminists who conceived of 'housework as *menial work*':

Cleaning, rightly understood, is a necessary and therefore honourable occupation and unless we are prepared to deny the necessity of clean well-kept homes, there really is no more important work than housework. The health of our national life is dependent on our home life.[101]

This gestured to that other current of feminist thought, which argued for domestic work to be revalued rather than renounced altogether. From this perspective it was possible to imagine that service could be brought up to date and made more like other kinds of waged work. Catherine Webb of the Women's Industrial Council, for example, concluded in 1903 that that there was nothing 'inherently' wrong with domestic service; '[h]ousework *per se* is not found to be distasteful to girls' and it could therefore be redeemed if the 'stigma of inferiority' was removed.[102] One common solution to the servant problem put forward in the feminist press was, therefore, to introduce formal training and qualifications in the hope that this would transform service into a highly skilled, more respected, and therefore better paid and more popular, occupation. A comparison was often made with nursing, a once-despised sphere of female labour that had been elevated by establishing training schools and professional qualifications.[103]

The Women's Industrial Council (WIC), founded in 1894 to investigate and ameliorate the conditions of industrial women workers, was a leading voice in calling for improved training for domestic servants. A research and campaigning organisation rather than a trade union, it

---

[100] *Common Cause* 19 Oct. 1911, p. 484.
[101] Oliver, *Domestic Servants and Citizenship*, pp. 14–15.
[102] Catherine Webb, 'An Unpopular Industry', *Nineteenth Century*, 53 (June 1903), 989–1001, p. 1000.
[103] *Common Cause* 19 Jan. 1911, p. 675; 24 Aug. 1911, p. 349; 19 Oct. 1911, p. 484; *Women's Industrial News* March 1900, pp. 153–155.

was led by women who nevertheless had strong links to the labour movement as well as various suffrage organisations.[104] Although its driving force, Clementina Black, was from a wealthy middle-class family, the WIC had been co-founded by Amie Hicks, a working-class trade unionist, member of the Social Democratic Federation and a long-standing supporter of women's suffrage. Her daughter, Frances Hicks, was also active in the organisation. Catherine Webb, secretary for the WIC from 1895 to 1902 in addition to taking a leading role in the Women's Co-operative Guild, also came from a working-class background. Webb studied at Morley College, and was made a member of its council in 1915, so it is likely that she knew its principal Mary Sheepshanks and perhaps even Sheepshanks' cook general, Kathlyn Oliver.[105]

The WIC worked to improve training for all kinds of industrial women workers, and it is noteworthy that it included domestic service within this remit.[106] Throughout its existence it consistently argued that the best way to 'make domestic service more popular and more in accordance with modern ideas' was to stop treating servants like 'serfs' and instead to raise their status by turning them into qualified skilled workers.[107] This was the main recommendation of its 1916 Report, based upon on a large survey of both domestic servants and mistresses, the research for which had been carried out before the outbreak of war.[108] Their interest in domestic service had begun much earlier. In 1898 the WIC founded the Association of Trained Charwomen, which offered training 'in all

---

[104] Ellen Mappen, *Helping Women at Work: The Women's Industrial Council, 1889–1914* (London: Hutchinson, 1985), pp. 11–13. See also Carol Dyhouse, *Feminism and the Family 1880–1939* (Oxford: Basil Blackwell, 1989), pp. 59–60; Krista Cowman, *Mrs Brown Is a Man and a Brother: Women in Merseyside's Political Organisations, 1890–1920* (Liverpool: Liverpool University Press, 2004), pp. 32–39.

[105] Mappen, *Helping Women at Work*, pp. 13–18; Karen Hunt, *Equivocal Feminists: The Social Democratic Federation and the Woman Question 1884–1911* (Cambridge: Cambridge University Press, 1996), pp. 153–157; June Hannam, 'Hicks, Amelia Jane [Amie] (1839–1917), Socialist and Trade Unionist', in *Oxford Dictionary of National Biography*, online edn. (Oxford University Press, 2004); Gillian Scott, 'Webb, Catherine (1859–1947), Co-operative Movement Activist and Writer', in *Oxford Dictionary of National Biography*. Amie and Frances Hicks should not be confused with another mother and daughter political duo, Lillian and Amy Hicks, who were members of the Women's Freedom League; Claire Eustance, '"Daring to Be Free": The Evolution of Women's Political Identities in the Women's Freedom League 1907–1930', PhD thesis, University of York (1993), p. 441.

[106] For example, *Women's Industrial News* Dec. 1902, pp. 333–340; March 1904, pp. 413–420.

[107] *Women's Industrial News* March 1900, pp. 153–155; June 1903, p. 378; Dec. 1907, p. 673.

[108] Butler, *Domestic Service*.

branches of house cleaning and plain cooking' in return for guaranteed rates of pay (2s. 6d. per day with food or 3s. 6d. without) and a maximum working day of ten hours.[109] By March 1907 this Association had seventy-five regular members and a further 139 women registered on their supplementary list, and in 1910 alone it found employment for 1,704 charwomen.[110] By 1912, however, it was struggling due to a lack of publicity and the difficulty of competing with Labour Exchanges that did not establish any minimum standard of wages.[111]

Domestic economy had been a compulsory subject (for girls) in all government-funded elementary schools since 1878, but the WIC maintained that state provision needed to be greatly expanded and conceived of as a form of industrial training for domestic servants.[112] In 1900 Mrs Percy Bunting published an article in the organisation's paper, the *Women's Industrial News*, recommending that all county councils offer a course with an examination which, if passed, would secure the student a certificate that could become a 'Hall mark' of skilled domestic servants.[113] When the WIC carried out a 'systematic inquiry' into the causes of the servant problem in 1903, many of the forty-four mistresses to whom questionnaires were sent believed that formal training was 'a prime necessity in restoring dignity to the industry'. Catherine Webb's report on the inquiry specified that scholarships and apprenticeships were needed to ensure that such technical education was affordable to 'the servant class'.[114] In 1904 Grace Oakeshott, honorary secretary of the WIC's Technical Training Committee, lobbied the London County Council's Technical Training Board to expand its evening, afternoon and day schools in domestic economy. She optimistically noted that their classes had already 'done much to raise the character of Domestic Service ... shown that this is an occupation demanding skill, intelligence and training'. From this point onwards the WIC expanded their focus to include 'the training of working-class girls as children's nurses'. In

---

[109] *Women's Industrial News* June 1898, p. 49; TWL, 'Circular for "The Association of Trained Charwomen"' (n.d.), Women's Industrial Council Letters Book, p. 10, WIC/D/3. The ATC was advertised frequently, with the same wage rates in place until at least 1906; *Women's Industrial News* March 1900, n.p.; March 1903, n.p.; Feb. 1905, n.p.; March 1906, n.p. In 1905 a further hourly rate was advertised: 6d. for the first hour and 4d. for further hours; Feb. 1905, n.p.; March 1906, n.p.

[110] *Women's Industrial News* March 1907, p. 618.

[111] *Common Cause* 29 Feb. 1912, p. 808.

[112] June Purvis, 'Domestic Subjects since 1870', in Ivor Goodson (ed.), *Social Histories of the Secondary Curriculum: Subjects for Study* (Lewes: Falmer Press, 1985), 145–176, pp. 149–151.

[113] *Women's Industrial News* March 1900, pp. 153–155.

[114] Catherine Webb, 'An Unpopular Industry', pp. 995, 998.

1909 it raised funds to pay the fees for two or three girls to be trained in some of London's day nurseries, in the hope that this would create a precedent for future scholarships funded by the London County Council.[115] The following year Clementina Black and Elsie M. Zimmern pursued an even more ambitious plan: setting up a day nursery in Hackney, East London, which finally opened in the summer of 1911. The aim was to provide working-class mothers with affordable childcare, while also training nursemaids on the job, although in the end the fees of £26 a year would have prohibited poorer students from applying.[116] This project was approvingly reported on in both the *Vote* and the *Common Cause*.[117]

Feminist historians have criticised the imposition of domestic economy upon students in state elementary schools, for 'wasting girls' time' and limiting the educational horizons of working-class women.[118] Similar criticism could be made of the training advocated by the WIC. Although social reformers and suffrage supporters maintained that it would solve the 'servant problem' from the servant's point of view, in that highly skilled workers would be able to demand better pay and conditions, some of them also clearly saw it as a solution to their own problem as mistresses in need of more competent domestic workers. It was a strategy that would ensure the continuation of a 'servant class'.[119] In this they were no different from the many conservative voices arguing that working-class girls should be compelled to have more training in domestic economy.[120] In particular, there was a growing unease amongst middle-class women about handing over the care of their children to untrained nurse-maids who, it was feared, might contaminate their offspring with bad habits.

At least some working-class women were aware of, not to mention irritated by, the disingenuous motives of the most enthusiastic advocates

---

[115] *Women's Industrial News* March 1904, pp. 413–420; Dec. 1908, pp. 92–94; April 1909, p. 6.

[116] *Women's Industrial News* April 1910, pp. 4–8; Oct. 1910, pp. 13–14; April 1911, p. 78; June 1911, pp. 93–95; Oct. 1911, p. 137.

[117] *Vote* 4 June 1910, p. 65; *Common Cause* 30 March 1911, pp. 833–834.

[118] Carol Dyhouse, *Girls Growing Up in Late Victorian and Edwardian England* (Abingdon: Routledge, 2012 [first published 1981]), chapter 3; Purvis, 'Domestic Subjects since 1870', pp. 145, 170; Dena Attar, *Wasting Girls' Time: The History and Politics of Home Economics* (London: Virago, 1990); Jane Martin, *Women and the Politics of Schooling in Victorian and Edwardian England* (London: Leicester University Press, 1999), pp. 81–82.

[119] Webb, 'An Unpopular Industry', p. 998; *Women's Industrial News* March 1900, pp. 153–155.

[120] For conservative support for training, Dyhouse, *Girls Growing Up*, pp. 82–83; Attar, *Wasting Girls' Time*, pp. 45–46.

of domestic training. At the National Conference on Industrial Training of Women and Girls in London in 1908, which gave over an entire afternoon to discussing training for children's nurses, the pioneering woman medical doctor Jane Walker complained that nurse-maids needed to be taught to take more care of their personal hygiene given that 'the relation between a nurse and a child, was a peculiarly sensitive one'. In response, a Mrs Gasson from the Women's Co-operative Guild politely reminded the conference 'that they were asking the working class, the class who are struggling for daily bread, to make a certain amount of self-sacrifice in order that their girls should be trained'. She thought it was a shame that there were fewer than six working-class women present at the conference, and reminded her middle-class audience how difficult it was for working people to practice personal hygiene when they were forced to live in insanitary conditions. A Mrs Knight, who described herself as a working woman from West Ham (London), was even more direct, protesting 'against the general idea of the daughters of the working class being specially trained for the purpose of looking after the children of the well-to-do ... What they had to do was alter the system so that the people who created the wealth of the country had proper leisure and opportunities of looking after their own children.'[121]

Nevertheless, the demand for better training could also have more radical implications. Not only did it treat domestic work as more akin to other kinds of skilled manual labour, it also challenged the notion that all women were naturally good at housework and that this was their true and proper role. The WIC complained of how, in periods of economic recession, both local government and middle-class people in general excused themselves from providing adequate relief for unemployed women on the basis that surely they could easily find work in service. In reality, they insisted, 'a jute worker cannot suddenly be transformed into a parlourmaid, or a South London widow, whose children depend on her, be transported to a situation of housemaid in Hampstead'.[122] Moreover, to argue that service should be made more like other forms of work was to open up the possibility of bringing it under the aegis of the labour laws that were increasingly regulating other kinds of manual labour. Esther Longhurst, a regular columnist in the *Woman Worker*, put forward the idea of a government training college for girls of sixteen to nineteen, offering a two-year course with a government diploma on completion. She went on to suggest that 'the employer must be obliged ... to treat her employee properly. We have been able to limit the hours of

---

[121] *Women's Industrial News* Dec. 1908, pp. 77–94.
[122] *Women's Industrial News* Dec. 1907, p. 673; Dec. 1905, pp. 472–478.

the factory workers ... Surely it is not, therefore, impossible to legislate for the domestic worker.'[123] Perhaps this accounts for why, although the DWU saw the need for higher wages and more rights at work as the priority, they also gave their general support to improved training in order to create a workforce of skilled domestic servants.[124]

The question of how far the government ought to intervene in the workplace of the home came to the fore once again when Lloyd George, Chancellor of the Exchequer, proposed to include servants in the National Health Insurance scheme of 1911. Servants, like any other worker, would be required to contribute a portion of their wages in order to qualify for sick pay; while mistresses, like any other employer, would have to match the contributions of each servant in their household.[125] Resistance to this so-called 'servant tax' soon emerged, with some opposed in principle to government intervention in the private sphere. The *Mirror* reported that thousands of mistresses opposed 'dictatorial interference between mistress and maids and this intrusion by the State on the sanctity of our very kitchens'. According to the *Mirror*, by compelling employers to pay for state insurance rather than trusting them to look after their sick servants themselves, the Bill undermined the 'kindly feeling between mistresses and maids' and eroded the maternal principles upon which the servant–employer relationship was supposedly founded.[126]

Given the conservative tenor of much of the opposition, it is perhaps surprising to find that the 'servant tax' was also criticised, at least initially, by several women's labour and suffrage organisations, including the DWU. The Women's Trade Union League, the National Federation of Women Workers, the Women's Industrial Council, the Women's Co-operative Guild, the Women's Labour League and the Anti-Sweating League formed a deputation to Lloyd George on 16 June 1911 in which they raised a number of concerns.[127] In July the NFWW held a

---

[123] *Woman Worker* 7 April 1909. See also *Woman Worker* 29 Sept. 1909, p. 396; 5 Jan. 1910, p. 602.

[124] Jessie Stephen continued to push for better training after the First World War; TUC, Press Cuttings, *Daily News* 9 April 1919, Box 21, Reel 10, 504e/3; *Brighton Herald* 28 June 1919, Box 21, Reel 10, 504e/5.

[125] Unemployment Insurance formed Part 2 of what became the National Insurance Act; Pat Thane, 'The Making of National Insurance, 1911', *The Journal of Poverty and Social Justice*, 19:3 (Oct. 2011), 211–219, p. 216. For the most detailed account of the inclusion of servants in the National Insurance Bill, see W. J. Braithwaite, *Lloyd George's Ambulance Wagon* (London: Methuen, 1957).

[126] *Mirror* 30 Nov. 1911, p. 3.

[127] Braithwaite, *Lloyd George's Ambulance Wagon*, pp. 232–243. Braithwaite incorrectly claimed that 'we heard nothing from the agitators or suffragettes' regarding women's

demonstration in Trafalgar Square against 'the existing form' of the National Insurance Bill.[128] That same month a protest meeting was organised by the National Industrial and Professional Suffrage Society, the Manchester Women's Trades Council, the Lancashire and Cheshire Women's Textile Workers' Representation Committee, the Women's Freedom League, the Fabian Women's Group, the DWU and the Constitutional Society for Women's Suffrage.[129] Criticism was also raised at the half-yearly meeting of the Council of the NUWSS, in the pages of the *Common Cause* and in numerous editorials and articles by Frederick and Emmeline Pethick-Lawrence in *Votes for Women*.[130] These women's organisations were critical of a number of aspects of the Bill: the way it discriminated against married women, the unfair cost of contributions that it placed upon the lowest paid women workers, and, especially, its impact on servants. As I discussed in Chapter 2, the Suffrage Atelier even produced a series of postcards that condemned the 'servant tax' on the principle of 'no taxation without representation', and pointed out that if the government could interfere in the feminine sphere of the home, then women ought to have a say in the laws that affected them.

One of the main objections was to the proposed arrangements for servants' sick pay. Lloyd George had worked on the assumption that in small households where there was only one servant (about 60 per cent of servant-employing homes by his calculation) it was common practice to dismiss the servant when she became ill.[131] This was not an unreasonable assumption, since most employers could not afford to continue to pay for their sick servant's board and lodging in addition to the labour they would have to buy in as cover. Even a relatively wealthy family such as the Blathwayts were keen to unburden themselves of servants with health problems that lasted longer than a couple of weeks.[132] The National Insurance Bill initially proposed that sick pay would be paid only to

---

insurance, perhaps failing to understand that many of the 'advanced leaders' of the women's labour organisations mentioned above were also active in the various suffrage societies; pp. 234–235. For the position of the Women's Co-operative Guild, see Gillian Scott, 'The Women's Co-operative Guild and Suffrage', in Boussahba-Bravard (ed.), *Suffrage Outside Suffragism*, 132–156, pp. 141–145.

[128] *Common Cause* 13 July 1911, pp. 252–253.
[129] *Manchester Guardian* 14 July 1911, p. 6; 24 July 1911, p. 3.
[130] *Manchester Guardian* 8 July 1911, p. 6; *Common Cause* 15 June 1911, p. 179; 13 July 1911, pp. 252–253; *Votes for Women* 12 May 1911, pp. 521–522; 19 May 1911, p. 542; 16 June 1911, p. 608; 23 June 1911, p. 624; 30 June 1911, p. 638; 14 July 1911, p. 670; 21 July 1911, p. 702; 11 Aug. 1911, pp. 729–731; 15 Sept. 1911, p. 794; 20 Oct. 1911, p. 42; 27 Oct. 1911, p. 52; 2 Nov. 1911, p. 67; 10 Nov. 1911, pp. 81–82.
[131] Braithwaite, *Lloyd George's Ambulance Wagon*, pp. 252–254.
[132] *Freewoman* 7 Dec. 1911, pp. 42–44; Horn, *The Rise and Fall of the Victorian Servant*, pp. 181–182.

workers *not* in receipt of board and lodgings, in the belief that this would apply to the majority of servants who needed to claim. This arrangement was criticised first because the payment of 7s. 6d. was wholly inadequate compensation for loss of board, lodgings and earnings, and second because it seemed to encourage mistresses to dismiss servants who they otherwise might have allowed to stay on with full pay for short periods of sickness.[133]

By November, Lloyd George had added a new clause to the Bill which gave mistresses the option of continuing to pay their servants' full wages for up to six weeks of illness, in which case their weekly contribution was reduced to 2½d., and their servant's lowered to 2d. If the mistress did not legally agree to this arrangement in advance, then the normal contributions of 3d. each would be made, and servants would now be eligible for sick pay of 7s. 6d. per week for the first twenty-six weeks of illness even if they continued to receive board and lodgings (but not full wages) from their employers.[134] Following this amendment, many withdrew their opposition to the 'servant tax'. The *Common Cause* published an article explaining the new clauses and subsequently gave its editorial support to the revised Bill. Radical suffragists and labour activists Eva Gore Booth and Esther Roper concluded that the Bill had been reformed to such an extent that it was better to fight to improve it further rather than resist it altogether. And the editors of the *Freewoman* now also publicly declared themselves in favour of National Health Insurance. The editors of *Votes for Women* remained sceptical, however, insisting that the Bill still discriminated against women to the advantage of male workers. The Women's Freedom League continued to oppose National Insurance after the Act had been passed, not because they were against state insurance or intervention between mistress and maid, but on the basis that, like the census which they also opposed, it constituted 'government without consent' imposed upon disenfranchised women.[135]

Opposition culminated in a 'monster meeting' at the Royal Albert Hall on 29 November 1911. The *Mirror* reported that the Hall was packed with 12,000 women, with a further 10,000 gathered outside. One of the

---

[133] *Manchester Guardian* 8 July 1911, p. 6; *Common Cause* 30 Nov. 1911, p. 588.
[134] *Common Cause* 23 Nov. 1911, pp. 569–570.
[135] *Common Cause* 30 Nov. 1911, p. 588; 7 Dec. 1911, p. 610; *Manchester Guardian* 30 Nov. 1911, pp. 3, 10; *Freewoman* 7 Dec. 1911, pp. 42–44; *Votes for Women* 2 Nov. 1911, p. 67; 10 Nov. 1911, pp. 81–82; *Vote* 6 July 1912, p. 188; Eustance, '"Daring to Be Free"', pp. 179–180; Laura E. Nym Mayhall, *The Militant Suffrage Movement: Citizenship and Resistance in Britain, 1860–1930* (Oxford: Oxford University Press, 2003), p. 112.

main speakers was Lady Desart (Ellen Cuffe), an Anglo Irish aristocrat and opponent of women's suffrage.[136] According to the *Manchester Guardian*, her speech did not acknowledge the recent concessions and instead opposed the Bill on principle, claiming that 'self-respecting servants did not want any state dole' and that insurance would merely set class against class and destroy the 'beautiful harmony' between mistress and maid.[137] Lady Desart's politics could not have been further from those of the socialist feminists heading up the DWU, and yet there, sitting beside her on the platform, was Grace Neal. Within just over a year of its formation, the agitation around the 'servant tax' had propelled this small union into the pages of the national press, placed its General Secretary in front of enormous audiences and even led to an invitation to join the servants' deputation to Lloyd George.[138] It must have been hard to turn down the opportunity for so much publicity despite the rather unlikely alliances it entailed, and this probably partly accounts for the union's continued involvement even after many leading feminists had accepted the amended Bill.

Grace Neal used her platform to attack domestic service more generally. 'The Bill would do nothing to improve the conditions of domestic servants, "many of whom"', she said, "are working for the sweating wage of a penny an hour."' She also argued that servants wanted '"not a national interference Bill but a compulsory character Bill"', drawing attention to another of the union's key demands. Grace Neal may have even stirred up divisions between the employers and the servants at the Albert Hall meeting, despite the claims of more conservative organisers that its moving spirit was one of unity. While the *Mirror* claimed that 'when they [the servants] were reminded how mistresses look after their servants in sickness they cheered and cheered again', the more sceptical *Manchester Guardian* insisted that 'some of the claims made for mistresses roused cries of opposition'. There are certainly no reports of Grace Neal giving in to the sentimental rhetoric of the 'kindly... mutual affection that existed between mistress and maid'.[139] Her opposition to

---

[136] Senia Pašeta, 'Cuffe [née Bischoffsheim], Ellen Odette, Countess of Desart (1857–1933), Philanthropist and Politician', in *Oxford Dictionary of National Biography*.

[137] *Manchester Guardian* 30 Nov. 1911, p. 10.

[138] The DWU demanded an audience with Lloyd George, although when they were invited to join the servants' deputation Grace Neal declined the offer; *Manchester Guardian* 30 Nov. 1911, p. 10.

[139] *Mirror* 30 Nov. 1911, p. 3; *Manchester Guardian* 14 July 1911; 30 Nov. 1911, p. 10.

the Bill rather derived from a particularly uncompromising radicalism, shared by some others in the labour movement, which viewed National Insurance as a capitalist compromise funded by workers' contributions rather than progressive taxation.[140]

A year after the agitation had begun, and once the Bill had become an Act, women such as Lady Desart continued to oppose it, forming the Insurance Tax Resisters' Defence Association.[141] Rebecca West wrote scornfully of such 'peeresses' in the *Daily Herald*, contrasting her encounter with these aristocratic law-breakers to her interview with the General Secretary of the DWU in June 1912.

REBECCA WEST: '"Do you approve of the Insurance Act as it applies to servants?"
GRACE NEAL: "I disapprove of the Act altogether ... I am a socialist. How could I approve of a contributory scheme?"

Ultimately the DWU accepted the amended version of the 'servant tax', imperfect though it was. 'We are going to take the half-loaf first, get the whole afterwards', Grace Neal told Rebecca West.[142] Neal became one of the 159 members appointed to the Advisory Committee which would be consulted on future alterations to the Act, and the union was approved as a Society through which servants could arrange for their payments and access their benefits.[143]

Grace Neal concluded in her interview with Rebecca West that '"If there is going to be an Insurance Act we domestic workers must be included. Our industry must be recognised like any other."'[144] This question of whether domestic service was or could be treated as comparable to other forms of work was returned to throughout this debate on National Insurance. The *Common Cause* approved of the amended Bill on the basis that it now treated servants the same other workers.[145] The editors of the *Freewoman* similarly welcomed 'any expedient which loosens the personal hold of mistress over maid, which will make it clear to the girls of the coming generation that they are to seek in domestic service just so much honour as comes from any other craft'.[146] That

---

[140] Pat Thane, 'The Working Class and State "Welfare" in Britain, 1880–1914', *Historical Journal*, 27:4 (1984), 877–900, pp. 896–897; Pat Thane, 'The Making of National Insurance, 1911', pp. 213–214.
[141] Pašeta, 'Cuffe'.
[142] Rebecca West, *Daily Herald* 18 June 1912, in Marcus, *The Young Rebecca*, pp. 353–356.
[143] *Manchester Guardian* 10 April 1912, p. 3; 25 June 1912, p. 9.
[144] Rebecca West, *Daily Herald* 18 June 1912, in Marcus, *The Young Rebecca*, pp. 353–356.
[145] *Common Cause* 30 Nov. 1911, p. 588.
[146] *Freewoman* 7 Dec. 1911, pp. 42–44. See also 29 Feb. 1912, pp. 296–297.

servants were included in the Act at all was significant, given that they had thus far been excluded from almost all labour legislation.[147]

However, few feminists found it possible to argue this consistently. Although the editors of the *Freewoman* wanted, in the case of National Health Insurance, for servants to be treated like other workers, they also wholly undermined this argument when they claimed elsewhere in their newspaper that housework was inherently lower grade work. Even those who argued most forcefully for domestic service to be raised to the level of industrial work found themselves coming up against the contradictions of this position. Despite the WIC's long-standing commitment to treating service as equal to other forms of women's work, the 1916 Report opposed suggestions made by the DWU for a national standard of wages. It claimed that domestic work was not 'definite' enough, and that it was too difficult to develop 'a standard of efficiency' for work that 'produces utilities and not commodities'.[148] The DWU's vision of future domestic service as entirely rationalised along the lines of industrial labour, in fact, proposed to transform it out of existence. The best course of action, maintained Kathlyn Oliver, was for the living-in system to be abolished in favour of the state employment or 'nationalisation' of domestic workers.[149] Grace Neal formulated a 'scheme for the establishment of hostels for working-women, whence the ordinary domestic could go to her work each day as does the typist, the shop girl or any other worker. Payment by the hour would be the rule' and servants would have their own domestic needs catered for by well-paid workers: 'Each hostel would have its own domestic staff so that the daily servant would not have several hours of drudgery before leaving for her work.'[150] Live-in domestic service would no longer exist.

Despite the best efforts of the DWU to maintain that the solution to the servant problem lay in the treatment of domestic work as a job like any other, it was far harder to articulate servants' *experience* of exploitation in these terms. Domestic work exceeded the parameters of an industrial model of labour, not only in refusing to be contained within a clearly delineated working day, but also because of how it seemed to seep into all aspects of the servants' existence. The language maids used to describe the frustrations of always being on call is in itself telling. More

---

[147] Einat Albin, 'From "Domestic Servant" to "Domestic Worker"', in J. Fudge, S. McCrystal and K. Sankaran (eds.), *Challenging the Legal Boundaries of Work Regulation* (London: Hart Publishing, 2012), 231–250. The only exception is the Apprentices and Servants Act (1851).

[148] Butler, *Domestic Service*, pp. 60, 82.

[149] Oliver, *Domestic Servants and Citizenship*, p. 18.

[150] TUC, Press Cuttings, *Weekly Dispatch* 5 Jan. 1913, Box 25, Reel 12, 609/21.

than one servant complained that they did 'not have half an hour to call their own'.[151] The problems of the 'living-in' system signalled servants' lack of space to express themselves independently of their work. Grace Neal pointed out that domestic work

brings with it so many worries that cannot occur when minding a loo, packing cornflour, or stitching trousers. In each of these mentioned trades the worker can, at a given time, put it all away and get home, outside of all cares of work. Not so the domestic.[152]

It was also almost impossible to have autonomy *over* their work, or to do it very well without their capability being further exploited. Jessie Stephen, for example, put in extra work in her post as a cook general 'cleaning all the black lead off all the steel parts of the kitchen range making them shine as they did when the range was first put in'. She was proud of her ability to make the otherwise dreary kitchen appear 'very much brighter', which helped her feel closer to her mother, who 'had the same ideas about keeping brasses and steel shining'. Her employer, Mrs Harvey, 'delighted with … how much nicer the whole place looked', had already recognised Stephen's exceptional competence, fired the second servant to save money and made Jessie responsible for the whole house with only a small increase in her wages.[153]

Servants often described domestic work as colonising one's entire existence, leading to a 'dwarfing' of their spiritual and mental lives. Many maids declared that they wanted 'not only their bodies fed but also their minds', and Kathlyn Oliver complained that too many mistresses failed to regard their servants 'as an intelligent being with a mind and a soul to cultivate and not merely a machine'.[154] Service, domestic workers claimed, prevented them from fulfilling their capacities as human beings. 'A Comrade' wishing the DWU 'every success' wrote of how she had worked as a maid for twelve years, during which time she 'never knew what an oratorio, grand opera, or scientific lecture was'. Having left service for factory work, she now had her evenings and weekends free to sing in a choir, ramble on the moorlands and 'enjoy the glory of a caravan holiday'.[155] Many servants agreed with the 'Greenwich domestic' who claimed that 'domestic service is simply stagnation to the intelligent mind'. This servant of twenty years' standing played on the double meaning of the term 'character' (as both employment reference and

[151] *Woman Worker* 2 June 1909, p. 518; *Glasgow Herald* 3 Oct. 1913, p. 5.
[152] *Common Cause* 23 Nov. 1911, p. 578.
[153] Stephen, 'Submission Is for Slaves', pp. 26–27.
[154] *Woman Worker* 2 June 1909, p. 518; 14 July 1909, p. 30; 25 Aug. 1909, p. 182.
[155] *Woman Worker* 12 Jan. 1910, p. 626.

personhood) to describe the manner in which many felt their work to
have eroded their very self: 'We want the legislature to come to our aid',
she explained in the *Common Cause*, 'so that we can retain our own
characters rather than being "given" one by one whose own will not bare
inspection very often'.[156]

'I think there is no other work which so crushes the soul out of
everyone and tends to make them worms indeed', Kathlyn Oliver wrote,
while simultaneously exhorting her fellow workers to take pride in such
work.[157] Oliver's indictment of domestic labour at times verged on the
self-loathing. She maintained that it was 'deadening and brutalising
work', causing 'anaemia, nervousness, ugliness and ill temper, prostitution, suicide and insanity'.[158] The problem turned again on the nature of
the work itself, and the fact that servants were employed to perform work
which their middle-class employers felt to be an 'unrefined, unpleasant
business'.[159] It was therefore hard even for the DWU to deny the fact that
only women with no other options would ever take it up.[160] By December 1910, about a year and a half after she had initiated the idea of a
union, Oliver had become partly disillusioned with servants' self-
organisation. The 'separated and isolated condition caused by the
living-in system' was, she felt, an almost insurmountable 'difficulty'
when considered alongside the fierce opposition from employers. She
now preferred to 'advocate the parliamentary vote as the best means of
improving the conditions of domestic labour'.[161] Oliver once again
pointed to a less tangible problem with service: the commonly held belief
that the servant was somehow inherently beneath the woman she served:

I say that if a girl cannot be a domestic worker and a lady at the same time, there is
something demoralising in the *work*, for money does not make a lady or a position
either, and if there is anything in the nature of domestic work which renders it
impossible for a girl or woman to be cultured and refined, then it is immoral for
any woman to employ another to do this work.

Here Oliver was discussing class differences between women, but she
was also referring to differing conceptions of womanhood (what it meant
for a woman to be 'cultured' and 'refined' regardless of income or status)
and the wider question of whether the identity of the servant could be

[156] *Common Cause* 9 Nov. 1911, p. 543; 28 Sept. 1911, p. 432.
[157] *Woman Worker* 20 Oct. 1909, p. 382; TUC, Press Cuttings, *Labour Leader* 20 May
1910, Box 25, Reel 12, 609/11.
[158] *Common Cause* 23 Nov. 1911, pp. 578–579.
[159] *Common Cause* 7 Dec. 1911, p. 610.
[160] *Woman Worker* 20 Oct. 1909, p. 382; Oliver, *Domestic Servants and Citizenship*, p. 14.
[161] *Labour Leader* 2 Dec. 1910, p. 765.

reconciled with that of the emancipated woman. The leaders of the DWU were familiar with, and indeed participants in, such discussions. The impossibility of reconciling the life of the average servant with the suffrage movement's vision of fulfilled womanhood made the union's task of generating pride in its members especially challenging. The very feminist politics that had spurred on the formation of the DWU, at the same time foreclosed the possibility of mobilising servants as both militant and modern women workers and agents of their own liberation.

6 Servants and Co-operative Housekeeping

In September 1910 the *Daily Mail* reported on a co-operative housekeeping colony, newly established by Alice Melvin. It was described as a garden village 'where tenants will be able to dispense with private servants' and enjoy a communal dining hall, public laundry and 'all the most modern labour-saving devices heating, hot water and so on'.[1] Melvin was keen to advertise this, and co-operative housekeeping more generally, as a solution to the 'servant problem', a boon for both mistresses and domestic workers. This did not mean an end to domestic service altogether. The newly organised housework would still be carried out by servants, but they would be employed by the community rather than individual mistresses. Various schemes for the collectivisation of domestic labour – most commonly referred to as 'co-operative housekeeping' – emerged in this period. With striking frequency advocates from a range of perspectives framed co-operative housekeeping as a solution to the 'ever recurring domestic servant problem'.[2] Yet histories of co-operative living have never before examined how servants experienced the new organisation of housework.

Co-operative housekeeping has caught the attention of only a small number of historians of 'first wave' feminism, perhaps because it was only ever fully endorsed by a minority of activists.[3] It was, however, often

---

[1] *Daily Mail* 1 Sept. 1910, p. 9.
[2] Listed as one of the key 'Objects' of Brent Garden Village; *Daily Mail* 7 Dec. 1911, p. 2.
[3] Carol Dyhouse, *Feminism and the Family in England 1880–1939* (Oxford: Basil Blackwell, 1989), pp. 111–133; Gillian Scott, *Feminism and the Politics of Working Women: The Women's Co-operative Guild, 1880s to the Second World War* (London: University College London Press, 1998), pp. 73–74; Sheila Rowbotham, *Dreamers of a New Day: Women Who Invented the Twentieth Century* (London: Verso, 2011), chapter 6.
Most historiography on co-operative housekeeping has tended instead to situate it within a history of architecture and social housing; Lynn F. Pearson, *The Architectural and Social History of Co-operative Living* (Basingstoke: Macmillan Press, 1988); Alison Ravetz, *Council Housing and Culture: The History of a Social Experiment* (London: Routledge, 2001). Investigations into working women's campaigns for the reform of housework have been situated within labour movement and socialist history rather than

discussed in both the feminist and mainstream press, and thus became familiar to large numbers of women, especially as a possible solution to the 'servant problem'. The origins of co-operative housekeeping can be traced back to Owenite socialist communities of the 1840s, where the collectivisation of household labour was part of a wider commitment to women's emancipation.[4] Experiments in communal living continued among socialists and advocates of the 'simple life' such as William Morris and Edward Carpenter in the second half of the nineteenth century, though without always fully interrogating the gendered power dynamics of household labour.[5] From the late nineteenth century onwards, feminists once again began to consider how collectivisation might work to free women from 'domestic drudgery'. Such projects acquired a new practical impetus as ever-larger numbers of single middle-class women began to leave their family homes to enter professional and clerical jobs in the cities. The suffrage movement highlighted the drastic shortage of suitable accommodation for this class of woman worker, as well as the difficulties of having to undertake one's own housework at the end of a busy day at the office. It called for innovative solutions in housebuilding and the reorganisation of domestic labour, with emphasis increasingly placed upon the socialisation of housework rather than communal living more generally.

This chapter uncovers the working conditions and organisation of domestic service in feminist-inspired plans for co-operative housekeeping. It examines blueprints put forward by Jane Hume Clapperton and Clementina Black, alongside schemes that were put into practice in Henrietta Barnett's Waterlow Court and Alice Melvin's Brent Garden Village. By focusing on the degree to which the boom in co-operative housekeeping was framed by the 'servant problem', I trace previously unrecognised connections between the housing schemes of middle-class feminists and the campaigns for public facilities spearheaded by the Women's Co-operative Guild, the East London Federation of the Suffragettes and the Women's Labour League. These working-class campaigns were informed not only by a critique of conditions endured by unwaged

the history of the women's movement; see Alistair Thomson, '"Domestic Drudgery Will Be a Thing of the Past": Co-operative Women and the Reform of Housework', in Stephen Yeo (ed.), *New Views of Co-operation* (London: Routledge, 1988), 108–127; Christine Collette, *For Labour and for Women: The Women's Labour League, 1906–1918* (Manchester: Manchester University Press, 1989), pp. 23, 161–162.

[4] Barbara Taylor, *Eve and the New Jerusalem: Socialism and Feminism in the Nineteenth Century* (London: Virago, 1983).

[5] Pearson, *The Architectural and Social History of Co-operative Living*, pp. 67–68; Sheila Rowbotham, *Edward Carpenter: A Life of Liberty and Love* (London: Verso, 2008), pp. 94–95, 214.

housewives, but also, I argue, by an awareness of the struggles of servants such as those involved in the Domestic Workers' Union (DWU).

Co-operative Housekeeping Schemes, 1880–1918

The belief that co-operative housekeeping would solve the 'servant problem' was common to advocates with otherwise diverse intellectual, political and practical agendas. Jane Hume Clapperton had been active in Freethinking feminist and suffrage-supporting circles since at least the 1870s, and subscribed to the WSPU in 1907 and the Women's Freedom League in 1908.[6] She advocated the collectivisation of housework in her philosophical treatises *Scientific Meliorism* (1885) and *A Vision of the Future* (1904), as well as making it the subject of an entire novel, *Margaret Dunmore or, A Socialist Home* (1888). These ideas had some reach within feminist circles; Clapperton corresponded with the Men and Women's Club and published a series of articles in the newspaper *Shafts* in 1893.[7] She believed that society was not yet ready for the communisation of the economy, as envisaged by socialists such as Robert Owen, but that a more modest form of co-operation in domestic life would help to generate a new outlook that would subsequently enable more radical social change. Her discussion of the 'servant problem', therefore, placed great ideological, moral and spiritual import upon what might otherwise appear to be a trivial or wholly practical question. According to Clapperton, the 'burden so many of my sex bear, in the management of domestic servants', was of a 'magnitude' that few men fully comprehended:

'Why don't you dismiss her at once?' a husband will say, when his wife complains of a servant, oblivious apparently to the fact that to obtain another entails effort, and that the chances of improving matters by this masterly policy are extremely small.

Clapperton was sympathetic not only to middle-class women unable to source the necessary labour to manage their homes, but also to a new generation of working-class girls affected by 'the restless spirit of the age', who, hating the 'monotony, dullness, [and] routine' of service 'flit rapidly from place to place'. In fact, she saw this as a sign that humanity had already 'evolved … beyond that stage of our history, when domestic masterhood and servitude of adults was an appropriate relation'. Now,

---

[6] Elizabeth Crawford, *The Women's Suffrage Movement: A Reference Guide 1866–1928* (London: University College London Press, 1999), p. 112; Laura Schwartz, *Infidel Feminism: Secularism, Religion and Women's Emancipation, England 1830–1914* (Manchester: Manchester University Press, 2013).

[7] Dyhouse, *Feminism and the Family*, pp. 111–114.

at the dawn of a new modern age, the institution of domestic service was nothing more than a vestige of a more backward time, and the shortage of servants was destined to become ever more acute as society continued to modernise. 'Associated homes' (communities of up to twenty families living together in a complex that would combine private bedrooms with a communal music room, art room, dancing room and schoolroom) were, for Clapperton, 'the only natural and adequate escape from this difficulty'.[8]

Charlotte Perkins Gilman, perhaps the best-known advocate of co-operative housekeeping in this period, was from the United States but her work was widely read and reported on in Britain, where she often undertook lecture tours.[9] Gilman had a slightly different vision from Clapperton, drawing upon a North American entrepreneurial spirit rather than a British utopian socialist tradition.[10] She believed that families should maintain their individual households but that the domestic work should be removed from the responsibility of the housewife and placed in the hands of public or commercial bodies of professional domestic workers. Charlotte Perkins Gilman also wanted to solve the 'servant problem', maintaining that the existing institution of domestic service was not only untenable but also morally repugnant: 'Strangers by birth, by class, by race, by education – as utterly alien as it is possible to conceive – these we introduce into our homes – into our very bed chambers; in knowledge of all the daily habits of our lives.' Gilman's rhetorical aim was to drive home the point that under present conditions the home utterly failed to live up to the myth of 'privacy' championed by its conservative proponents. Her belief that housework was valuable work, which should be performed by skilled experts, was addressed to

---

[8] Jane Hume Clapperton, *Scientific Meliorism and the Evolution of Happiness* (London: Kegan Paul, 1885), pp. 287–288. See also Jane Hume Clapperton, *A Vision of the Future Based on the Application of Ethical Principles* (London: Swan Sonnenschein, 1904), p. 274.

[9] For Charlotte Perkins Gilman's influence in Britain, *National Review* March 1909, pp. 139–148; *Anti-Suffrage Review* April 1909, p. 3; Pearson, *The Architectural and Social History of Co-operative Living*, pp. 69–72; Dyhouse, *Feminism and the Family*, pp. 114–117; Claire Eustance, '"Daring to Be Free": The Evolution of Women's Political Identities in the Women's Freedom League 1907–1930', PhD thesis, University of York (1993), pp. 208–209. There is a large historiography on Perkins Gilman; recent works include Judith Allen, *The Feminism of Charlotte Perkins Gilman: Sexualities, Histories, Progressivism* (Chicago: University of Chicago Press, 2009); Cynthia J. Davis, *Charlotte Perkins Gilman: A Biography* (Stanford: Stanford University Press, 2010); Sheryl L. Meyering (ed.), *Charlotte Perkins Gilman: The Woman and Her Work* (Rochester: University of Rochester Press, 2010).

[10] Some British reviewers were critical of Gilman's more commercial vision; *Freewoman* 29 Feb. 1912, pp. 296–297.

mistresses rather than maids – the assumed 'we' of the above quotation. Nor did it prevent her from reinscribing common prejudices regarding 'the average servant' of the present day, whom she described as 'an ignorant young woman' possessing an 'empty', 'uncultivated mind ... prone to unguarded gossip'. Gilman believed that the conditions under which the majority of servants presently laboured were in urgent need of reform, which could only be provided by the collectivisation of housework.[11]

Feminist advocacy of co-operative housekeeping as a solution to the 'servant problem' was thus relatively well established by the time that Alice Melvin came to put some of these ideas into practice. Between 1909 and 1914, Alice Melvin initiated several schemes, including Brent Garden Village (est. 1909–1910) in Finchley, North West London, which was initially intended to provide 114 houses and flats of varying sizes, alongside a co-operative kitchen, dining hall and laundry. Residents would benefit from privacy in their living arrangements combined with the convenience of collectivised housework. Melvin did not foreground the entrepreneurial possibilities of co-operative housekeeping as much as Gilman had, but she did intend for her schemes to function as viable commercial entities. Brent Garden Village was advertised as 'a well secured 4.5% investment', although it struggled to find people willing to advance the capital.[12] Melvin went on to found the 'Society for the Promotion of Co-operative Housekeeping and House-Service' (1911) and the Melvin Hall Co-operative Housekeeping and Service Society (1912), before her retirement in 1914.[13] Promoting her schemes in both the feminist and the national press, Melvin also presented them first and foremost as a solution to the 'servant problem'. For example, the series of articles in which she introduced co-operative housekeeping in the feminist newspaper the *Freewoman* focused specifically upon 'Co-operative Housekeeping and the Domestic Worker'. Like Clapperton and Gilman, Melvin saw the 'servant problem' as having two sides to it – both the 'labour and anxiety' of the middle-class housewife struggling with a shortage of competent servants, and the bad and unhealthy conditions endured by servants themselves.[14]

---

[11] Charlotte Perkins Gilman, *The Home: Its Work and Influence* (Walnut Creek: AltaMira Press, 2002 [first published 1903]), pp. 42, 105; Charlotte Perkins Gilman, *What Diantha Did* (n.p.: Read How You Want, 2010 [first published 1909–1910]), pp. 110–113.

[12] *Daily Mail* 7 Dec. 1911, p. 2.

[13] Pearson, *The Architectural and Social History of Co-operative Living*, chapter 7.

[14] *Freewoman* 7 March 1912, p. 312; 4 April 1912, pp. 386–387; *Woman Worker* 13 April 1910, p. 880; *Daily Mail* 1 Sept. 1910, p. 9.

Feminist interest in co-operative housekeeping continued during and after the First World War, and, as we shall see, was even boosted by women's experience of changes to domestic life that wartime necessitated. Despite all these upheavals, the 'servant problem' remained at the centre of arguments for the collectivisation of domestic labour. Clementina Black's *A New Way of Housekeeping* (1918) declared that: 'Labour unrest ... is, among domestic servants, chronic', a problem that Black had first identified in 1893. This, she argued, created serious problems not just for middle-class housewives and mothers, but also for the single professional woman compelled to spend 'her own hours of freedom, which are not very ample ... in the endeavour to supplement her servant's inefficiency'. Clementina Black, however, maintained that the 'servant problem' ran much deeper and lay in the nature of the work itself. She was one of those who believed that domestic labour was 'primitive and undeveloped' and had failed to progress in line with the technological advances, specialisation and collectivisation that had transformed all other forms of work since the onset of industrialisation.[15]

Co-operative housekeeping was widely promoted as the only way to bring housework, and therefore domestic service, up to date.[16] In 1885 Jane Hume Clapperton was already arguing that collectivisation would bring about much-needed modernisation: 'economy of labour would result, not only from union of function, but from the superior amount of thought bestowed upon the problem of how to work efficiently. Labour-saving machinery may also come into service.'[17] Charlotte Perkins Gilman argued that domestic labour could only be truly professionalised, skilled and technologically advanced if it was collectivised and undertaken in the public sphere.[18] It is possible that Clapperton's *Margaret Dunmore* influenced Gilman's novel *What Diantha Did*, published two decades later, since both provided minutely detailed accounts of the rational and efficient organisation of domestic labour in its socialised form. Clappterton described her 'Unitary Home' at length:

The spacious gallery has every appliance for work, on modern methods. The floor, on which stands the plate racks, slopes into a sink, which renders drying unnecessary. Small mops are provided for washing dishes, and waterproof gloves

---

[15] Clementina Black, 'The Dislike to Domestic Service', *The Nineteenth Century and After: A Monthly Review*, 33:193 (1893), 454–456; *Common Cause* Aug.–Sept. 1916; Clementina Black, *A New Way of Housekeeping* (London: W. Collins Sons, 1918), pp. 3, 8, 13–16.

[16] *Common Cause* 12 Sept. 1919, pp. 393–394.

[17] Clapperton, *Scientific Meliorism*, p. 289. See also Clapperton, *A Vision of the Future*, p. 275.

[18] Gilman, *The Home*, pp. 106–109, 183.

for paring potatoes and cleansing vegetables ... To facilitate service at table, the light refectory is next to the kitchen, and a service window between precludes all burdensome carrying of cooked meats to and fro.[19]

This belief in the potential for modern technology to instigate radical social change remained undiminished in Clementina Black's *A New Way of Housekeeping*, which was not a fictionalised utopian fantasy but intended as a practical guide for postwar reconstruction. Wartime, however, had added further urgency to the co-operative cause, with its emphasis on the need for thrift highlighting the 'extravagant' wastefulness of individual households owning their own sets of brooms and saucepans and purchasing food in small quantities. Black's preface to the book, written just before the end of the First World War, moreover predicted that the future of the nation would depend upon the female workforce, most of whom would need to be released from the labours of the home to engage in 'economically profitable' work.[20]

Despite their critique of the present conditions of housework and domestic service, few proponents of co-operative housekeeping envisaged a world in which everybody undertook domestic labour for themselves or shared in it equally. Jane Hume Clapperton probably came closest to this position, yet also retreated from it somewhat once the details of this arrangement were given full consideration. Her novel about a 'Unitary Home' initially presented it as a house with no servants, where instead an 'executive committee, consisting of two male and two female members – elected by ballot every six-months – meets each evening to arrange the work of the following day and appoint the members required to perform the work'. Clapperton was very unusual, even among feminists, in proposing that there was to be no distinction between male and female employments in the 'Unitarian Home' (although her novel acknowledges how much this transgressed acceptable gender norms by depicting some male residents as decidedly resistant to performing tasks they see as 'essentially feminine'). For the female residents, the important distinction is between those tasks acceptable to a 'lady', such as looking after the children, or even waiting at table, and the 'dirty housework', fit only for working-class women. 'I will

[19] Jane Hume Clapperton, *Margaret Dunmore or, a Socialist Home* (Milton Keynes: Lightening Source UK, n.d. [first published 1888]).

[20] Black, *A New Way of Housekeeping*, p. xi, chapter 6. Black unsuccessfully argued for some system of co-operative housekeeping to be included within the proposals put forward in the *Report of the Women's Advisory Committee on the Domestic Service Problem Together with Reports by Sub-Committees on Training, Machinery of Distribution, Organisation and Conditions* (London: Ministry of Reconstruction, 1919), pp. 32–33.

not be one of the housemaids, please!' cries Lucy, one of the fictional occupants of the 'Unitary Home', although eventually her 'prejudices melted away'. Later on in the novel, however, the narrator seems to endorse such distinctions, accepting that domestic servants might be brought in in an emergency, 'but only to assist in the kitchen, in housework etc., and not to perform any of the *higher domestic functions*'.[21]

Charlotte Perkins Gilman had no problem with a division of labour that necessitated a certain class of worker to undertake all domestic labour for other sections of society. Instead she hoped for the transformation of the work and the people who performed it through a process of professionalisation, whereby it would 'cease to be domestic service – and become world service'. The eponymous heroine of *What Diantha Did* eventually succeeds in establishing a 'House Worker's Union'. This is not a trade union, but a company, 'a group of 30 girls, picked and trained', who live together in a large complex and are hired out on an hourly basis by individual households, enabling employers to do away with resident servants entirely. 'You are not servants – you are employees', the manager of the House Worker's Union tells her new staff. Traditional servants' uniforms, those 'liveries' and 'labels' of status, are done away with. Servants simply carry about their own cap and apron, to be worn only when practically necessary such as during cooking and sweeping. A new kind of skilled worker is thus born, one who works with speed, accuracy and economy, possessing a 'pleasant, quiet, assured manner' very different from 'the old slipshod methods of the ordinary general servant'. It was this transformation of domestic service into a 'business' 'involving a high degree of skill' that Gilman believed was key to improving the conditions of domestic workers. In the novel, domestic 'employees' work an agreed number of hours, are paid for every hour they work and receive a much higher rate than they had previously earned as ordinary servants. Moreover, each has her own private bedroom and own domestic needs catered for by two resident 'housemaids'.[22]

Writing almost ten years later, Clementina Black believed a similar kind of arrangement to be a realistic prospect for postwar Britain. By this point, Black felt able to declare most definitively that 'communal living arrangements' attempted in the decades leading up to the war had failed: 'People do not want to pool their lives. They only want to get their food and their service properly organised.' She recommended instead Domestic Federations of about fifty households, catered for by a staff of servants

[21] Clapperton, *Margaret Dunmore*, pp. 25–26, 24, 34. My emphasis.
[22] Gilman, *What Diantha Did*, pp. 167, 177–178.

supervised by a 'well-paid manageress'. Most of the work would consist of cooking and serving public meals in a common dining room, though the residents of the Federation might also hire domestic workers to come into their homes for a set number of hours each week. Most servants would live together in the 'Centre' where meals were served, and have their own bed-sitting room in which they were free to do exactly as they pleased. Like Gilman, Black also emphasised that Federation servants would be better paid than they were at present, and that they would be answerable not to individual mistresses but instead to the general managers.[23]

Clementina Black and Charlotte Perkins Gilman offer an interesting comparison. Black was more rooted in trade union activism and working-class women's movements, and avoided the sneering assessments of the 'average' domestic servant that appear in Gilman's work.[24] Yet Black's blueprint for a reformed system of service was in some ways more conservative. She still termed domestic workers in the proposed new scheme 'servants' and referred to their work as 'serving'; she still insisted that they needed to wear a uniform (although she did concede that 'it will be wise not to include a cap as part of it'); and though she hoped that in the long term they would be able to discipline themselves, in the short term '[p]ertness, insubordination, or persistent carelessness' on the part of servants would be taken most seriously and the 'offender' subjected to 'the ordeal of having to "go before the committee"'.[25] Perhaps Clementina Black was simply trying to be more realistic than the utopian novelists Clapperton and Gilman, and we should not forget that even apparently limited reforms, such as servants being allowed to do as they liked in the privacy of their own bedrooms, represented a radical departure from existing practices. Nonetheless, the rules and regulations that Black believed should continue under this new regime of housekeeping certainly undermined her and fellow advocates' claim that co-operative housekeeping would be a satisfactory solution for *all* women.

---

[23] Black, *A New Way of Housekeeping*, pp. 55, 60–69, 70–73.

[24] For Gilman's relationship with the labour movement, Davis, *Charlotte Perkins Gilman*, pp. 150–151.

[25] Black, *A New Way of Housekeeping*, pp. 60, 70, 75. Black's views appear to have become slightly more conservative on this question between writing a series of articles for the *Common Cause* in 1916 and the subsequent book. In the former she declared, 'Very few and elementary rules will be imposed, a good tone being secured rather by very careful selection of the first servants than by external regulations'; *Common Cause* 1 Sept. 1916, pp. 263–264. The disciplinary procedures referred to in the book do not appear in the articles.

Domestic Workers' Experiences of Co-operative Housekeeping

In 1912 Kathlyn Oliver, recently retired from her position on the executive of the DWU, responded to Alice Melvin's proposal for 'co-operative colonies' in the *Freewoman*. 'When the words "abolition from domestic drudgery" caught my eye', wrote Oliver, 'I eagerly went over Mrs Melvin's scheme, but alas! I found that the abolition of domestic drudgery was not for me, but was for "middle-class people".' As far as Oliver could see, co-operative housekeeping offered nothing more radical than a system whereby 'people who individually could not afford the luxury of a domestic drudge, can, by combination with others in similar circumstances, share this luxury'. This might well be a very sensible solution to the 'servant problem' as experienced by the progressive middle classes, 'But me thinks that this common ownership of domestic drudgery will not be quite so satisfactory from the domestic drudge's point of view.' Alice Melvin replied in the same issue, insisting that she too was strongly opposed to the poor conditions currently endured by domestic workers. However, the co-operative system would, she insisted, offer an ideal solution. Servants would no longer be at the mercy of unfair employers, but would be able to lodge complaints with the colony's central committee. Moreover, if servants were to be hired by the hour, day or month, and live, not in the homes of their employers, but in their own quarters, the problem of loneliness – which afflicted so many present-day domestic workers – would be solved. Kathlyn Oliver wrote once more to the *Freewoman*, acknowledging that, for most servants, Melvin's proposed arrangements would be an improvement on their current conditions. But she remained wholly unconvinced that co-operative housekeeping would remove the stigma attached to this form of work, and she strongly objected to the hierarchical implications of retaining a domestic staff separate from the residents. 'I suppose that if I were employed under this system as a domestic I should be known and addressed as "Kate" by every man, woman and child on the co-operative estate?' According to Oliver, the distinction between staff and residents and the division of labour it entailed would reinforce rather than undermine the assumption that some people existed 'to do the dirty work' for another group of '"superior" people who were above such work'. Unless such hierarchies were broken down, other attempts at reform would have little effect. For example, although Kathlyn Oliver wanted servants to be able to approach their relationship with their mistress as an employment contract rather than a personal arrangement, she was concerned that Melvin's proposal to completely de-personalise the employment of servants could backfire.

If employers were to be freed from the personal obligations that came with keeping their own live-in servants, the more anonymous workers who came into their homes for a few hours each day might, in their eyes, 'degenerate into a machine' – simply a pair of hands to do the work they did not wish to do.[26]

While Clapperton and Gilman's vision of co-operative housekeeping remained theoretical and utopian, and Black's more practical guide was never embodied in a particular scheme, Alice Melvin's co-operative colonies did become a reality. How did 'co-operatised' domestic workers fare in comparison to those employed in private households? Were Kathlyn Oliver's fears borne out? When Alice Melvin was writing in the *Freewoman*, she had already begun to put these ideas into practice in Brent Garden Village in the suburbs of North West London. At the centre of the village lay Brent Lodge, a former stately home, which had been converted into a co-operative kitchen, dining hall, laundry and accommodation for domestic staff. The Lodge was connected to the surrounding residents' homes by a covered walkway, allowing servants to move easily back and forth between their own dwellings and those they cleaned. Melvin supervised the design of the residents' houses, which bore a close resemblance to the 'kitchenless homes' advocated by Gilman, although they did have a small combined scullery and kitchen containing a gas stove in case their tenants wanted occasionally to cook simple meals for themselves.[27] An article on the proposed community appearing in the *Daily Mail* in 1910 claimed that its servants would be required to work only a ten-hour day, 'thus doing away with one of the chief objections to domestic service'.[28] None of the articles promoting the co-operative scheme specified exactly how much servants would be paid. It was initially proposed that residents could hire servants from the Lodge for 4½d. per hour.[29] This is considerably more than the 1d. per hour that the DWU calculated as the wage of the average servant – though there is no evidence to suggest that the Brent Garden Village servants received this sum in full.

One of the few pieces of evidence offering an insight into life as a domestic servant in Brent Garden Village is a series of photographs published in the *Daily Sketch* in November 1911, when the first tenants moved in, and the communal kitchen and dining hall was opened (see Figure 11). The residents featured in these pictures are well-enough

[26] *Freewoman* 20 June 1912, p. 98; 4 July 1912, p. 137.
[27] Pearson, *The Architectural and Social History of Co-operative Living*, pp. 119–120.
[28] *Daily Mail* 24 Aug. 1910, p. 3.
[29] Pearson, *The Architectural and Social History of Co-operative Living*, p. 121.

Figure 11 Servant at Brent Garden Village.
Daily Sketch 16 Nov. 1911, p. 16 (reproduced by permission of the British Library)

dressed to confirm Alice Melvin's aspiration (and Kathlyn Oliver's concern) that co-operative housekeeping would cater primarily to the middle classes. Brent Garden Village charged rents at £32–£63 per year, certainly beyond the means of working-class women. Moreover, the fact that two out of the four publicity photographs appearing in the *Daily Sketch* featured domestic servants suggests that their presence was used as an important indicator of respectability and social status to prospective residents.

Although allowances must be made for the likelihood that these images were posed by the photographer, the formality of the servants' stance and appearance is also revealing. In the dining hall a servant stands to attention, not simply serving the residents their food but waiting on them as if they were in a private middle-class home. Both she and her counterpart in the kitchen wear traditional servants' uniforms including the hated cap.[30] What slim evidence exists, therefore, does seem to support

<hr>

[30] *Daily Sketch* 16 Nov. 1911, p. 16; *Daily Mail* 24 Aug. 1910, p. 3. Brent Garden Village continued to grow, attracting thirty-three households by 1914, but began to move away

Kathlyn Oliver's prediction that, although co-operative housekeeping schemes might solve the 'servant problem' from the perspective of the middle-class housewife, they would fail to challenge the hierarchies of power and status that constituted a large part of the problem as servants viewed it.

The same was true for Alice Melvin's subsequent co-operative colonies. In November 1911 the 'Society for the Promotion of Co-operative Housekeeping and House-Service' was reported in the press under the rather more snappy title 'Society for the Abolition of Housework'. At the inaugural meeting of the Society, two new housing schemes were proposed. The first was an ambitious plan to found a 'miniature town' in Ruislip on the outskirts of West London:

> inhabitants shall hand over all the cares of housekeeping to a trained corps of universal servants. Experienced cooks will prepare any food desired in the common kitchen, trained nurses will take care of children in the common nursery ... And chambermaids will relieve tenants of all the remaining details of household 'drudgery', leaving those, however, who wish to cook, sew, or make their own beds to enjoy housework within reasonable limits.[31]

Servants themselves never appeared as subjects of the schemes' publicity or planning. A newspaper report on the Society's founding meeting refers to servants only in the stereotyped context of 'the vagaries of "Mary Ann," her genius for smashing things, and her strange theories of domestic science'.[32] This 'miniature town' was never built, but Melvin did succeed in setting up a more modest, co-operative colony in Hampstead, North West London, which came to be known as the Priory. It consisted of five houses on Priory Road, each of which had about ten tenants who were provided with meals, although it is not known whether a central kitchen or dining room existed.[33] Servants at the Priory were employed not by individual residents but by a committee that was also responsible for fixing their duties, salaries and other remuneration. The Priory continued to provide co-operative residences until 1937, but its various rule books, which specified such details as whether tenants were allowed to keep pets (no), or allowed to play musical instruments in their flats (not after 10:30 p.m.), do not contain any information on how domestic service was to be organised. This suggests that, contrary to Alice Melvin's

---

from a commitment to collectivised housework; Pearson, *The Architectural and Social History of Co-operative Living*, p. 121.

[31] *Standard* 15 Nov. 1911, p. 12.   [32] *Standard* 16 Nov. 1911, p. 4.

[33] The Priory was established under the auspices of the 'Second Melvin Co-operative Housekeeping Society' (which became the 'Melvin Co-operative Residential Society' by the time it was registered as a friendly society in March 1914); Pearson, *The Architectural and Social History of Co-operative Living*, p. 126.

assurances in the *Freewoman*, no special attention was paid to restructuring and improving the conditions of domestic workers to ensure that they too reflected the modernising aspirations of co-operative colonies. The silence of the Priory's records on the topics of working hours, salaries or living conditions for servants indicates that they simply followed normal practices which did not require any special rules or clarification. Had the arrangements been any more innovative or an exception to conditions in private households, surely these would have been recorded in the Society's rules in a similar manner to how, in 1923, it was specified that a 'married woman may be a member and hold and deal with shares or other interest in the Society as if she were unmarried'.[34]

While Alice Melvin's co-operative housekeeping schemes were open to families, many other similar housing projects were more directly targeted at single professional women. The women's movement had been campaigning for more housing, especially in London, for this new class of 'lady' workers since the 1880s. In 1888 the Ladies' Dwellings Company opened Sloane Gardens House in Lower Sloane Street, and the following year the Ladies' Residential Chambers opened Chenies Street Chambers, designed by Millicent Garrett Fawcett's sister, Agnes Garrett.[35] This housing needed not only to be respectable, safe and affordable, but also to solve the 'servant problem' for women whose waged work prevented them from meeting their own domestic needs yet who might only be able to afford to employ an inexperienced young girl requiring more supervision than they had time for. When in 1899 the Women's Industrial Council established a committee to investigate 'the housing needs of ladies living and working in London', it emphasised that such women needed to be free 'to devote themselves to their various callings undeterred by domestic worries'. Extensive discussion of how to organise the necessary domestic service ensued.[36] Co-operative housekeeping was

---

[34] National Archives, London, 'Priory Residential Society Ltd. No. 5757 R', 'The Melvin Co-operative Residential Society (Hampstead) Ltd: Rules' (2 March 1914), FS 17/246.

[35] Martha Vicinus, *Independent Women: Work and Community for Single Women, 1850–1920* (London: Virago, 1985), pp. 295–296; Elizabeth Crawford, *Enterprising Women: The Garretts and Their Circle* (London: Frances Boutle, 2002), pp. 206–217; Lisa Catherine Robertson, 'New and Novel Homes: Women Writing London's Housing', PhD thesis, University of Warwick (2016), p. 120.

[36] The Women's Library at the London School of Economics, London, 'Circular for the Housing of Educated Working Women in London' (Nov. 1899), Women's Industrial Council Letters Book, p. 208, WIC/D/3; *Women's Industrial News* Dec. 1899, pp. 148–151; March 1900, pp. 159–160; Oct. 1910, pp. 14–15. Emily Hobhouse, the honorary secretary of this committee, summarised its findings in 'Women Workers: How They Live, How They Wish to Live', *Nineteenth Century* 27 (March 1900), 471–484. See also Emily Gee, '"Where Shall She Live?" The Accommodation of Working Women in

widely viewed as the most sensible solution, and almost all flats that came to be built specifically for 'working ladies' included communal dining rooms and a collectivised domestic staff.[37] The model to which they looked was not so much commercial hotels or managed flats, but the residential women's colleges, especially at the ancient universities, which were designed with the explicit intention of liberating middle-class women from domestic duties by providing 'a room of one's own' serviced by 'scouts' and 'bedders'.[38]

Another block of 'spinster flats' was built as part of Hampstead Garden Suburb, North West London, in 1911.[39] The Suburb had been founded in 1905 by social reformer and philanthropist Henrietta Barnett, who wanted to both preserve the open countryside around Hampstead Heath from 'mediocre' suburban development and create a community in which a mixture of social classes could live in healthy, attractive and rationally designed surroundings.[40] The majority of housing in Hampstead Garden Suburb was intended for families, but Barnett also had a particular interest in the housing problems faced by single professional women.[41] She worked with architect Baillie Scott to design Waterlow Court, comprising forty-nine one- to three-bedroom flats arranged around a quad. Waterlow Court was built by the Industrial Dwellings

the Capital 1875–1925', thesis for diploma in building conservation, Architectural Association (2007).

[37] Pearson, *The Architectural and Social History of Co-operative Living*, pp. 49–51.

[38] Laura Schwartz, *A Serious Endeavour: Gender, Education and Community at St Hugh's, 1886–2011* (London: Profile Books, 2011), chapter 4. See also Jane Hamlett, '"Nicely Feminine, Yet Learned": Student Rooms at Royal Holloway and the Oxbridge Colleges in Late Nineteenth-Century Britain', *Women's History Review*, 15:1 (2006), 137–161; William Whyte, 'Halls of Residence at Britain's Civic Universities, 1870–1970', in Jane Hamlett, Lesley Hoskins and Rebecca Preston (eds.), *Residential Institutions in Britain, 1725–1970: Inmates and Environments* (London: Pickering & Chatto, 2013), 155–166, p. 165.

[39] This is what they were initially termed by the Suburb's General Purposes Committee; London Metropolitan Archive (hereafter LMA), Hampstead Garden Suburb Archive, 'Sub-Committee Minute Book' (May 1906–March 1913), p. 55, ACC/3816/01/03/001. Henrietta Barnett's husband also referred to them as such; Henrietta Barnett, *Canon Barnett: His Life, Work and Friends* (London: John Murray, 1921), p. 718.

[40] Henrietta Barnett, 'The Garden Suburb at Hampstead', *Contemporary Review*, 87 (1 Jan. 1905), 231–237. For the history of Hampstead Garden Suburb, see Alison Creedan, *'Only a Woman' Henrietta Barnett: Social Reformer and Founder of Hampstead Garden Suburb* (Chichester: Phillimore & Co., 2006); Micky Watkins, *Henrietta Barnett: Social Worker and Community Planner* (n.p., 2011); Kathleen M. Slack, *Henrietta's's Dream: A Chronicle of the Hampstead Garden Suburb 1905–1982* (n.p.: Calvert's North Star Press, 1982).

[41] Queen's Court was opened at Hampstead Garden Suburb in 1927, and offered similar but more downmarket accommodation for 'thrifty working women' (typists, clerks and nurses) but without the communal staff of servants; Watkins, *Henrietta Barnett*, p. 159.

Company and completed in 1909. Intended for unmarried or widowed women, the flats contained a living room, bathroom and lavatory but only a very small scullery. Instead, residents took regular meals in the communal dining room where they were served by domestic workers employed not by individual residents but by the community at large. The professions of its early residents suggest that it attracted both the kind of women that Clementina Black and Alice Melvin wanted to emancipate from housework, and those who made up the suffrage movement's key constituency: school mistresses, artists, typists, stenographers, secretaries, lecturers, 'statistical researchers', lady inspectors and even one 'teacher of Swedish gymnastics'.[42] Hampstead Garden Suburb formed its own contingent on the Women's Suffrage Procession in June 1911, and the Women's Freedom League and the Women's Labour League held regular meetings at the Suburb's Institute.[43] Waterlow Court was viewed by many as part of wider campaigns for women's rights and in particular emancipation from housework. In the socialist newspaper the *Clarion*, Julia Dawson reported on Waterlow Court's experiment in 'simplified housekeeping' in the same column in which she wrote about the need for better designed and easier-to-clean houses. In the same breath she reprimanded her readers to stop obsessing about domestic matters and instead attend to the sound of 'rain ... pattering on the roses, and the corn-crake ... calling in the long grass'.[44] Waterlow Court thus featured as part of what we now know to be familiar feminist trope: to demand that housework be made more professional and 'scientific' while simultaneously implying that it was the least worthwhile of all activities a woman may devote her time to.

---

[42] For example, Amelia Charlotte Hindley listed her occupation as 'headteacher'; Ethel Dorothy East as 'assistant school mistress'; Deborah Commins as 'artist sculptor'; Alice Elizabeth Holdsworth as 'typist'; Alice Harriet Hall as 'stenographer'; Amy Hunter as 'secretary to editor of trade paper'; Harriet Christine Newcomb as 'lecturer'; Annie Jackson as 'statistical research'; Maria Jane Hildreth as 'Inspector Public Control Dept.' and Rose Victoria Davies as 'teacher of Swedish gymnastics'; England and Wales Census (1911), Waterlow Court, Hendon, Middlesex.

[43] *Town Crier* June 1911, p. 35; Dec. 1911, p. 115; Jan. 1912, pp. 127–128; Oct. 1912, p. 101; Dec. 1912, p. 130; March 1913, p. 181. Rebecca West, Margaret Bondfield and the birth control advocate and Freethinking feminist Bessie Drysdale were all Suburb residents in the years before the First World War; Slack, *Henrietta's Dream*, p. 27; Kathryn Laing (ed.), *The Sentinel: An Incomplete Early Novel by Rebecca West* (Oxford: European Humanities Research Centre, 2002), xiii–liii, p. xvii. Mrs Drysdale placed an advertisement in the *Town Crier* Aug. 1912, p. 82, giving her address as 49 Rotherwick Road. Although, as a member of the Women's Freedom League, Bessie Drysdale boycotted the 1911 census, the Registrar confirmed that she was resident at this address; England and Wales Census (1911), 49 Rotherwick Road, Hendon, Middlesex.

[44] *Clarion* 16 July 1909, p. 6. See also *Woman Worker* 13 Jan. 1909, p. 42.

In 1911, a total of fourteen servants served seventy-seven tenants. The only male servants were John Stockhausen, the superintendent of the flats, and his brother-in-law, John Enright, who was employed as the 'House Porter'. The rest of the staff was entirely made up of women:

> Florence Hogg, aged forty-seven (lady superintendent)
> Violet Cecil Russell, aged thirty-two (cashier)
> Agnes Hawker, aged fifteen (scullery maid domestic)
> Alice Emma Porter, aged twenty-five (between maid)
> Alice Laura Hatt, aged nineteen (domestic housemaid)
> Jessie E. Wright, aged twenty-one (scullery maid)
> Ellen Moore, aged twenty-one (cook)
> Mabel Annie Giddings, aged twenty-one (housemaid)
> Ethel Maud Wrackham Powditch, aged twenty-three (waitress)
> Florence Dawkins, aged twenty (domestic housemaid)
> Annie Ethel Welling, aged eighteen (domestic housemaid)
> Annie Florence Heather, aged sixteen (domestic housemaid)[45]

A 1909 advertisement for Waterlow Court claimed that 'Servants are provided for the use of tenants at an additional charge of three shillings per week.' It did not clarify whether this included personal service, such as cleaning individual flats, as well as meals in the communal dining room.[46] Using 1911 figures, this would have generated £11 11s. per month to pay a staff of fourteen. Assuming that this entire sum went directly into servants' wage packets, and that all servants were paid the same (both of which are unlikely), servants would have received £9 18s. a year – a poor wage even for relatively low-level servants in London. There are so many variables when attempting to calculate wages according to this fragmented evidence, however, that no firm conclusions can be drawn. For example, perhaps servants' wages were topped up from some other source of income, or perhaps they only worked half-days. What these figures do suggest is that working at Waterlow Court was not an obvious choice for a woman seeking well-paid full-time work. And this is starkly at odds with the claims made by so many advocates of co-operative housekeeping that this new way of organising domestic labour and the servant–employer relationship would create a more professional-ised and higher-status class of domestic worker.

The 1911 census lists all the female servants as living together in flat number 24, part of the same quadrangle as the lady residents. At Water-low Court the servants' quarters occupied the first and second floors

---

[45] England and Wales Census (1911), 24 Waterlow Court, Hendon, Middlesex.
[46] *Garden Cities and Town Planning* Nov. 1909, p. 246.

above the communal dining room on the ground floor. They were provided with their own 'hall' (equivalent to, though smaller than, the residents' 'common room'), larder, scullery and pantry. The large kitchen was used to prepare meals for their employers rather than reserved for their own private use. The servants' bedrooms were roughly the same size as the residents': 12 ft × 10 ft on the first floor and 10 ft × 8 ft on the second floor (the most common-sized bedroom found in the residents' flats was 10 ft × 10 ft). But if the census information is correct, the eleven female servants must have been sleeping three and four to a room, whereas all seventy-seven residents are listed as having their own bedrooms. The domestic workers also had to share a single bath and toilet.[47] It is possible that servants objected to such conditions, or that by 1911 more servants were employed than the architect had originally envisaged. Either way, by 1910 plans were already under way to extend the servants' quarters into an annex that was subsequently built alongside, but external to, the quadrangle. The annex was an improvement in that it offered two toilets, a separate bathroom with a bath-tub and seven sleeping 'cubicles' of 10 ft × 6 ft, although it is unclear exactly how many domestic workers were expected to share these facilities.[48]

What do these bare facts and figures tell us about the status and treatment of servants at Waterlow Court? What can we find out about the nature of their relationship with the Swedish gymnastics teachers, stenographers and lady artists that they served? In 1909 it cost £1 14s. per month to rent a one-bedroom flat at Waterlow Court, with two-bedroom flats costing between £2 5s and £2 14s. Julia Dawson thus concluded that Waterlow Court was intended for 'professional women whose incomes run into three figures', rather than lower-middle-class women workers who, she believed, were more in need of suitable housing.[49] Waterlow Court servants lived in the same block as these better-off women professionals, free from the frustrations of 'living-in'. Clementina Black and Alice Melvin believed that providing domestic workers with their own accommodation was one of the main ways in which co-operative housekeeping schemes would improve the conditions of service. It is possible that this organisation of space at Waterlow Court

---

[47] The housekeeper, Florence Hogg, had her own bedroom and sitting room. LMA, Hampstead Garden Suburb Archive, Architectural Drawings, 'First Floor Plan' (1908), ACC/3816/P/01 0390/G, 'Second Floor Plan' (1908) ACC/3816/P/01 0390/H.
[48] LMA, Hampstead Garden Suburb Archive, Architectural Drawings, 'Annex: Elevations and Ground Plan' (1910), ACC/3816/P/01 0391/F.
[49] *Garden Cities and Town Planning* Nov. 1909, p. 246; *Clarion* 16 July 1909, p. 6. Julia Dawson gives a slightly different figure for the rent – maintaining that a one-bedroom flat cost £1 19s per month including attendance.

reflected similarly egalitarian aspirations on the part of Baillie Scott and Henrietta Barnett. Yet Scott and Barnett were also inspired by the architecture of the Oxbridge women's colleges, where the fact of servants living alongside yet separate from students did nothing to challenge rigid class hierarchies between these groups of women.[50] Moreover, once the annex was built, a much clearer demarcation between the 'ladies' flats' and the servants' quarters was established. Servants may have gained greater privacy, but they were now much more completely excluded from the central focus of Waterlow Court.

The ideas about social status built into the architecture of Waterlow Court were in keeping with attitudes towards servants expressed by residents of the Suburb at large. This self-consciously progressive community combined a probably higher-than-average degree of philanthropic concern for the conditions of domestic servants, while continuing to view them as a class apart. Henrietta Barnett may have envisaged a community where different social classes lived in harmony and enjoyed the same public space, but she never argued for an end to a class distinction. In the article in which she laid out her plans for Hampstead Garden Suburb, she even pointed to the servant–employer relation as a positive example of mutual aid between the classes.[51] Likewise, the first generation of residents did not pause to question their reliance upon the domestic labour of working-class women, acknowledging it only when lamenting, along with the rest of the British middle class, the perceived shortage of suitable servants. In 1911 the Suburb's local newspaper, the *Town Crier*, complained that 'The demand for domestic help is as constant in the Garden Suburb as elsewhere.' The issue became so pressing that the following year a subcommittee of the Residents' Council set up its own servants' registry for 'housewives in difficulties for workers'.[52]

The *Town Crier* claimed that many of London's domestic workers were deterred from taking up posts in Hampstead Garden Suburb because of its distance from the entertainments and working-class neighbourhoods of the city centre.[53] This, combined with the fact there were no public houses in the Suburb, would also have made it difficult for servants to meet potential lovers or husbands among their own class and thus to pursue one of the most common routes out of service favoured by

[50] Schwartz, *A Serious Endeavour*, chapter 4.
[51] Barnett, 'The Garden Suburb at Hampstead', p. 236.
[52] *Town Crier* Nov. 1911, p. 98; Aug. 1912, p. 75; Sept. 1912, p. 85; Oct. 1912, p. 97. See also *Town Crier* Aug. 1914, p. 57; *Record* April 1915, p. 112.
[53] *Town Crier* Dec. 1911, p. 109; Nov. 1912, p. 117.

unhappy domestics. It would have been particularly hard for those at Waterlow Court to pursue romantic or sexual relationships with men, since the porter in his Lodge monitored all the comings and goings of this 'Adamless Eden'.[54] When Suburb residents discussed the 'servant problem', they did not look to Waterlow Court for the solution. Perhaps this was because it did not turn out to be the panacea that had been hoped for. Instead, the committee in charge of running the servants' registry focused on the need for 'steady supply, good pay, [and] good work', encouraging (though not compelling) employers to pay servants 2s. 6d. per day and providing half-day chars with a lunch at the end of their morning's work. They also reminded employers to account for the time and expense endured by charwomen commuting from poorer areas of London.[55] Concern to avoid the worst excesses of low wages and bad conditions was not the same, however, as a commitment to equality; and it should not be assumed that all the facilities available to residents of Hampstead Garden Suburb in general, including the suffrage meetings, were automatically open to domestic servants. Indeed, in March 1915 some 'Ladies of the Suburb' advertised a club for young domestic servants 'seeking wholesome recreation', which suggests that the numerous other clubs and entertainments on offer to residents were either inaccessible to these young women or rarely frequented by them.[56] Servants may have been cause for concern and even compassion among forward-thinking Suburb residents and supporters of women's rights, but they were still viewed as a wholly separate and different type of woman – the object rather than the subject of movements for social reform.

In November 1914 a Hampstead Garden Suburb branch of the DWU was announced, supported by a Cyril Harding of 27 Erskine Hill, next door to the Suburb's own servant registry at number 29.[57] Despite, or perhaps encouraged by, their close geographical proximity, they took different approaches. The DWU was unique in consistently placing servants as the agents of their own destiny and struggles for improved working conditions. Kathlyn Oliver's critique of co-operative housekeeping encapsulates the difference in approach. In her letters to Alice Melvin and the *Freewoman*, Oliver persisted in decentring the middle-class housewife as the feminist subject. In fact, Oliver and Melvin had already exchanged sharp words on this very issue two years previously in the

---

[54] *Clarion* 16 July 1909, p. 6.
[55] Prior to the establishment of this registry, the Suburb's local paper had advertised the Women's Industrial Council's Association of Trained Charwomen; *Town Crier* Oct. 1911, p. 88; Nov. 2011, p. 98.
[56] *Record* March 1915, p. 94.   [57] *Town Crier* Nov. 1914, p. 103.

correspondence pages of the *Woman Worker*. In 1910 Alice Melvin had attended one of the founding meetings of Kathlyn Oliver's DWU, but was sorely disappointed to discover that 'the note struck was one of class war' rather than encouraging 'the true spirit of cooperation and understanding between employer and worker'. In response to this, Kathlyn Oliver reiterated that her union existed not for the convenience of mistresses, but to further the interests of servants. What this brief exchange reveals, in the same manner as Oliver and Melvin's correspondence two years later, is how difficult it was for even socialist and feminist middle-class reformers to accept that their interests might be directly counter-posed to those of working-class women, at least when it came to the workplace of the home.[58] As a result, co-operative housekeeping – an otherwise innovative, radical and well-thought-out attempt to end the backbreaking labour and isolation endured by both waged and unwaged women in the home – failed to challenge the unequal power relations that lay at the heart of the 'servant problem'.

Working-Class Women's Organisations and Co-operative Housekeeping

The co-operative housekeeping schemes discussed thus far were aimed at middle-class housewives and professional working women. Some forms of co-operative housekeeping did, however, appeal to more working-class elements in the wider suffrage movement, even if enthusiasm was never as great as in more middle-class circles.[59] Proposals for co-operative housekeeping began to circulate in the Women's Co-operative Guild almost as soon as it was established, though support was not as unanimous as the name of the organisation might suggest. Some leading Guildswomen made the case for co-operative kitchens and cost-price restaurants, for public wash-houses where women could make use of up-to-date technology to wash their own clothes and for better-designed houses. Rank-and-file members would have had access to theories of co-operative housekeeping via the Guild's popular circulating library and the 'Women's Corner' of the movement's paper, the *Co-operative News*. Moreover, working-class women already had experience of the benefits of some form of collectivised housework, for neighbours and extended family often helped each other out on wash day or with childcare. There were sometimes tensions between the visions of co-operative

---

[58] *Woman Worker* 13 April 1910, p. 880; 4 May 1910, pp. 942–943. Alice Melvin referred to her membership of a 'Socialist Society' in this exchange.

[59] Dyhouse, *Feminism and the Family*, pp. 132–138.

housekeeping advocated by more middle-class Guildswomen, and the practical needs and desires of the working-class membership. But some aspects of co-operative housekeeping, such as campaigns for local councils to build public wash-houses, did gain widespread support.[60]

The East London Federation of the Suffragettes was much smaller and much more radical than the Women's Co-operative Guild. It was in some ways more successful in putting co-operative housekeeping ideas into practice in working-class communities, at least in the extreme poverty of the East End.[61] Whereas the Guild never managed to establish co-operative kitchens, despite some level of support among its members, Sylvia Pankhurst's idea for a Cost Price Restaurant (serving 'two-penny two course meals to adults, penny meals to children, at midday; and each evening a pint of hot soup and a chunk of bread for a penny') was made a reality at the end of August 1914 and proved so popular that three more were established. The First World War unwittingly created the conditions for some of these more working-class visions of co-operative housekeeping to be realised, as food shortages, the entry of women into munitions work and the loss of the male breadwinner made more traditional domestic arrangements difficult to maintain. Sylvia Pankhurst recollected how, in the weeks following the outbreak of war, when the government delayed paying out the 'separation allowance' to the families of working-class men who had enlisted, many women and children in London's East End were left destitute and greatly in need of cheap, nourishing food.[62] Later, cost-price restaurants were also established by charitable organisations and by the Ministry of Food as a way to ensure that women munitions workers received the nutrition they needed to get them through long and exhausting days. The suffrage movement remained alert to their wider political potential to liberate women from the home and rationalise the inefficient and backward conditions of housework.[63] Pre-war feminist thinking on

---

[60] Thomson, '"Domestic Drudgery Will Be a Thing of the Past"', pp. 127, 112.

[61] Patricia W. Romero, *E. Sylvia Pankhurst: Portrait of a Radical* (New Haven: Yale University Press, 1987); Barbara Winslow, *Sylvia Pankhurst: Sexual Politics and Political Activism* (London: University College London Press, 1996); Mary Davis, *Sylvia Pankhurst: A Life in Radical Politics* (London: Pluto Press, 1999); Shirley Harrison, *Sylvia Pankhurst: The Rebellious Suffragette* (Newhaven: Golden Guides Press, 2012); Katherine Connelly, *Sylvia Pankhurst: Suffragette, Socialist and Scourge of Empire* (London: Pluto Press, 2013); Rosemary Taylor and Sarah Jackson, *East London Suffragettes* (Stroud: History Press, 2014). By the First World War there were 'no more than a few hundred people actively involved'; Winslow, *Sylvia Pankhurst*, pp. 77–78.

[62] E. Sylvia Pankhurst, *The Home Front: A Mirror to Life in England during the First World War* (London: Cresset Library, 1987 [first published 1932]), pp. 22–29, 43–44.

[63] *Common Cause* 4 Aug. 1916, p. 219; Pankhurst, *The Home Front*, p. 43.

co-operative housekeeping informed some of these wartime endeavours, such as the National Kitchen, established in 1917 on Westminster Bridge Road and based on a design by Ada Nield Chew, who had in turn been influenced by Charlotte Perkins Gilman. This kitchen was supported by the Women's Labour League which began to look into limited forms of co-operative housekeeping more seriously after 1918.[64] Clementina Black believed that these wartime canteens and public kitchens had made working-class women more open to considering other forms of co-operative housekeeping. Although the scheme in *A New Way of Housekeeping* was intended for middle-class women, she hoped that in time such a model would appeal to 'the poorer classes ... women who are at the same time wage-earners, mothers of children and servants of all work'.[65]

This history of co-operative housekeeping has tended to be treated separately from that of the more middle-class schemes discussed in this chapter. However, if we locate all of these varied attempts to collectivise domestic labour within wider feminist debates on housework and domestic service, their histories begin to be revealed as more interconnected. Although advocates of co-operative housekeeping in these working-class women's organisations focused on housewives, rather than servants and mistresses, many of them were aware of and had contributed to debates on the 'servant problem'. Catherine Webb of the Women's Co-operative Guild had been a leading proponent of co-operative housekeeping since 1894 when she presented a paper to the Guild's annual meeting on 'co-operation as applied to domestic work'.[66] Some of her arguments were very similar to those of Jane Hume Clapperton and Clementina Black, describing the collectivisation of housework as part of 'the still onward march of civilisation' and arguing that industrial economies of scale should be applied to domestic labour. She also wrote the report for the Women's Industrial Council 1903 enquiry into the 'servant problem', and would likely have been aware of the DWU.[67] Margaret Bondfield, a founding member of the Women's Labour League and the President of the People's Suffrage Federation, possibly learned some of her support

---

[64] Dyhouse, *Feminism and the Family*, p. 117; Collette, *For Labour and for Women*, pp. 161–162; Krista Cowman, '"From the Housewife's Point of View": Female Citizenship and the Gendered Domestic Interior in Post–First World War Britain, 1918–1928', *English Historical Review*, 130:543 (2015), 352–383.

[65] Black, *A New Way of Housekeeping*, pp. 110–111.

[66] Gillian Scott, 'Catherine Webb (1859–1947), Co-operative Movement Activist and Writer', in *Oxford Dictionary of National Biography*, online edn. (Oxford University Press, 2004); Thomson, '"Domestic Drudgery Will Be a Thing of the Past"', p. 117.

[67] Catherine Webb, 'An Unpopular Industry', *Nineteenth Century*, 53 (June 1903), 989–1001.

for co-operative housekeeping during her time as a resident of Hampstead Garden Suburb.[68] She was also active in the National Federation of Women Workers, to which the DWU belonged. She attended at least one of the DWU's meetings, when in 1910 she unfurled a banner that had been presented to it by the radical Countess of Warwick.[69] Just after the First World War, Bondfield published a pamphlet titled 'Women as Domestic Workers', denouncing those who called upon newly unemployed munition workers to return to service. 'For the majority', she asserted, 'waged domestic service is an unregulated, sweated industry' blighted by 'poor pay, the petty tyranny of little minds, and above all consciousness of inferior status'. Bondfield referred to the work of the pre-war Glasgow-based branch of the DWU whose organiser, Jessie Stephen, she also knew from the Labour Party.[70] Like the DWU, Bondfield wanted to turn domestic service into 'a well regulated industry, in which the social status of its workers will be equal to that of any other section of labour'. In order to achieve this, she advocated that the living-in system must be abolished and domestic workers unionised. In this pamphlet Bondfield moved seamlessly from discussing the conditions of waged domestic workers to discussing those of the unwaged housewife. Using an anecdote to explain the way in which their conditions represented two sides of the same coin, she referred to a recent conference in the West Country that had been debating 'the future development of domestic work':

a trade union comrade arose and impatiently dismissed the subject with 'why do we waste time discussing domestic service – we workers never have domestic service – we can't afford it!' He was properly told by the housewives present that he got domestic service, alright, but he paid nothing for it![71]

Thus, just as Margaret Bondfield argued for an eight-hour day for centrally employed domestic workers, she also advocated that 'the intolerably long working day of the average house mother ... [should] be reduced to about one third of the time' through 'co-operation': communal kitchens, co-operative wash houses and nurseries.[72] For her,

[68] Slack, *Henrietta's Dream*, p. 27; Collette, *For Labour and for Women*, p. 76.
[69] *Labour Leader* 2 Dec. 1910, p. 765.
[70] Margaret Bondfield, 'Women as Domestic Workers', in Ellen Malos (ed.), *The Politics of Housework* (London: Alison & Busby, 1980 [first published 1919]), 83–87. Jessie Stephen described how she and Bondfield fell out at some point in the 1920s, after Stephen publicly criticised Bondfield for advocating that British women emigrate to Canada to take up jobs as domestic servants; Working Class Movement Library, Salford, Jessie Stephen, 'Submission Is for Slaves' (unpublished manuscript), pp. 151–152.
[71] Bondfield, 'Women as Domestic Workers', p. 86.   [72] Ibid., p. 86.

waged domestic workers and unpaid working-class wives and mothers operated within the same spectrum of exploitation.

Working-class women probably couldn't have cared less when Jane Hume Clapperton, Clementina Black and Alice Melvin complained about a shortage of cooks and parlour-maids, but their view of housework was also shaped by the 'servant problem'. Many working-class house-wives would have worked as servants before marriage and as charwomen afterwards, and all of them would have known a close family member who had done so. Three out of seven autobiographical testimonials published by members of the Women's Co-operative Guild, for example, were by women who had been servants.[73] Their critique of the drudgery and isolation of housework, and campaigns for some form of co-operative housekeeping, must therefore be understood as part of a dia-logue with domestic worker militancy. The socialist and suffragette Hannah Mitchell has become well known for her critique of how working-class wives and mothers like herself had their political aspir-ations severely circumscribed by housewifely duties, forced to campaign for the Cause 'between tea and dinner' with 'one hand tied behind us'. Yet her loathing of housework did not begin with marriage, but was already alive and well when she entered domestic service at age thirteen. Mitchell's memoir recalled how her younger self had not only hated the work itself, but also the inferior status attached to it:

I was expected to wear a cap and apron to wait at table ... but this I flatly refused to do; having cooked and served the meal I felt it was too much to be expected to stay in the dining room to 'hand the dishes round'. I wore an apron at work of course, but absolutely refused to don the muslin badge of servitude.[74]

Hannah Mitchell had left home at a young age, provoked by a difficult relationship with her mother who imposed on her daughter an unendur-able domestic burden, subscribing to standards of cleanliness she, in turn, had learnt during her own time in service.[75]

---

[73] 'Memories of Seventy Years, by Mrs Layton', 'A Plate Layer's Wife, by Mrs Wrigley', 'In a Mining Village, by Mrs F. H. Smith', in Margaret Llewelwyn Davies (ed.), *Life as We Have Known It by Co-operative Working Women* (London: Virago, 1977 [first published 1931]).

[74] Hannah Mitchell, *The Hard Way Up: The Autobiography of Hannah Mitchell, Suffragette and Rebel* (London: Virago, 1977), pp. 67–68.

[75] Ibid., pp. 39, 42–43, 54–56, 63.

Conclusion

The idea for this book began a long time ago, when I was writing the history of an Oxford women's college and trying to find ways of understanding the often-ignored presence of domestic workers in this feminist-minded institution. During that time, I read Alison Light's *Mrs Woolf and the Servants* and was compelled by her argument that 'the history of service is the history of British women'. Thinking about the wider social and political context within which Virginia Woolf's subjectivity had been forged, I wanted to explore further both a feminised articulation of class relations and the role of waged domestic labour in the formation of 'first wave' feminism. The 'fantasy' of independence and autonomy that was so central to Woolf's vision of herself as a modern woman, the prioritising of the intellectual over the emotional, and the high-minded over domestic trivialities, resonated in many ways with the female communities I was researching. It was no coincidence that Virginia Woolf's essay 'A Room of One's Own' was first given as a lecture at Girton and Newnham, Cambridge colleges founded in the belief that young women, in order to realise their intellectual potential, must be freed from the domestic duties expected of them at home. That is not to say that every student passing through these often rather politically cautious institutions embraced the kind of lifestyle advocated by Woolf, nor that Woolf was representative of 'first wave' feminism. But when it came to attitudes towards servants and domestic labour, many of the themes that Light identified in bohemian Bloomsbury I also came across in suburban Oxford – in particular, the identification of servants as the 'other' to the modern emancipated woman, symbolising old-fashioned or passive models of femininity.[1] Where had these ideas and associations come from? What political perspectives underpinned them? How much

---

[1] Alison Light, *Mrs Woolf and the Servants* (London: Penguin Books, 2008), pp. xiv–xv, xx, 55, 76, 151, 203–205; Laura Schwartz, *A Serious Endeavour: Gender, Education and Community at St Hugh's 1886–2011* (London: Profile Books, 2011), chapter 4; Virginia Woolf, *A Room of One's Own* (London: Hogarth Press, 1929).

purchase did they have across a broader and longer-standing current of feminist thought and action? And what did working-class feminists, including those who worked as servants, have to say about it all?

Asking these questions of the 'first wave' as a whole quickly brought me to the debates on the 'servant problem' that exercised many women engaged in suffrage activism at the turn of the twentieth century. My research revealed a much more varied and complex range of thinking than I had originally envisaged. Many in the suffrage campaign engaged sympathetically with servants, some of them were servants, and this movement developed a sophisticated analysis of reproductive labour that often strove to reform and revalue it. At the same time, Woolf's reservations, her hesitancy about those who could be dismissed as having a 'housemaid's mind', as well as Oxford's first women students' desire to clearly differentiate themselves from the women who cooked and cleaned for them, proved to be far from idiosyncratic.[2] Such attitudes must be located within a much broader current of thought: the feminist work ethic. Sometimes this ethic crystallised into a coherent renunciation of the 'servant attributes' of submissive womanhood; at others it was incorporated into more positive attempts to re-envisage the domestic sphere. Most interestingly, I found domestic workers participating in these debates, challenging those who deemed household labour nothing more than 'menial work' while at the same time internalising many of the beliefs that made it difficult for servants to identify as part of a feminist movement.

Underpinning much discussion of the 'servant problem' were two central questions: was domestic service a job like any other and was housework equal to other kinds of work? The suffrage movement never arrived at a unanimous answer, nor did it ever agree upon a definitive solution. The Domestic Workers' Union (DWU), however, took the debate in a new direction, highlighting the inherently exploitative nature of the employment contract and the gendered and classed division of labour. They forced these issues onto the pages of the suffrage press, despite considerable resistance from many mistresses in that movement. Often their critiques remained at the margins of debates on the 'servant problem'; they were rarely coherently theorised nor fully incorporated into the various solutions that emerged. But they persist as a counter-voice, as a point of tension, in the suffrage archive.

Grace Neal and Kathlyn Oliver's proposal for servants to live together in hostels and go out to work in a number of different houses for limited

---

[2] Light, *Mrs Woolf and the Servants*, p. 147.

periods of time was about more than simply improving pay and conditions. Crucial to this vision was the severing of mistress and maid so that servants would be employed by the state rather than by the people who used their services. Moreover, their insistence that servants should have their own domestic needs catered for was a way of recognising that they too had to deal with the housework problem and, just like middle-class women who went out to work, should be relieved of this double burden. The DWU always insisted that servants were part of the wider working class, cognisant of the conflict of interest between themselves and their employers and capable of class struggle. It was this understanding of class exploitation that remained at the heart of their various proposals to reform domestic service, a kernel of contradiction that sometimes seemed to point more towards a desire to eradicate the industry altogether. On the one hand, the DWU argued that servants simply needed to be treated as skilled workers, adequately trained and remunerated for undertaking an important job, and protected by labour legislation in the same manner as factory workers. On the other, Kathlyn Oliver and Jessie Stephen's insistence that their union existed to represent the interests of the workers, and that these might not be the same as those of their employers, made their vision of professionalisation quite different from that put forward by middle-class reformers who hoped to solve the 'servant problem' for mistresses as well as maids. The DWU's feminist politics, their understanding of the need to transform women's relationship to the home and domestic labour more generally, and to liberate them to undertake other forms of work, mitigated against a more straightforward or moderate trade unionist position which merely argued for an improvement in workers' conditions within the existing social and economic system. Kathlyn Oliver's critique of Alice Melvin's co-operative housekeeping might in some ways be seen as a churlish response to a genuine attempt to make concrete improvements to the lives of domestic workers. But Oliver's sense of herself as a woman with an equal claim to the emancipatory politics that informed such projects meant that she could not accept the idea that her middle-class sisters might be able to free themselves of the burdens of the home while she, 'a domestic drudge', would continue to perform work that others wished to avoid.

The First World War abruptly curtailed the activities of the DWU, and although organising efforts continued sporadically in the inter-war years, they never fulfilled the radical hopes of its founders. Subsequent agitation in the 1970s bore a closer resemblance to Stephen and Oliver's union, when militant cleaners and Women's Liberationists formed campaign alliances – though these focused on organising cleaners in offices and university colleges rather than in private homes.[3] *Feminism and the Servant Problem* therefore argues for a longer and more continuous history of domestic worker organising in Britain, stretching from New Unionism to present-day cleaners' struggles, a new area of British labour history in which much research remains to be done.[4] The persistence of the 'servant problem' into the inter-war period, and the fact that many aspects remain unresolved in the twenty-first century, should caution against easy triumphalist narratives of feminist progress over the last hundred years. In particular, the exclusion of servants from the 1918 Representation of the People Act serves as an important reminder of some of the limitations of the suffrage movement and which women's rights it managed to secure. To argue that servants occupied a difficult position within 'first wave' feminism is not, however, the same as saying that they were not present, and this book has shown what an important role they and other working-class women played. It also demonstrates how many suffrage activists were equally committed to socialism and trade unionism and how these movements often overlapped. I therefore aim to nuance a tendency within some currents of today's intersectional feminism to disavow the feminism of the past as white and middle-class. This, I believe, sometimes compounds the problems it seeks to highlight by assuming a homogeneous political perspective on the part of previous movements and thus erasing the counter-voices and contributions made by more marginalised activists. Nor should analyses of the class politics of the suffrage movement begin and end with the question of 'inclusivity'. We must also interrogate the content of the political ideas emerging from that movement, to ask which competing currents eventually won out and why this was the case. We need more research, for example, on the feminist work ethic, how it developed over the course of the twentieth century and was eventually co-opted by neo-liberalism. Finally, I hope that this book can act as a corrective to over-determined claims regarding the novelty of the twenty-first-century service economy and the supposed accompanying demise of the working class. Important changes have, of course, occurred in Britain since the 1970s as service sector jobs increasingly displaced those in manufacturing. But a feminist approach to this history, which takes account of more than just the male working class, not only highlights the long-standing economic significance of the service

---

[3] For 1970s campaigns, Sheila Rowbotham, 'Cleaners' Organising in Britain from the 1970s: A Personal Account', *Antipode*, 38:3 (2006), 608–625; Delap, *Knowing Their Place*, pp. 91–92; Schwartz, *A Serious Endeavour*, pp. 133–134.

[4] For more recent initiatives, Jane Wills, 'Making Class Politics Possible: Organising Contract Cleaners in London', *International Journal of Urban and Regional Research*, 32:2 (June 2008), 305–323.

industry, but also reveals how, although it was difficult to organise domestic workers, the impulse for collective struggle never was and never can be limited to the factory.

In the spring of 2017, I, along with other members of the Feminist Fightback collective, became involved in support work for what turned out to be a successful strike by cleaners at the London School of Economics. Mildred Simpson, a cleaner at the university of sixteen years' standing, summed up the strikers' demands (for the same right to pensions, sick pay, holiday and parental leave as other LSE employees) with the words: 'All we are asking for is equality.'[5] On one of the strike days I was invited to speak about the history of the DWU at a teach-in that took place outside the Women's Library (now housed at the LSE) where I had undertaken much of my research. The struggles of more than 100 years ago were only too familiar to the twenty-first-century domestic workers that were present that day – not just because of continued resistance to treating cleaners on an equal basis with other workers, but also because of the irony of LSE having recently appointed its first woman director while failing to extend its interest in gender equality to ensuring decent wages and conditions for the women who cleaned its offices, libraries and classrooms.

   Often, when I present my research, people tell me how struck they are by the similarities between the complaints of early twentieth-century servants and mistresses and the concerns that plague many women's lives in the twenty-first century. Some express outrage that 'this stuff is still going on today!' Others, always women, tell me somewhat furtively that they feel guilty about employing a cleaner, but are not really sure what else to do given the demands of their own jobs. Sometimes men inform me that they and their wives share all the housework, before going onto mention that there is, in fact, another woman who comes in each week to shoulder part of that burden. It's hard not to feel as if we're going round and round in circles: domestic labour is still mainly women's work, it is still undervalued and underpaid, and therefore it is still mainly women's work. Yet I also think it's crucial that we don't simply cry '*plus ça change*'. To reduce domestic labour to 'the problem that will always be with us' is to reinscribe a wholly incorrect notion of it as timeless and outside of history.

---

[5] United Voices of the World, 'London School of Economics', www.uvwunion.org.uk; Feminist Fightback, 'Supporting the LSE Cleaners' Strike from the Picket Lines' (24 June 2017), www.thefword.org.uk.

In fact, the twentieth century witnessed profound changes to the organisation of housework and its related employment practices, shaped by wider historical developments. The First World War radically, if only temporarily, disrupted traditional patterns of service. Not only did many servants enter munitions factories or step into jobs vacated by men at the front, leaving many mistresses to run their homes single-handed, some middle-class women's war duty required them to undertake domestic labour in hospitals and canteens. The inter-war years saw intensifying levels of anxiety among the middle classes about the future of service, more working-class women choosing light manufacturing and shop work, and increasing reliance upon daily help rather than live-in servants in lower-middle-class households.[6] Some feminist and labour movement activists also began to note slow and uneven improvements in servants' working conditions.[7] All of these trends were not simply the result of the disruptions of the war but also influenced by the agitation of the militant servants who appear in this book.

Nevertheless, domestic service exhibited remarkable resilience in the face of all of these challenges. Middle-class women remained vocal about their need for competent domestic servants.[8] In 1936 Ray Strachey surveyed the changes to women's employment since the granting of the franchise in 1918, and remarked upon the rapid expansion of 'paid employment of women in occupations other than home-making':

[I]f this state of affairs is not to impose an intolerable and dangerous strain upon the female sex, one of two things must happen. Either men must take on a greater share of the tasks of home-making or the intensity of the hours of competitive conditions of labour must be reduced. Or both.[9]

The difficulties articulated by middle-class mistresses in the suffrage movement, struggling to combine professional work with the need to maintain comfortable homes, thus persisted. Although by the 1930s Strachey was offering some solutions to the 'servant problem' that had seldom been put forward in the pre-war debates, she certainly did not propose an end to domestic service altogether. The numbers of women employed as servants had quickly recovered in the 1920s as women were pushed out of so-called men's jobs, and by 1931 service still accounted

[6] Delap, *Knowing Their Place*, pp. 12–14. See also Pamela Horn, *The Rise and Fall of the Victorian Servant* (Stroud: Alan Sutton Publishing, 1990), pp. 188–190.
[7] London Metropolitan University: Trades Union Congress Library, '10th Report for the Years 1918 and 1919'; TUC, 'The Annual Report and Balance Sheet of the National Federation of Women Workers'.
[8] Delap, *Knowing Their Place*, p. 99.
[9] Ray Strachey, 'Changes in Employment', in Ray Strachey (ed.), *Our Freedom and Its Results* (London: Hogarth Press, 1936), 117–172, pp. 169–170.

for 24 per cent of all women in waged work.[10] Inter-war governments actively sought to ensure the continuation of a servant class, even while highlighting the need to improve the conditions and status of the industry. The 1923 Ministry of Labour's *Report on the Supply of Female Domestic Servants* once again identified professionalisation as a solution, and many new training programmes were funded and promoted by the Ministry of Labour's Central Committee of Women's Training and Employment. Meanwhile, the unemployment benefits system was designed to coerce women into service. After 1922 those receiving the dole were required to accept any job available to them and, because demand for servants remained high even during the postwar economic slump and the Depression of the 1930s, unemployed women often had their benefits discontinued if they refused to take up a domestic post. Some former suffrage activists and Labour Party women, including Margaret Bondfield and the Women's Industrial Council, ended up supporting these inter-war government training drives, in spite of the way the wider policy severely restricted working-class women's employment choices. Some of them did so reluctantly, feeling there was little alternative in times of such severe economic hardship, but their complicity also reveals the inherent limitations of pre-war visions of professionalisation as a solution to the 'servant problem'.[11]

A more profound watershed in the history of British service came with the social and political upheavals following the Second World War. This book focuses on a relatively short period of time, but of course its subjects lived on long after the point at which my research has left them. Many of the women who grew up in a period when domestic service was the norm (even if it was coming in for ever-greater scrutiny) and who were active in a feminist movement in which class difference was a constant (if troublesome) presence, were still alive in the 1950s and 1960s to witness the high point of social democracy. Jessie Stephen thrived in this new atmosphere: revelling in the unlikely relationships that were thrown up by the war years, and ending her days as respected Labour Party activist in a comfortable council house. In an interview recorded in 1977, she comes across as happy with her choice to remain independent of the nuclear family and proud she had lived a life that would have been unimaginable

---

[10] Delap, *Knowing Their Place*, p. 13

[11] Diane Aiken, 'The Central Committee on Women's Training and Employment: Tackling the Servant Problem, 1914–1945', PhD thesis, Oxford Brookes University (2002); Pamela Horn, *Life below Stairs: The Real Lives of Servants, 1939 to the Present* (Stroud: Amberley, 2014), chapter 3; Cathy Hunt, *The National Federation of Women Workers, 1906–1921* (Basingstoke: Palgrave Macmillan, 2014), pp. 99–101.

to her own mother.[12] Mary Blathwayt lived until 1961, although her involvement in politics did not continue beyond the suffrage movement. On a visit to Eagle House in 2017, I spoke with Colin Frayling, whose grandfather had purchased it after Mary Blathwayt's death. A young man at the time, Frayling recalled how the household that had once been filled with servants and suffragettes had shrunk to just the one room that Mary Blathwayt inhabited before she died while the rest of the building crumbled around her. The 'Suffragette Arboretum', the trees planted by each suffrage activist who had stayed with the Blathwayts, was buried under a new housing estate, and Eagle House was converted into flats. Its new owner, Frederick William Hawker, was a local man, the managing director of a joinery and building business founded just across the road in 1919. His wife, Edith Annie (née Onslow), had been a servant at Field End House, Batheaston, during the First World War.[13]

The effects of postwar social democracy were felt not only in terms of class, but also gender. By the end of the Second World War the age of the 'live-in' domestic servant had passed. The stay-at-home housewife with sole responsibility for her family's domestic needs became the normative model, if not always the reality, and the social unit upon which both consumer capitalism and the welfare state was founded.[14] A subsequent generation of feminists was rightly critical of the isolation and limited social horizons that these gender roles entailed. Nevertheless, free health care, some elder care and social housing meant the state taking responsibility for many aspects of reproductive labour that had weighed so heavily upon the early twentieth-century working-class wives who feature in this book. The welfare state also created the political and demographic conditions for the emergence of a 'second wave' of feminism in the 1970s and 1980s. And if the Women's Liberation Movement no longer had to grapple with a 'servant problem', they certainly did have to struggle against the gendered division of labour in the home. One of the most striking

---

[12] The Women's Library at the London School of Economics, London, 'Oral Evidence on the Suffragist and Suffragette Movements: The Brian Harrison Interviews', (1974–1981), interview with Jessie Stephen (1977), 8SUF/B/157, Disc 32–33.

[13] The Hawkers' connection with Eagle House began in the 1920s, when they rented first the gardener's cottage and then the old servants' quarters from the Blathwayts. Field End House is now known as Tower House. This information is based on conversations with Colin Frayling in September 2017 and Freda Roberts (née Hawker, daughter of Frederick William and Edith Annie Hawker) in September 2018. Freda Roberts stressed how Mary Blathwayt remained alert and kind right up to her death, always remembering the Hawker family birthdays with a gift of 5s.

[14] Some regional studies have in fact revealed a rise in working-class women undertaking part-time work outside the home; Selina Todd, 'Affluence, Class and Crown Street: Reinvestigating the Post-War Working Class', *Contemporary British History*, 22:4 (Dec. 2008), 501–518, p. 506.

contrasts between the 'first' and 'second wave' critiques of housework was that the latter was far more forceful in demanding that men take on their fair share. Women's Liberationists' arguments for the socialisation of domestic labour via state-funded childcare and communal living also highlight important continuities within feminism across the century.

The legacies of the early twentieth-century debates on housework and the 'servant problem' with which this book is concerned were not lost entirely, but the role of domestic labour in contemporary capitalism has been determined by many other factors. In 1973 the left-wing North American sociologist Lewis A. Coser was able to declare fairly uncontroversially that the forces of modernisation had made domestic service an obsolete occupational role.[15] From today's perspective such a statement appears ludicrous. Paid domestic labour in both the public sphere and private homes has returned with a vengeance since the 1980s and become a central feature of neo-liberalism and globalisation. As welfare states have been attacked and the vast majority of women in the global north are now employed outside the home (over 70 per cent in Britain), some reproductive labour has been outsourced to the commercial sphere (convenience food, private childcare), and more and more middle-class families have once again begun to employ domestic workers in their own homes.[16] According to International Labour Organisation statistics, the number of domestic workers globally grew by almost 20 million between 1995 and 2010.[17] In the United Kingdom around 448,400 people worked as cleaners across the industry in 2010, employed by as many as one in ten British households, and 30 per cent of those in England were migrant workers.[18] Global inequality has thus been key to delivering

---

[15] Quoted in Rafaella Sarti, 'Historians, Social Scientists, Servants and Domestic Workers: 50 Years of Research on Domestic and Care Work', in Dirk Hoerder, Elise van Nederveen Meerkerk and Silke Neunsinger (eds.), *Towards a Global History of Domestic and Caregiving Workers* (Leiden: Brill, 2015), 25–60, p. 39.

[16] In 2017, 70.7 per cent of women aged sixteen to sixty-four were in paid employment, compared with 79.5 per cent of men, the highest female employment rate since records began in 1971 when the figure was at 52.8 per cent; Office for National Statistics, 'Statistical Bulletin: UK Labour Market' (Dec. 2017), www.ons.gov.uk.

[17] Elise van Nederveen Meerkerk, Silke Neunsinger and Dirk Hoerder, 'Domestic Workers of the World: Histories of Domestic Workers as Global Labor History', in Hoerder et al. (eds.), *Towards a Global History of Domestic and Caregiving Workers*, 1–24, pp. 12–15.

[18] Institute for Employment Research, 'Labour Market Information Future Trends', www.warwick.ac.uk; Selina Todd, 'Domestic Service and Class Relations in Britain 1900–1950', *Past and Present*, 203 (2009), 181–204, p. 181. Other studies have suggested that it is even larger, and that the unregulated nature of much of the cleaning industry make exact calculations difficult; Linda McDowell, *Working Bodies: Interactive Service Employment and Workplace Identities* (Oxford: Wiley-Blackwell, 2009), pp. 38, 81.

cheap labour back into British homes, and many migrant domestic workers are enmeshed in a global chain of care that requires them to outsource the care of their own homes and families in their countries of origin. Immigration controls, fear of deportation among undocumented workers and those whose visas are sponsored by their employers, in addition to a more general hostile environment also affecting European Union workers, make it difficult to assert even the limited employment rights currently in place.[19] Yet many migrants have become involved in, and indeed spearheaded, a resurgence in domestic workers' unions and pressure groups demanding governmental and international legislative intervention. These organising efforts began in the global south in the 1980s and were brought to the global north in the early twenty-first century primarily by migrating Caribbean, Latin America and Asian domestic workers.[20] In Britain, some of the most significant gains made by cleaners in the last decade or so have been won by small grass-roots migrant workers' unions such as the Cleaners and Allied Independent Workers Union, the Independent Workers of Great Britain and United Voices of the World, although these have tended to focus on workers in offices and public institutions rather than private homes.[21] On a global scale, trade unions have begun to give greater recognition to domestic workers, and in 2011 the International Labour Organisation passed Convention 189 Concerning Decent Work for Domestic Workers.[22] At the time of writing, this Convention is now in force in twenty-four nations, but has not been ratified in Britain where cleaners on average earn around £7–£8 per hour, still less than the national living wage.[23]

Feminists continue to debate the rights and wrongs of employing a cleaner in one's own home. Much important work is being done to highlight the sexism and racism that structure this labour market, theorising the particularities of its exploitative form and pointing out that

[19] Lucy Delap, '"Yes Ma'am": Domestic Workers and Employment Rights', *History and Policy*: Policy Papers (3 Sept. 2012) www.historyandpolicy.org.

[20] Nederveen Meerkerk et al., 'Domestic Workers of the World', pp. 15–17.

[21] Kelly Rogers, 'Precarious and Migrant Workers in Struggle: Are New Forms of Trade Unionism Necessary in Post Brexit Britain?', *Capital and Class*, 41:2 (2017), 336–343.

[22] Celia Mather, '*Yes We Did It!' How the World's Domestic Workers Won International Rights and Recognition* (Cambridge, MA: WIEGO, 2013); Eileen Boris and Jennifer N. Fish, 'Decent Work for Domestics: Feminist Organising, Worker Empowerment and the ILO', in Hoerder et al. (eds.), *Towards a Global History of Domestic in Caregiving Workers*, 530–552.

[23] International Labour Organisation, 'Ratifications of C189 – Domestic Workers Convention, 2011 (No. 189)', www.ilo.org; PayScale, 'Cleaner Salary', www.payscale .com; McDowell, *Working Bodies*, p. 85. In 2017–2018 the national living wage was £8.75, rising to £10.20 in London; www.livingwage.org.uk.

cleaners are frequently employed to sidestep men's continued failure to take on their share of the housework.[24] Barbara Ehrenreich has argued that even if decent wages and tolerable conditions are provided, outsourcing housework still reproduces oppressive gender and race relations and hierarchies between women since the cleaner is only there because her employer has something 'better to do'.[25] Likewise, Bridget Anderson has suggested that there is no such thing as a fair wage for domestic work, given the social relations which currently define its commodification and the relative powerlessness of the domestic worker vis-à-vis their employer.[26] Vanessa May, by contrast, argues that it is far more useful to focus on supporting domestic workers' efforts to organise and campaigning for improved employment legislation. Lotika Singha has similarly critiqued what she believes to be the assumption underpinning much feminist concern regarding paid domestic labour – that the work itself is inherently worse than other forms of work – and instead asks us to think harder about how it might be professionalised so that it can become a respected and decently remunerated career.[27] May and Singha's arguments have many merits, not least in resisting an idea of domestic workers as victims and instead emphasising their agency, their ability to organise to transform their own conditions, and the important contribution they make to the economy and society at large. Tracing the long history of these debates, however, has suggested to me that it is worth continuing to probe further the ambivalence that many feminists feel about paying someone else to do their domestic work. A focus on pay and conditions and, especially, worker self-organisation must be the starting point of any feminist project to overcome the oppression and exploitation embedded in actually existing domestic labour practices. Yet the early twentieth-century DWU has taught me that this cannot be the end-point. Servants such as Kathlyn Oliver, Grace Neal and Jessie Stephen were active in a historical moment when the aspirations of working-class militancy frequently exceeded ameliorative trade unionism and began to imagine a world in which all forms of labour and related power relations would be much more fundamentally transformed.

---

[24] The Equal Opportunities Commission reported in 2007 that women still undertook 75 per cent of all unwaged work in the home; McDowell, *Working Bodies*, p. 82.
[25] Barbara Ehrenreich, 'Maid to Order', *Harper's Magazine*, 300:1799 (April 2000), 59–70.
[26] Bridget Anderson, *Doing the Dirty Work? The Global Politics of Domestic Labour* (London: Zed Books, 2000), pp. 25–26.
[27] Vanessa H. May, *Unprotected Labour: Household Workers, Politics, and Middle-Class Reform in New York, 1870–1940* (Chapel Hill: University of North Carolina Press, 2011), pp. 180–182; Lotika Singha, 'The Problem That Has No Name: Can "Paid Domestic Work" Be Reconciled with Feminism?', PhD thesis, University of York (2017).

This book has argued for the need to become more alert to the limitations and lacunae of the feminist political traditions that we have inherited, especially with regard to class and work. But throughout the research I have never ceased to be amazed by the rich and varied imagination of this movement. In particular, feminism has long offered a powerful critique of economically reductive and masculinist visions of class struggle and, in pushing for the personal to be incorporated into the political, has occasionally brought to life more radical alternatives. Some of the suffrage movement's suggestions for solving the 'servant problem', when considered alongside radical servants' insistent critique of the division of labour and the private employment contract, must, I think, continue to inform today's feminist debates on reproductive labour. Surely, in addition to advocating better employment rights for domestic workers and a levelling-up with other industries within the current economic system, we can also continue to make the case for this form of work and the power relations that structure it to be transformed out of existence. Can we not revisit arguments in favour of state-funded community kitchens (as a more healthy and more sociable alternative to convenience food?), for housing designed around the collectivisation of housework (as a way to save not just time and money but also the environment?), and for the state to recognise work in the home as real work and offer some form of remuneration (a basic income?) in return? More than this, can we not argue for the radical reduction of all hours worked in paid employment, so that we have more time to attend not just to our domestic needs but also our mental health and the emotional connections we build with friends and families? Can we not dismantle the division of labour even further, demanding time in professional jobs, for example, to clean our own offices and use this as an opportunity to gain a greater sense of ownership over our workplaces and build better relationships with our colleagues? Can we not consider what would be necessary to truly end the racial divisions that structure modern domestic labour by placing resistance to immigration controls at the centre of union organising? Such demands may appear utopian, but perhaps this is exactly what we need in these unstable political times when, despite the hate and fear that has erupted in the last few years, radical change has at the very least revealed itself as possible. It is worth remembering that demands that today would seem moderate, not least the vote, were once inconceivable to the majority of people. I end then, with a much more modest wish: that this book may offer an excavation of a historical moment that might help us continue to struggle for a world where nobody is a 'drudge', where every woman gets to 'think her own thoughts' and where we all understand that if the mind and the heart is to flourish, the body needs to be cared for by each other and by all of us.

Select Bibliography

Primary Sources

Archives

Alfred Gillett Trust (C&J Clark Ltd.), Street; Millfield Papers

Cumbria Archive, Carlisle; Catherine Marshall Papers

Gloucestershire Archives, Gloucester; Blathwayt Family of Dyrham Collection

London Metropolitan Archive; Hampstead Garden Suburb Archive, Court Registers

London Metropolitan University: Trades Union Congress Library; Gertrude Tuckwell Collection

National Archives, London; Home Office Records, Priory Residential Society Ltd.

Sheffield Archives; Edward Carpenter Collection

UK Censuses

University of Warwick: Modern Records Centre, Trades Union Congress Archive; Trade Union Correspondence Regarding the Organisation of Domestic Workers 1926–36

Wolverhampton Archive; Emma Sproson, 'Autobiography' (unpublished manuscript, n.d.), Sproson Correspondence

The Women's Library at the London School of Economics, London: Autograph Letter Collection, Pamphlet Collection, Suffrage Postcard Collection, Oral Evidence on the Suffragette and Suffragist Movements: the Brian Harrison Interviews

Working Class Movement Library, Salford; Jessie Stephen, 'Submission Is for Slaves' (unpublished manuscript, n.d.)

Newspapers

Clarion
Common Cause
Daily Express
Daily Herald
Daily Mail
Englishwoman

Freewoman
Garden Cities and Town Planning
Glasgow Herald
Labour Leader
Manchester Guardian
Mirror
New Age
Observer
Record
Rochdale Observer
Standard
Suffragette
Telegraph
The Times
Town Crier
Woman Worker
Woman's Dreadnought
Women's Franchise
Women's Industrial News
Vote
Votes for Women

Published Sources

A. J. R., *The Suffrage Annual and Women's Who's Who* (London: Stanley Paul, 1913).

Barnett, Henrietta, 'The Garden Suburb at Hampstead', *Contemporary Review*, 87 (1905), 231–237.

Benson, M. E., 'In Defence of Domestic Service: A Reply', *Nineteenth Century*, 28 (1890), 616–626.

Black, Clementina, 'The Dislike to Domestic Service', *Nineteenth Century and After: A Monthly Review*, 33:193 (1893), 454–456.

A New Way of Housekeeping (London: W. Collins Sons, 1918).

Bodichon, Barbara Leigh Smith, *Women and Work* (London: Bosworth & Harrison, 1857).

Bondfield, Margaret, 'Women as Domestic Workers', in Ellen Malos (ed.), *The Politics of Housework* (London: Alison & Busby, 1980 [first published 1919]), 83–87.

Braithwaite, W. J., *Lloyd George's Ambulance Wagon* (London: Methuen, 1957).

Bulley, A. Amy, 'Domestic Service: A Social Study', *Westminster Review*, 135:2 (1891), 177–186.

Butler, C. Violet, *Domestic Service: An Enquiry by the Women's Industrial Council* (New York: Garland, 1980 [first published 1916]).

Chew, Doris Nield (ed.), *Ada Nield Chew: The Life and Writings of a Working Woman* (London: Virago, 1982).

Clapperton, Jane Hume, *Scientific Meliorism and the Evolution of Happiness* (London: Kegan Paul, 1885).

Margaret Dunmore or, A Socialist Home (Milton Keynes: Lightening Source UK, n.d. [first published 1888]).

A Vision of the Future Based on the Application of Ethical Principles (London: Swan Sonnenschein, 1904).

Colmore, Gertrude, *Suffragette Sally* (Toronto: Broadview Press, 2008 [first published 1911]).

Darwin, Ellen W., 'Domestic Service', *Nineteenth Century*, 28 (1890), 286–296.

Davies, Margaret Llewelyn, *Maternity Letters from Working Women* (London: Virago, 1978 [first published 1915]).

Drake, Barbara, *Women in Trade Unions* (London: Virago, 1984 [first published 1920]).

Foley, Winifred, *A Child in the Forest* (London: Ariel Books, 1974).

Frazer, Mrs J. G., *First Aid to the Servantless* (Cambridge: W. Heffer & Sons, 1913).

Furniss, Averil Sanderson, and Marion Phillips, *The Working Woman's House* (London: Swarthmore Press, 1920).

Gilman, Charlotte Perkins, *The Home: Its Work and Influence* (Walnut Creek: AltaMira Press, 2002 [first published 1903]).

What Diantha Did (n.p.: Read How You Want, 2010 [first published 1909–1910]).

Glasier, Katharine Bruce, *Socialism and the Home* (London: Independent Labour Party, n.d.).

Hobhouse, Emily, 'Women Workers: How They Live, How They Wish to Live', *Nineteenth Century*, 27 (March 1900), 471–484.

Jermy, Louise, *The Memories of a Working Woman* (Norwich: Goose & Son, 1934).

Kenney, Annie, *Memories of a Militant* (London: Edward Arnold, 1924).

Lockwood, Florence, *An Ordinary Life 1861–1924* (London: Mrs Josiah Lockwood, 1932).

Marx, Karl, *Grundrisse* (Harmondsworth: Penguin, 1973 [first published 1939]).

Capital: A Critique of Political Economy, 3 vols. (London: Penguin Books, 1976 [first published 1867]), vol. I.

Maud, Constance Elizabeth, *No Surrender* (New York: John Lane, 1912 [first published 1911]).

Mitchell, Hannah, *The Hard Way Up: The Autobiography of Hannah Mitchell, Suffragette and Rebel* (London: Virago, 1977).

Oliver, Kathlyn, *Domestic Servants and Citizenship* (London: People's Suffrage Federation, 1911)

Pankhurst, Sylvia, *The Suffragette Movement* (London: Virago, 1977 [first published 1931]).

The Home Front: A Mirror to Life in England during the First World War (London: Cresset Library, 1987 [first published 1932]).

Papworth, L. Wyatt, 'Charwomen', in Clementina Black (ed.), *Married Women's Work* (London: Virago, 1983 [first published 1915]).

Powell, Margaret, *Below Stairs* (London: Pan Books, 1968).

Reeves, Maud Pember, *Round about a Pound a Week* (London: Persephone, 2008 [first published 1913]).

Robins, Elizabeth, *The Convert* (London: Macmillan, 1913 [first published 1907]).

Strachey, Ray (ed.), *Our Freedom and Its Results* (London: Hogarth Press, 1936).

Swanwick, H. M., *I Have Been Young* (London: Victor Gollancz, 1935).

Webb, Catherine, 'An Unpopular Industry', *Nineteenth Century*, 53 (1903), 989–1001.

West, Rebecca, *The Sentinel: An Incomplete Early Novel by Rebecca West*, ed. Kathryn Laing (Oxford: European Humanities Research Centre, 2002).

Woolf, Virginia, *A Room of One's Own* (London: Hogarth Press, 1929).

Secondary Sources

Unpublished

Dussart, Fae, 'The Servant/Employer Relationship in 19th Century India and England', PhD thesis, University College London (2005).

Eustance, Claire, '"Daring to Be Free": The Evolution of Women's Political Identities in the Women's Freedom League 1907–1930', PhD thesis, University of York (1993).

Gee, Emily, '"Where Shall She Live?" The Accommodation of Working Women in the Capital 1875–1925', thesis for diploma in building conservation, Architectural Association (2007).

Howell, Carys, 'Wales' Hidden Industry: Domestic Service in South Wales, 1871–1921', PhD thesis, University of Swansea (2014).

Jenkins, Lyndsey, 'From Mills to Militants: The Kenney Sisters, Suffrage and Social Reform c. 1890 to 1970', PhD thesis, University of Oxford (2018).

Robertson, Lisa Catherine, 'New and Novel Homes: Women Writing London's Housing', PhD thesis, University of Warwick (2016).

Robinson, Olivia (2016), 'Out of Sight and Over Here: Foreign Female Domestic Servants in London 1880–1939', conference poster presented at the Social History Society Conference, University of Lancaster (2016).

Singha, Lotika, 'The Problem That Has No Name: Can "Paid Domestic Work" Be Reconciled with Feminism?', PhD thesis, University of York (2017).

Walters, Susan Pauline, 'Emma Sproson (1867–1936): A Black Country Suffragette', MA dissertation, University of Leicester (1993).

Published

Anderson, Bridget, *Doing the Dirty Work? The Global Politics of Domestic Labour* (London: Zed Books, 2000).

Attar, Dena, *Wasting Girls' Time: The History and Politics of Home Economics* (London: Virago, 1990).

Beetham, Margaret, 'Domestic Servants as Poachers of Print: Reading Authority and Resistance in Late Victorian Britain', in Lucy Delap, Ben Griffin and Abigail Wills (eds.), *The Politics of Domestic Authority in Britain since 1800* (Basingstoke: Palgrave, 2009), 185–203.

Bland, Lucy, 'Heterosexuality, Feminism and the *Freewoman* Journal in Early Twentieth-Century England', *Women's History Review*, 4:1 (1995), 5–23.

  Banishing the Beast: English Feminism and Sexual Morality 1885–1914 (London: Tauris Parke Paperback, 2001).

Blodgett, Harriet, *Centuries of Female Days: Englishwomen's Private Diaries* (Gloucester: Alan Sutton, 1989).

Bonnett, Alistair, 'How the British Working Class Became White: The Symbolic (Re)Formation of Racialised Capitalism', *Journal of Historical Sociology*, 11:3 (Sept. 1998), 316–340.

Boris, Eileen, 'Class Returns', *Journal of Women's History*, 25:4 (Winter 2013), 74–87.

Boris, Eileen, and Jennifer N. Fish, 'Decent Work for Domestics: Feminist Organising, Worker Empowerment and the ILO', in Dirk Hoerder, Elise van Nederveen Meerkerk and Silke Neunsinger (eds.), *Towards a Global History of Domestic in Caregiving Workers* (Leiden: Brill, 2015), 530–552.

Boris, Eileen, and Premilla Nadasen (eds.), 'Historicizing Domestic Labor: Resistance and Organising', Special Issue *International Labor and Working-Class History*, 88 (Fall 2015).

Boston, Sarah, *Women Workers and the Trade Unions* (London: Lawrence & Wishart, 2015 [first published 1980])

Bourke, Joanna, *Husbandry to Housewifery: Women, Economic Change, and Housework in Ireland, 1890–1914* (Oxford: Clarendon Press, 1993).

  Working-Class Cultures in Britain 1890–1960: Gender, Class and Ethnicity (London: Routledge, 1994).

  'Housewifery in Working-Class England 1860–1914', in Pamela Sharpe (ed.), *Women's Work: The English Experience 1650–1914* (London: Arnold, 1998), 332–358.

Boussahba-Bravard, Myriam (ed.), *Suffrage Outside Suffragism: Women's Vote in Britain, 1880–1914* (Basingstoke: Palgrave Macmillan, 2007).

Bressey, Caroline, 'Black Women and Work in England, 1880–1920', in Mary Davis (ed.), *Class and Gender in British Labour History: Renewing the Debate (or Starting It?)* (Pontypool: Merlin Press, 2011), 117–132.

Buettner, Elizabeth, *Empire Families: Britons and Late Imperial India* (Oxford: Oxford University Press, 2004).

Bush, Julia, *Women against the Vote: Female Anti-Suffragism in Britain* (Oxford: Oxford University Press, 2007).

Caine, Barbara, *English Feminism, 1780–1980* (Oxford: Oxford University Press, 1997).

Canning, Audrey, 'Stephen, Jessie (1893–1979)', in *Oxford Dictionary of National Biography*, online edn. (Oxford University Press, 2004).

Chaudhuri, Nupur, 'Memsahibs and Their Servants in Nineteenth-Century India', *Women's History Review*, 3:4 (1994), 549–562.

Clark, Anna, *The Struggle for the Breeches: Gender and the Making of the British Working Class* (Berkeley: University of California Press, 1995).

  'E. P. Thompson and Domestic Service', *Labor: Studies in Working-Class History of the Americas*, 10:3 (2013), 41–44.

Collette, Christine, *For Labour and for Women: The Women's Labour League, 1906–1918* (Manchester: Manchester University Press, 1989).

Connelly, Katherine, *Sylvia Pankhurst: Suffragette, Socialist and Scourge of Empire* (London: Pluto Press, 2013).

Cook, Kay, and Neil Evans, '"The Petty Antics of the Bell-Ringing Boisterous Band"? The Women's Suffrage Movement in Wales, 1890–1918', in Angela V. John (ed.), *Our Mothers' Land: Chapters in Welsh Women's History, 1830–1939* (Cardiff: University of Wales Press, 1991), 159–188.

Costa, Mariarosa Dalla, and Selma James, *The Power of Woman and the Subversion of the Community* (Bristol: Falling Wall Press, 1975).

Cott, Nancy F., *The Grounding of Modern Feminism* (New Haven: Yale University Press, 1987).

Cowman, Krista, '"Incipient Toryism": The Women's Social and Political Union and the Independent Labour Party, 1903–1914', *History Workshop Journal*, 53 (2002), 128–148.

Mrs Brown Is a Man and a Brother: Women in Merseyside's Political Organisations, 1890–1920 (Liverpool: Liverpool University Press, 2004).

Women of the Right Spirit: Paid Organisers of the Women's Social and Political Union, 1904–1918 (Manchester: Manchester University Press, 2007).

'"From the Housewife's Point of View": Female Citizenship and the Gendered Domestic Interior in Post–First World War Britain, 1918–1928', *English Historical Review*, 130:543 (2015), 352–383.

Cowman, Krista, and Louise A. Jackson (eds.), *Women and Work Culture: Britain c. 1850–1950* (Aldershot: Ashgate, 2005).

Crawford, Elizabeth, *The Women's Suffrage Movement: A Reference Guide* (London: University College London Press, 1999).

Creedan, Alison, *'Only a Woman': Henrietta Barnett: Social Reformer and Founder of Hampstead Garden Suburb* (Chichester: Phillimore, 2006).

Davidoff, Leonore, *Worlds Between: Historical Perspectives on Gender and Class* (Cambridge: Polity Press, 1995).

Davidoff, Leonore, Megan Doolittle, Janet Fink and Katherine Holden, *The Family Story: Blood, Contract and Intimacy, 1830–1960* (Harlow: Longman, 1999).

Davidoff, Leonore, and Catherine Hall, *Family Fortunes: Men and Women of the English Middle Class, 1780–1850* (London: Hutchinson, 1987).

Davidson, Caroline, *A Woman's Work Is Never Done: A History of Housework in the British Isles 1650–1950* (London: Chatto and Windus, 1982).

Davin, Anna, 'Imperialism and Motherhood', *History Workshop Journal*, 5 (1978), 9–65.

Davis, Mary, *Sylvia Pankhurst: A Life in Radical Politics* (London: Pluto Press, 1999).

Davis, Mary (ed.), *Class and Gender in British Labour History: Renewing the Debate (or Starting It?)* (Pontypool: Merlin Press, 2011).

Delap, Lucy, 'Feminist and Anti-Feminist Encounters in Edwardian Britain', *Historical Research*, 78:201 (2005), 377–399.

Knowing Their Place: Domestic Service in Twentieth-Century Britain (Oxford: Oxford University Press, 2011).

Delap, Lucy, Maria Dicenzo and Leila Ryan (eds.), *Feminism and the Periodical Press, 1900–1980*, 3 vols. (Abingdon: Routledge, 2006).

Dicenzo, Maria, 'Militant Distribution: *Votes for Women* and the Public Sphere', *Media History*, 6:2 (2000), 115–128.

Dicenzo, Maria, Lucy Delap and Leila Ryan (eds.), *Feminist Media History: Suffrage, Periodicals and the Public Sphere* (Basingstoke: Palgrave Macmillan, 2011).

Doughan, David, 'Chew, Ada Nield (1870–1945) Labour Organiser and Suffragist', in *Oxford Dictionary of National Biography*, online edn. (Oxford University Press, 2004).

Doughan, David, and Denise Sanchez, *Feminist Periodicals 1855–1984: An Annotated Critical Bibliography of British, Irish, Commonwealth and International Titles* (Brighton: Harvester Press, 1987).

Dussart, Fae, '"To Glut a Menial's Grudge": Domestic Servants and the Ilbert Bill Controversy of 1883', *Journal of Colonialism and Colonial History*, 14:1 (2013), n.p.

'"Strictly Legal Means": Assault, Abuse and the Limits of Acceptable Behaviour in the Servant–Employer Relationship in Metropole and Colony 1850–1890', in Victoria K. Haskins and Claire Lowrie (eds.), *Colonisation and Domestic Service: Historical and Contemporary Perspectives* (Abingdon: Routledge, 2015), 153–171.

Dyhouse, Carol, *Feminism and the Family in England 1880–1939* (Oxford: Basil Blackwell, 1989).

Girls Growing Up in Late Victorian and Edwardian England (Abingdon: Routledge, 2013).

Ehrenreich, Barbara, 'Maid to Order', *Harper's Magazine*, 300:1799 (April 2000), 59–70.

Eley, Geoff, *A Crooked Line: From Cultural History to the History of Society* (Ann Arbor: University of Michigan Press, 2005).

Eley, Geoff, and Keith Nield, *The Future of Class in History: What's Left of the Social?* (Ann Arbor: University of Michigan Press, 2007).

Fauve-Chamoux, Antoinette (ed.), *Domestic Service and the Formation of European Identity: Understanding the Globalisation of Domestic Work, 16th–21st Centuries* (Bern: Peter Lang, 2004).

Federici, Silvia, *Wages against Housework* (New York: Falling Wall Press, 1975).

Revolution at Point Zero: Housework, Reproduction and Feminist Struggle (Oakland, CA: PM Press, 2012).

Feminist Fightback, 'Cuts Are a Feminist Issue', *Soundings*, 49 (Winter 2011), 73–83.

Fleming, Susie, and Gloden Dallas, 'Jessie', *Spare Rib*, 32 (Feb. 1975), 10–13.

Frank, Billy, Craig Horner and David Stewart (eds.), *The British Labour Movement and Imperialism* (Newcastle: Cambridge Scholars, 2010).

Garner, Les, 'Marsden, Dora (1882–1960)', in *Oxford Dictionary of National Biography*, online edn. (Oxford University Press, 2004).

Giles, Judy, *The Parlour and the Suburb: Domestic Identities, Class, Femininity and Modernity* (Oxford: Berg, 2004).

Glew, Helen, *Gender, Rhetoric and Regulation: Women's Work in the Civil Service and the London County Council, 1900–55* (Manchester: Manchester University Press, 2016).

Gordon, Eleanor, *Women and the Labour Movement in Scotland, 1850–1914* (Oxford: Clarendon, 1991)

Green, Barbara, *Feminist Periodicals and Daily Life: Women and Modernity in British Culture* (Basingstoke: Palgrave Macmillan, 2017).

Gullace, Nicoletta, 'Christabel Pankhurst and the Smithwick Election: Right-Wing Feminism, the Great War and the Ideology of Consumption', *Women's History Review*, 23:3 (2014), 330–346.

Hannam, June, '"Suffragettes Are Splendid for Any Work': The Blathwayt Diaries as a Source for Suffrage History', in Claire Eustance, John Ryan and Laura Ugolini (eds.), *A Suffrage Reader: Charting Direction in British Suffrage History* (London: Leicester University Press, 2000), 53–69.

Hannam, June, and Karen Hunt, *Socialist Women: Britain, 1880s to 1920s* (London: Routledge, 2002).

Hardyment, Christina, *From Mangle to Microwave: The Mechanisation of Household Work* (Cambridge: Polity Press, 1988).

Harrison, Brian, *Separate Spheres: The Opposition to Women's Suffrage in Britain* (London: CroomHelm, 1978).

Haskins, Victoria K., and Claire Lowrie (eds.), *Colonisation and Domestic Service: Historical and Contemporary Perspectives* (Abingdon: Routledge, 2015).

Hearn, Mona, *Below Stairs: Domestic Service Remembered in Dublin and Beyond, 1880–1922* (Dublin: Lilliput Press, 1993).

Higgs, Edward, 'Domestic Servants and Households in Victorian England', *Social History*, 8:2 (1983), 201–210.

Hoerder, Dirk, Elise van Nederveen Meerkerk and Silke Neunsinger (eds.), *Towards a Global History of Domestic and Caregiving Workers* (Leiden: Brill, 2015).

Holcombe, Lee, *Victorian Ladies at Work: Middle-Class Working Women in England and Wales 1850–1914* (Hamden, CT: Archon Books, 1973).

Holden, Katherine, *Nanny Knows Best: The History of the British Nanny* (Stroud: History Press, 2013).

Holgersson, Ulrika, *Class: Feminist and Cultural Perspectives* (Abingdon: Routledge, 2017).

Holton, Sandra Stanley, *Feminism and Democracy: Women's Suffrage and Reform Politics in Britain 1900–1918* (Cambridge: Cambridge University Press, 1986).

Quaker Women: Personal Life, Memory and Radicalism in the Lives of Women Friends, 1780–1930 (Abingdon: Routledge, 2007).

'Challenging Masculinism: Personal History and Microhistory in Feminist Studies of the Women's Suffrage Movement', *Women's History Review*, 20:5 (2011), 829–841.

'Friendship and Domestic Service: The Letters of Eliza Oldham, General Maid (c. 1820–1892)', *Women's History Review*, 24:3 (2014), 429–449.

Horn, Pamela, *The Rise and Fall of the Victorian Servant* (Stroud: Alan Sutton Publishing, 1990).

Life below Stairs in the Twentieth Century (Stroud: Amberley, 2001).

Hunt, Cathy, *The National Federation of Women Workers, 1906–1921* (Basingstoke: Palgrave Macmillan, 2014).

Hunt, Karen, *Equivocal Feminists: The Social Democratic Federation and the Woman Question 1884–1911* (Cambridge: Cambridge University Press, 1996).

'Women, Solidarity and the 1913 Dublin Lockout: Dora Montefiore and the "Save the Kiddies" Scheme', in Francis Devine (ed.), *A Capital in Conflict: Dublin City in the 1913 Lockout* (Dublin: Dublin City Council, 2013), 107–128.

James, Selma, *Sex, Race, and Class – The Perspective of Winning: A Selection of Writings 1952–2011* (Oakland, CA: PM Press, 2012).

Joannou, Maroula, 'The Angel of Freedom: Dora Marsden and the Transformation of the *Freewoman* into the *Egoist*', *Women's History Review*, 11:4 (2002), 595–611.

John, Angela V., 'Radical Reflections? Elizabeth Robins: The Making of Suffragette History and the Representation of Working-Class Women', in Owen Ashton, Robert Fyson and Stephen Roberts (eds.), *The Duty of Discontent: Essays for Dorothy Thompson* (London: Mansell Publishing, 1995), 191–211.

Jordan, Ellen, *The Women's Movement and Women's Employment in Nineteenth-Century Britain* (London: Routledge, 1999).

Leneman, Leah, *A Guid Cause: The Women's Suffrage Movement in Scotland* (Aberdeen: Aberdeen University Press, 1991).

Lewenhak, Sheila, *Women and Trade Unions: An Outline History of Women in the British Trade Union Movement* (New York: St. Martin's Press, 1977).

Lewis, Jane (ed.), *Labour and Love: Women's Experience of Home and Family, 1850–1940* (Oxford: Basil Blackwell, 1986).

Liddington, Jill, *Rebel Girls: Their Fight for the Vote* (London: Virago, 2006).
Vanishing for the vote: Suffrage, Citizenship and the Battle for the Census (Manchester: Manchester University Press, 2014).

Liddington, Jill, and Jill Norris, *One Hand Tied behind Us: The Rise of the Women's Suffrage Movement* (London: Virago, 1984).

Light, Alison, *Mrs Woolf and the Servants* (London: Penguin Books, 2008).

Mappen, Ellen, *Helping Women at Work: The Women's Industrial Council, 1889–1914* (London: Hutchinson, 1985).

Mather, Celia, '*Yes We Did It! How the World's Domestic Workers Won International Rights and Recognition*' (Cambridge, MA: WIEGO, 2013).

May, Vanessa H., *Unprotected Labour: Household Workers, Politics, and Middle-Class Reform in New York, 1870–1940* (Chapel Hill: University of North Carolina Press, 2011).

Mayhall, Laura E. Nym, *The Militant Suffrage Movement: Citizenship and Resistance in Britain, 1860–1930* (Oxford: Oxford University Press, 2003).

McBride, Theresa, *The Domestic Revolution: The Modernisation of Household Service in England and France 1820–1920* (London: CroomHelm, 1976).

McClintock, Anne, *Imperial Leather: Race, Gender, and Sexuality in the Colonial Contest* (London: Routledge, 1995).

McDermid, Jane, 'The Making of a "Domestic" Life: Memories of a Working Woman', *Labour History Review*, 73:3 (Dec. 2008), 253–268.

McDowell, Linda, *Working Bodies: Interactive Service Employment and Workplace Identities* (Oxford: Wiley-Blackwell, 2009).

McIvor, Arthur J., *A History of Work in Britain, 1880–1950* (Basingstoke: Palgrave, 2001).

Merchant, Jan, '"An Insurrection of Maids": Domestic Servants and the Agitation of 1872', in Louise Miskell, Christopher A. Whatley and Bob Harris (eds.), *Victorian Dundee: Image and Realities* (East Lothian: Tuckwell Press, 2000), 104–121.

Meyering, Sheryl L. (ed.), *Charlotte Perkins Gilman: The Woman and Her Work* (Rochester: University of Rochester Press, 2010).

Moriarty, Theresa, '"Who Will Look after the Kiddies?": Households and Collective Action during the Dublin Lockout, 1913', in Jan Kok (ed.), *Rebellious Families: Household Strategies and Collective Action in the 19th and 20th Centuries* (New York: Berghahn, 2002), 110–124.

Morton, Tara, 'Changing Spaces: Art, Politics, and Identity in the Home Studios of the Suffrage Atelier', *Women's History Review*, 21:4 (2012), 623–637.

Muggeridge, Anna, 'The Missing Two Million: The Exclusion of Working-Class Women from the 1918 Representation of the People Act', *Revue Française de Civilisation Britannique*, 23:1 (2018), 1–15.

Myall, Michelle, '"No Surrender!": The Militancy of Mary Leigh, a Working-Class Suffragette', in Maroula Joannou and June Purvis (eds.), *The Women's Suffrage Movement: New Feminist Perspectives* (Manchester: Manchester University Press, 1998), 173–187.

Nadasen, Premilla, *Household Workers Unite: The Untold Story of African American Women Who Built a Movement* (New York: Beacon Press, 2015).

Neale, R. S., 'Working-Class Women and Women's Suffrage', *Labour History*, 12 (1967), 16–34.

Offen, Karen, 'Defining Feminism: A Comparative Historical Approach', in Gisela Bock and Susan James (eds.), *Beyond Equality and Difference: Citizenship, Feminist Politics and Female Subjectivity* (London: Routledge, 1992), 69–88.

Oldfield, Sybil, *Spinsters of this Parish: The Life and Times of F. M. Mayor and Mary Sheepshanks* (London: Virago, 1984).

Park, Jihang, 'The British Suffrage Activists of 1913: An Analysis', *Past and Present*, 120 (1988), 147–162.

Pearson, Lynn F., *The Architectural and Social History of Co-operative Living* (Basingstoke: Macmillan, 1988).

Pooley, Sian, 'Domestic Servants and Their Urban Employers: A Case Study of Lancaster, 1880–1914', *Economic History Review*, 62:2 (2009), 405–429.

Purvis, June, 'Domestic Subjects since 1870', in Ivor Goodson (ed.), *Social Histories of the Secondary Curriculum: Subjects for Study* (Lewes: Falmer Press, 1985), 145–176.

'The Prison Experiences of the Suffragettes in Edwardian Britain', *Women's History Review*, 4:1 (1995), 103–133.

Emmeline Pankhurst: A Biography (London: Routledge, 2002).

'Emmeline Pankhurst: A Biographical Interpretation', *Women's History Review*, 12:1 (2003), 73–102.

Christabel Pankhurst: A Biography (London: Routledge, 2018).

Ramadin, Ron, *The Making of the Black Working Class in Britain* (Aldershot: Gower Publishing, 1987).

Ross, Ellen, *Love and Toil: Motherhood in Outcast London, 1870–1918* (Oxford: Oxford University Press, 1993).

Rowbotham, Sheila, 'Cleaners' Organising in Britain from the 1970s: A Personal Account', *Antipode*, 38:3 (2006), 608–625.

Dreamers of a New Day: Women Who Invented the Twentieth Century (London: Verso, 2011).

Schwartz, Laura, *A Serious Endeavour: Gender, Education and Community at St Hugh's, 1886–2011* (London: Profile Books, 2011).

Scott, Gillian, *Feminism and the Politics of Working Women: The Women's Co-operative Guild, 1880s to the Second World War* (London: University College London Press, 1998).

Shiach, Morag, *Modernism, Labour and Selfhood in British Literature and Culture, 1890–1930* (Cambridge: Cambridge University Press, 2004).

Slack, Kathleen M., *Henrietta's's Dream: A Chronicle of the Hampstead Garden Suburb 1905–1982* (n.p.: Calvert's North Star Press, 1982).

Smith, Dorothy E., *The Everyday World as Problematic: A Feminist Sociology* (Milton Keynes: Open University Press, 1988).

Smith, Harold L., *The British Women's Suffrage Campaign 1866–1928* (Harlow: Pearson Education, 2010).

Steedman, Carolyn, *Master and Servant: Love and Labour in the English Industrial Age* (Cambridge: Cambridge University Press, 2007).

Labours Lost: Domestic Service and the Making of Modern England (Cambridge: Cambridge University Press, 2009).

An Everyday Life of the English Working Class: Work, Self and Sociability in the Early Nineteenth Century (Cambridge: Cambridge University Press, 2013).

Summers, Ann, 'Public Functions, Private Premises: Female Professional Identity and the Domestic-Service Paradigm in Britain, c. 1850–1930', in Billie Melman (ed.), *Borderlines: Genders and Identities in War and Peace, 1870–1930* (London: Routledge, 1998), 353–376.

Sutherland, Gillian, *In Search of the New Woman: Middle-Class Women and Work in Britain 1870–1914* (Cambridge: Cambridge University Press, 2015).

Thane, Pat, 'Women in the British Labour Party and the Construction of State Welfare, 1906–1939', in Seth Koven and Sonya Michel (eds.), *Mothers of the New World: Maternalist Politics and the Origins of Welfare States* (New York: Routledge, 1993), 343–377.

'The Making of National Insurance, 1911', *The Journal of Poverty and Social Justice* 19:3 (Oct. 2011), 211–219.

Thom, Deborah, 'The Bundle of Sticks: Women, Trade Unionists and Collective Organisations before 1918', in Angela V. John (ed.), *Unequal Opportunities: Women's Employment in England 1800–1918* (Oxford: Basil Blackwell, 1986), 261–289.

Thomson, Alistair, '"Domestic Drudgery Will Be a Thing of the Past": Co-operative Women and the Reform of Housework', in Stephen Yeo (ed.), *New Views of Co-operation* (London: Routledge, 1988), 108–127.

Tickner, Lisa, *The Spectacle of Women: Imagery of the Suffrage Campaign, 1907–1914* (London: Chatto & Windus, 1987).

Todd, Selina, 'Domestic Service and Class Relations in Britain 1900–1950', *Past and Present*, 203 (2009), 181–204.

'People Matter (Feature: The Making of the English Working Class Fifty Years On)', *History Workshop Journal*, 77 (2013), 259–265.

The People: The Rise and Fall of the Working Class, 1910–2010 (London: John Murray, 2014).

Thomas, Zoe, and Miranda Garrett (eds.), *Suffrage and the Arts: Visual Culture, Politics and Enterprise* (London: Bloomsbury, 2018).

Ugolini, Laura, '"It's Only Justice to Grant Women's Suffrage": Independent Labour Party Men and Women's Suffrage, 1893–1905', in Claire Eustance, Joan Ryan and Laura Ugolini (eds.), *A Suffrage Reader: Charting Directions in British Suffrage History* (London: Leicester University Press, 2000), 126–144.

Vellacott, Jo, *Pacifists, Patriots and the Vote: The Erosion of Democratic Suffragism in Britain during the First World War* (Basingstoke: Palgrave, 2007).

Visram, Rozina, *Ayahs, Lascars and Princes: Indians in Britain 1700–1947* (London: Pluto Press, 1986).

Wallace, Ryland, *The Women's Suffrage Movement in Wales* (Cardiff: University of Wales Press, 2009)

Walter, Bronwen, 'Strangers on the Inside: Irish Women Servants in England, 1881', *Immigrants and Minorities*, 27:2–3 (2009), 279–299.

Wilson, Nicola (2015), *Home in British Working-Class Fiction* (Farnham: Ashgate).

Winslow, Barbara (1996), *Sylvia Pankhurst: Sexual Politics and Political Activism* (London: University College London Press).

Index

For EU product safety concerns, contact us at Calle de José Abascal, 56–1°,
28003 Madrid, Spain or eugpsr@cambridge.org.

www.ingramcontent.com/pod-product-compliance
Ingram Content Group UK Ltd.
Pitfield, Milton Keynes, MK11 3LW, UK
UKHW020353140625
459647UK00020B/2449